Contradiction and Conflict

THE POPULAR CHURCH IN NICARAGUA

DEBRA SABIA

The University of Alabama Press

Tuscaloosa and
London

Copyright © 1997
The University of Alabama Press
Tuscaloosa, Alabama 35487-0380
All rights reserved
Manufactured in the
United States of America

∞

The paper on which this book is printed
meets the minimum requirements of
American National Standard
for Information Science-Permanence of Paper
for Printed Library Materials,
ANSI Z39.48-1984.

Library of Congress Cataloging-in-Publication Data

Sabia, Debra, 1957–
Contradiction and conflict : the popular church in Nicaragua /
Debra Sabia.
p. cm.
Includes bibliographical references and index.
ISBN 0-8173-0873-3 (alk. paper)
1. Basic Christian communities—Nicaragua—History. 2. Catholic
Church—Nicaragua—History—20th century. 3. Nicaragua—Church
history—20th century. 4. Nicaragua—Politics and
government—1979–1990. 5. Nicaragua—Politics and government—1990–
6. Socialism and Catholic Church—Nicaragua—History—20th century.
I. Title.
BX2347.72.N5S23   1997
282′.7285′09048—dc21   96-46304

British Library Cataloguing-in-Publication Data available

To my parents, in loving memory

CONTENTS

PREFACE

THIS WORK EXPLORES the rich history, ideology, and development of the popular church in Nicaragua. Examined within the revolutionary period of Nicaragua's history (1970s–1990s), the study investigates the historical conditions that worked to unify members of the Christian faith and those subsequent factors that fragmented the popular coalition.

Based on research conducted in Nicaragua, and primarily focused on three Christian base communities in Managua, the book gathers an assembly of voices that offer understanding into the development and nature of the popular church. Yet the eloquence of those voices belies a fundamental problem: Divergent notions of the popular church exist in Nicaragua. While a generalized conception of this church and its characteristics exists, it has not escaped the effects of local interpretations and doctrinal elaborations.

In dealing with the complexity of this problem, this book presents a typology as a means for exploring and thinking about the religious and political differences, contradictions, and conflicts evident among the progressive sector of Catholics. The typology constructed for this study has borrowed from the work and contribution of Max Weber's methodological approach of ideal types.

The popular church in Nicaragua has been conceived of and

understood as a community of faithful that fragmented into at least four different ideal types: (1) the Marxist, (2) the Revolutionary Christian, (3) the Reformist, and (4) the Alienated Christian type. Each of the ideal types is differentiated by its members' general orientation to spiritual and political beliefs and practices. These types have been derived from the author's observation and assessment of the evolutionary changes evident in the progressive community.

This book provides discourse on the subject of religion and politics. It explores the impact of the popular church on the Nicaraguan Revolution and, conversely, the effect that Nicaraguan politics have had on the popular church. By examining these dynamics the study offers some tentative conclusions for assessing the future viability of the popular church in the counterrevolutionary state.

Some acknowledgments and expressions of gratitude are in order. I would like to express sincere appreciation to Professors Morris Blachman and Joan Meznar at the University of South Carolina for their assistance throughout the research process. Special thanks are due to the friends I left behind in Nicaragua and especially to Dr. William McIntosh, who was always there for me, offering encouragement with his words of wisdom.

Contradiction and Conflict

CHAPTER ONE

Introduction

TODAY AROUND THE world and especially in Latin America we are witnessing the struggle for greater democratization. Since the fall of dictator Anastasio Somoza in 1979, the Nicaraguan people have sought to bring a new way of life and a new political vision to their tiny nation. In the last two decades Nicaragua has experienced a popular revolution, a civil war, and the international effects of an emerging new world order. Within this context progressive Christians have played a dynamic role in working for change. For an overwhelmingly large number of Christians, political struggle appears to have been inspired by a new form of faith: liberation theology.

Liberation theology is a theological current of Catholicism that originated in the region at the end of the 1960s. In the following decade this religious current appears to have evolved from a strictly theological endeavor to one that included a powerful social movement for change.

In Nicaragua, the liberation movement took life from the establishment and proliferation of *comunidades eclesiales de base* (Christian base communities, or CEBs). In the 1970s the communities flourished and gave rise to a new type of grass-roots church where Catholics came together to study, discuss, and reflect on their biblically oriented faith. Out of this reflection Nicaraguans came to discover a powerful political inspiration. In the

1

following years many would devote their lives to a political struggle that focused on demands for greater social justice.

This book is an attempt to understand the rise, growth, and fragmentation of the popular church in Nicaragua. The term *iglesia popular* (the popular church) is often used interchangeably in Latin America with its other common identifying names, including the grass-roots church, Christian base communities, the people's church, the progressive church, and/or the church of the poor. The intent here is to examine the historical conditions that gave rise to the progressive Christian coalition and to the development, growth, and ultimate fragmentation of the grass-roots church. How might we understand the dynamics that nurtured the base communities? How might we account for and understand the conditions for change? What effect have these events had on religion, on politics, and on Nicaragua's social revolutionary experiment?

FORMAT

The events and issues with which this book deals began with a unique historical moment, the meeting of the world's bishops at the Second Vatican Council in Rome, 1962–65. The council was the watershed that brought revolutionary change to the private and public spheres of Latin society. Indeed, Vatican II unleashed forces for change that impacted the region greatly, perhaps as significantly as had the arrival to the region of the Spanish conquistadors five hundred years before.

Previous studies have documented the historical import and power of the Catholic Church that was brought to Latin America by its Spanish representatives. It is beyond the scope or intent of this book to repeat that history here. Nevertheless, it is important to understand the birth of the contemporary popular church particularly as it has been understood as arising within—and then apart from—the established, universal church.

Much of the previous literature has offered an analysis of this history from a dual-model perspective. The first model has understood the Latin American church institutionally. The second model (the popular church) has often been understood as one

2

constituted by antagonists or more radicalized Catholics who separated themselves from the universal institution. Within this framework there has been a tendency toward understanding the two models of church as being in competition and conflict with each other. In the case of the *iglesia popular* there has also been a predilection toward understanding these radical, antagonistic Catholics as a unified, monolithic group. In Nicaragua, understanding the nature and ideology of the popular sector is not so simple a matter.

We shall see that in Nicaragua the notion of a breakaway church remains highly dubious. We shall also see that while there has existed a generalized conception of a separate people's church there exists a number of distinct trends and ideological differences in it. This study will examine these differences and ultimately suggest that one universal (Catholic) church still exists in Nicaragua. Within this institution, however, we shall see that several competing tendencies and internal divisions are clearly evident.

In addition to the radicalized tendency within the Nicaraguan Catholic Church, both traditional and reform sectors exist as well. A key issue distinguishing the radicalized sector from the reform and traditional ones has been that of partisan politics. In Nicaragua, differences have emerged in the Catholic community based on the support or nonsupport of the former revolutionary government, the Sandinista National Liberation Front (FSLN), the guerrilla movement that led the popular insurrection in 1979.

While many studies of the popular church have focused on these political differences within the radicalized Catholic sector, most have failed to address the spiritual dissimilarities among Catholic peoples. The intent of this book is to supplement this understanding by suggesting that to comprehend the political differences that are evident among them, we must focus more closely on the spiritual differences that also divide the Catholic community. The typology developed for this book presents a new way of exploring and thinking about these religious and political differences, contradictions, and conflicts.

3

Introduction

In recent years significant growth has occurred in Protestant churches throughout Latin America and particularly in Nicaragua. Indeed, some Protestant churches played a crucial role in the popular insurrection of 1979. Many others worked cooperatively with Catholics in the revolutionary process of the following decade. The primary objective here, however, remains focused on the Catholic sector of the popular church, the sector represented by the radicalized and reformed faithful who are working both in and outside the Christian base communities. Nonetheless, the subject of Protestantism is treated where appropriate, particularly in the history of the fragmentation of the Christian base communities.

This book is organized into three focal points. The first, which includes chapters 2–5, is devoted to an introductory review of Latin American Catholicism, the birth of the popular church, the growth and maturation of the Christian base communities, and finally the conditions that led to the fragmentation of the Catholic coalition.

The second focal point examines more closely that fragmentation. Chapters 6–9 analyze the resulting schisms of the popular sector and the effects on religion, politics, and the social life of Nicaraguan society.

Finally in the third focal point, in chapter 10, the significance of these experiences for Nicaraguans is assessed and some final thoughts are offered on the likely impact of those experiences for Catholicism, for the church of the poor in particular, and more generally, for the future viability of the liberation struggle.

METHODOLOGY

The popular church in Nicaragua is marked by heterogeneity and internal divisions. Such schisms, however, have not always been clearly discernible or readily obvious. Often there have only been hints of division and only subtle, whispered nuances. As this project unfolded it became apparent that a particular research approach was crucial in making sense of these distinctions and capturing these subtleties. Thus I found it invaluable to borrow from the contribution of the great social scientist, Max

4

Weber, in utilizing his methodological approach of the ideal type.

Weber's introduction of the ideal type proposes a way to give meaning and coherence to human behavior. Ideal types are logical constructions that the social scientist creates in order to conceptualize and analyze socially observed phenomena. For analytical purposes, ideal types furnish a standard in terms of which actual forms of social organization can be classified and compared. The method, however, is not without its difficulties. Ideal types are artificial constructs created by scholars as useful fictions against which to test the utility of categorizations. While they can prove quite useful in helping to elucidate directly observed phenomena, the propositions they generate must remain tentative.

For the purpose of this book, the popular church in Nicaragua is here conceived and understood as a community of faithful made up of four distinct ideal types. The construction of ideal types was developed incrementally following my first research trip to Nicaragua in spring 1990. Early in the research the typology began to take shape out of initial visitations to several Christian base communities. The two-month research trip also included meetings with Christian institutes and centers that had distinguished themselves as participants of the popular church. They were identified by people working within the CEBs in Nicaragua and in other cases by my own recognition of their work in the United States.

Both structured and unstructured methods of observation continued to be employed in subsequent research trips to Nicaragua, including a three-month trip to the country in summer 1991 and an eight-week visit in winter 1992. Both structured and unstructured strategies were deliberately selected as a means for dealing with the reactivity problem of direct observational research. Special care was given to collect data from a variety of sources. In this way the data could be cross-checked with other resources. Use of a variety of sources served as a means for reducing the potential bias of the researcher's presence while providing a strategy for gaining alternative perspectives.

The structured method employed for this research included

formal interviews with populations both in and outside the popular church, with governmental leaders, business elites, and officials of the Catholic hierarchy, including the cardinal of Nicaragua, Miguel Obando y Bravo. In some cases where formally planned and structured interviews were utilized, preplanned questions led to other insights. Thus it was necessary to be more flexible, dropping questions that did not work or deviating from a structured agenda. Instances when data agreed with other studies on the popular church have been indicated in the research where possible.

Another strategy employed for this project was the participant-observer method, a largely unstructured process that included direct observation, actual participation in CEB events, and informal conversations with people both in and outside the Christian base communities, including people at Protestant churches, at public celebrations, and at neighborhood events.

The central activity was the recording of observations and interviews. Great care was given to obtain accurate descriptions of actual events and the culturally significant beliefs and attitudes that appeared to guide the social action observed. During these activities it was not uncommon to rely heavily upon written notes, photographs, and taped interviews. It was also of great value to maintain a personal journal to record reactions and general impressions.

Field aides were Nicaraguans who were always present at the research sites. Their assistance was invaluable for providing feedback, for facilitating improved communication, for checking the accuracy of observations and interpreted materials, and for double-checking one another's impressions and recorded work.

The collection of data led to the development of a taxonomy of political and spiritual ideologies around which interviewees were eventually grouped. These classifications or ideal types developed primarily from the participant-observer method, the core of which focused around three primary Christian base communities in the capital city of Managua: the communities of San Pablo, San Judas, and Adolfo Reyes. These three communities

The "people's art"—revolutionary art depicting the popular insurrection of 1979.
The painting shown in this photograph is in the parish of San Pablo and is approximately eight feet high.

are among the CEBs that collectively constitute the heart of the
popular church, and they were selected for a variety of reasons.

First, they are among the oldest, the largest, and the most active of the Christian base communities in the capital city. Managua, the largest city in Nicaragua, is the place where half of the
country's four million citizens reside. It was also the city where
the heart of the revolutionary struggle against the Somoza dictatorship took place. Today, it is the city where affiliates of the
popular church continue to be the most active.

For reasons of history, region, and political culture, the three
focal communities are quite likely to operate in a manner very
similar to one another and very different from those outside the
capital. Indeed, findings suggest such a conclusion. Despite this
difficulty, selecting the oldest Christian base communities in Managua was considered important not only to examine the birth
of the popular church but also to understand its development

and evolution over time. With their rich histories of growth and change, it was deemed essential to draw on the earliest established CEBs within the country.

Second, it was important that the communities be selected based on the number of their participants. All three communities offered a large membership in barrios with stratified socioeconomic levels. These differences offered a greater distribution of personal attributes.

There were other reasons for selecting the communities of San Pablo, San Judas, and Adolfo Reyes. These communities continued to be identified by a large number of independent sources outside the popular sector. When asked about the work of the CEBs in Managua, the Catholic hierarchy and governmental and business leaders consistently cited all three as being among the most active in the capital city. Because the work of these communities has evolved over time and because all three continue to be vital, it was deemed important to study each of them.

The decision to study San Pablo, San Judas, and Adolfo Reyes was also made easier by their research accessibility. Each of the communities extended personal invitations to visit, live, and research with neighborhood families. The opportunity to live in the homes of CEB members and to watch the unfolding of their daily lives provided rich insights.

Potential weaknesses, however, do exist. First, in no way is this particular work intended to imply that it is solely representative of the larger progressive Christian sector that exists in Nicaragua. The decision to select three primary communities for intensive study makes generalizing to the larger population difficult. In theory and practice the study of the evolution and fragmentation of the popular church—as illustrated by the case studies of these three CEBs—is only intended to serve as a microcosm.

From the beginning, the ideal types that evolved were used as tentative theoretical tools for capturing the variegated ideologies and religious conflicts that were observed in the communities. Specific behaviors, attitudes, and beliefs continued to be assessed as an ongoing process. The strategy was to build theory from the ground up, by abstracting from particular observations more general and complex descriptions. Explanations of behavior could then be developed. In the case of each ideal type, past observations constituted the building blocks for future observations.

The construction of the ideal types, then, was extrapolated from the totality of the research experience. To guard against inferences in interpreting an individual's behavior or opinions, collected data were used throughout the project in a working hypothesis that could then be checked against the opinions of other researchers and other CEB members. The ideal type classifications that emerged were then compared and contrasted with each other in the search for variations, not only between the types but within each category as well. The final product ultimately developed from the final assessment of the data. The ideal types that evolved, however, may not necessarily be the final positions into which Nicaraguans might place themselves.

A primary purpose of these ideal types is to help expand the focus of existing research. What has been attempted here is to move beyond the issue of partisan politics. For this reason each of the types is differentiated by its general orientation to spiritual beliefs and practices; each has been developed by drawing upon peoples' religious practices and their self-conceptions of their beliefs. In this respect the conclusions rely heavily on the input from the community of faithful. Accordingly, there is less emphasis on the self-conceptions and perspectives of church officials who remain outside the progressive Christian movement.

It is hoped that the constructs developed here will assist in elucidating the prevailing conceptions of the popular church in Nicaragua. This typology does not, however, pretend to be inclusive of all interpretations and ideologies that may exist in the country. Rather, it seeks to provide a greater understanding of the spiritual differences exhibited within the popular sector. Recognizing these differences is important for distinguishing progressive Christians from one another.

As already noted, the second focus of this book deals specially with each of the types. The first of these is the Marxist type, the party faithful who worked in concert with the Sandinistas in building a classless society. The process for them was highly radicalizing and in some cases led to their complete alienation from the Catholic Church and from all religious practice.

The second type is that of the Christian Revolutionary. These Nicaraguans also had faith in the class option of the Sandinista party. However, unlike their Marxist counterparts, their motivation is cast in highly spiritual terms. Today, they remain serious religious people.

The third type is that of the Reformist Christian. These Catholics embrace notions of social justice but are critical of any ideology that seeks to defend one class interest over another. Finally, the Alienated Christian type includes Nicaraguans who criticize what they believe has been an overly politicized religion and who ultimately reject politics and further involvement in the base community movement.

The reader is again reminded that while this research is not meant to be representative of the macrolevel of Nicaraguan society it deals with some important groups at the microlevel within the country. These types help to elucidate the dynamics of the revolutionary experience on the popular church, and they offer some important insights into religion and human behavior, generally.

It is simplistic and misleading to believe that all people are alike, even those men and women who share similar values and commitments. This book hopes to demonstrate that people continue to learn from their life experiences and that they adapt their attitudes, values, and behaviors according to the lessons derived from those experiences. Social, political, economic, and psychological factors worked in concert in the process of these peoples' learning. Learning is a dialectical process. People make choices based on their individual and shared experiences and they continue to learn from their successes and their failures. This fact challenges the conventional wisdom that people do not change once they are committed to a particular idea or world view.

The interviewees' willingness to elaborate on and share their experiences assists in recognizing the variegated nature of the progressive Christian sector in Nicaragua. Thus, their story helps us to understand how it is that the perceived homogeneity of the popular church evolved toward a marked heterogeneous organization. By understanding their stories of the conflict and contradictions of the progressive sector, we might discern the fragmentation of the Christian base communities in a more meaningful way.

What is glaringly obvious in this research is the fact that members of the progressive Catholic sector have been constantly assimiliating the lessons of their revolutionary experiences. As so many members of the popular church have argued, it is a matter of seeing, judging, and acting—and requiring, in the end, a return to greater reflection.

Finally, this study should offer caution to those of us who seek to increase our understanding, study, and conceptualization of the church of the poor. We must remain sensitive to the fact that the community of faithful is a living entity, evolving and growing in reaction to its constituent members' individual and collective experiences. The same may be true of any human organization.

CHAPTER TWO

The Second Vatican Council

IN LATIN AMERICA, the establishment and rise to power of the Roman Catholic Church have been characterized by a close, often turbulent relationship with wealthy elites and traditional authoritarian regimes. Throughout its history the Catholic Church has been far better at preserving antidemocratic traditions in Latin America than it has been at promoting them.

The history of the Catholic Church is well documented elsewhere and will not be repeated here. Studies of Catholicism in Latin America remind us that while the church enjoyed an uneven, albeit privileged, status in society, it had in no way escaped its own internal divisions and conflicts. Its history is of a house divided. From its founding in Latin America there existed clergy critical of the institution's alliance with repressive regimes. Dissension, however, was not generally tolerated, and radical priests were sometimes defrocked and executed (Cockcroft 1989).

The environment of intolerance began to shift in the modern period. The historic Second Vatican Council that took place in Rome between 1962 and 1965 was a watershed for change. The Roman council was convened by a liberal pope, John XXIII. The Holy See called the world's bishops together, setting the stage for remarkable change.

In the Catholic world a climate of unrest and secularization had lent an urgency to inviting the church's leaders to the holy

12

city. By the middle of the twentieth century more than half of the world's Catholics were living in underdeveloped countries in conditions of crushing poverty and spiritual decay. It was a period of contradictions. In the nations of the north, economic revitalization followed the post–World War II era. In the nations of the south, however, people continued to suffer the effects of economic regression, material deprivation, and spiritual crisis.

In light of these realities, Pope John's decision to host the historic and monumental conference should not have been particularly surprising. Catholicism has always been a religion explicitly concerned with the public order (Mainwaring and Wilde 1989), and in many parts of the Catholic world public order appeared to be breaking down. Most troubling to the bishops in Latin America was the revolutionary triumph of Castro's Cuba. Indeed, the revolution had sent a shock wave through the Catholic community. Its victory had come on the heels of increasing criticism of traditional seats of power, including regional oligarchies and military dictatorships and their allies associated with the church. In many sectors of Latin society the triumph of the revolution appeared to increase enthusiasm for radical solutions to the problems of the region.

In the postwar period in Latin America the problems of underdevelopment and antidemocratic regimes provided an environment that helped to nurture and promote the establishment of Christian democratic parties (PDCs). Yet in spite of church support for the PDCs, and despite the early enthusiasm and optimism of many, the Christian parties had little success in addressing the problems of their countries. In many cases PDC members were targeted for repression and death. In other instances their leaders were co-opted by the very regimes they hoped to challenge.

In light of these concerns, Pope John called his spiritual leaders to Rome. Christian Smith (1991) and Walter LaFeber (1984) have argued that the Second Vatican Council was exceptional, particularly in its openness to elements outside the Catholic Church. Beyond inviting the world's bishops to Rome, Pope John extended an invitation to other members of the ecumenical community, including social scientists and nontheological scholars.

13

He challenged his guests to address the social and cultural malaise. How might the church understand the problems of underdevelopment? What was the responsibility of the clergy in these changing times? How might the church better understand its role in an increasingly troubled and de-Christianized world?

The reevaluation of the church's role that began at Vatican II marked a historic turning point for Catholicism worldwide. It called the church to conversion and set in motion a revolutionary process, perhaps one unanticipated by the majority of the bishops who participated in the conference (Gutiérrez 1990).

The tenor of Vatican II recognized the perceived failures of Christian leadership throughout the world. In doing so it also challenged the church's bishops to promote a new, more active strategy for resurrecting spiritual values in the structures of their states and societies (Brown 1966; Boff 1985). In particular, the conference advocated a more participatory model in working for human rights. It especially argued the need for greater social responsibilities among all sectors of the Catholic community (Mainwaring and Wilde 1989). In doing so the council acknowledged the coresponsibility of clergy and laity in these endeavors, and it challenged the faithful to search together for new sociopolitical solutions to the problems of mass poverty and deprivation (Núñez 1985).

Perhaps for the Latin American church the most profound effect of Vatican II was that it opened the opportunity for greater clerical reflection. In time an environment evolved in which the clergy could openly acknowledge past errors, including the church's long-standing relationship with corrupt institutions of power (Smith 1991). Vatican II legitimized the right of theologians to criticize the church, and it likewise fostered an openness to debate that included participants both in and outside the traditional structures of the church. Its impact for the region was revolutionary.

THE LATIN AMERICAN BISHOPS CONFERENCE

Shortly following the Vatican Council the Latin American bishops were called together to address how to deal pastorally and theologically with the mandates of Rome. The issues of mass deprivation and human suffering became the theme at the Latin American Bishops Council that met at Medellín in Colombia in 1968 (Christian 1986; Arellano 1990). There, the bishops came together to ask how the church would define its role in working for sociopolitical change. How would it define human rights and what would the church's strategy be for expanding the participation of clergy and laity in resurrecting spiritual values in the life of the Latin American state (Mulligan 1990)?

To address these issues the Medellín conference brought together a group of young, dynamic, and enthusiastic theologians who dominated the conference's discourse (Smith 1991: 100–101). Among them was a young Peruvian priest named Gustavo Gutiérrez. Gutiérrez had been educated at the University of Louvain in Belgium, and he brought with him to the conference his own extensive European education and Latin experience. He had helped to prepare the working papers for the ecclesiastical conference and his work was the first to speak of an indigenous, liberating theology. Thus, Gutiérrez has come to be viewed as the father of liberation theology (Christian 1986).

The working papers at the Medellín conference included the work and reflection of ecclesiastics who were at that time researching and writing on the Cuban Revolution. Protestant ministers from North and South America had traveled to the island nation in the early 1960s to study the revolution in action. At that time an intellectual cross-fertilization was taking place between Catholic and Protestant camps (Planas 1986).

The achievements of the Cuban Revolution in improving the life of the poor majority was of growing interest to young theologians like Gutiérrez. Indeed, the period between the Cuban Revolution and the Medellín conference was truly significant for the Latin American church. According to Gutiérrez (1990: 14), it marked a time when the bishops awakened to discover the true reality of the region—it was a time when consciousness of poverty grew. And unlike the intolerant practices of the past, clerical discussions, debates, and dissension were allowed, even encouraged. For the first time in the church's history the subject of human deprivation was permitted and pursued "without fear or apprehension" (ibid.).

15

The openness of the post–Vatican II climate was also significant because it continued to invite the use of social science analysis in rendering an understanding of the Latin American reality.
Scholarly openness was furthered by growing frustration among
some religious groups who were at this time seriously questioning the nonscientific conceptions of social Christianity (Cleary
1992). In particular, many had become critical of the methods
and practices employed by the PDCs in South America. These
critics accused the Christian parties of employing methods that
lacked scientific rigor, and they rejected as grossly inadequate a
purely electoral approach toward addressing the problems and
conflicts of Latin societies (Cáceres 1989). These same critics
were increasingly convinced that social transformation could
never be achieved by elites alone, and they advanced arguments
for greater grass-roots organizational initiatives in addressing the
needs of their communities.

The working papers prepared by the Gutiérrez group thus embraced a more inclusive, scientific, and critical understanding of
the region's reality. As a consequence, the Medellín papers provided an alternative analysis to the problems of Latin society that
was clearly socialist in orientation (Planas 1986). Based on observations of the Cuban Revolution and on a class analysis of
Latin society, the young theologians cited the international and
external legacy of a system of dependency as the major source
of human deprivation in Latin America. The documents were
predicated on a historical review of the region's development,
and they specifically identified the structure of social injustice
and mass inequality as capitalist in orientation. Indeed, the documents denounced the system of dependency as well as capitalism.
The Gutiérrez group thus blamed the capitalistic structure for
creating a class-based society motivated by profit and rooted in
human and resource exploitation.

These denunciations had revolutionary implications for the
Latin American church. By recognizing structural inequality the
Medellín documents challenged the church to work for the active transformation of the capitalist system. For the first time in
the church's history, the bishops announced an unprecedented

16

commitment on the part of the clergy to lead a challenge to the structures of oppression and injustice (McGrath 1990; Lernoux 1979).

At the Medellín conference, Christian liberation came to be understood as freeing people not only from individual, spiritual sin but also from the effects of human, structural sin imposed by a history of exploitation (Gutiérrez 1986). Within this context the church's role was clear: The clergy was being challenged to work for radical sociopolitical change. Thus the theology of liberation was born, and it evolved as a highly Christ-focused faith. Gutiérrez (1990) has suggested that at the Medellín conference the Latin American church acknowledged the life and work of Jesus as providing the example of what one's attitude and action might be. The constant link with Jesus as the example for Christian action became crucial to the later development of the liberation movement.

Medellín's focus on the life and work of Christ was exceptional. This Christology argued the church's mission to be one of solidarity with the poor and oppressed (Levine 1990a; McGrath 1990; Neal 1990). Indeed, the intense focus on the life and work of Christ mandated a call for the church likewise to adopt a preferential option for the poor—as Christ did under conditions of poverty and deprivation.

The church's acknowledgment of Jesus' mission to be the proclamation and fulfillment of the liberation of oppressed peoples fostered a new perspective and place of the church in the Latin world (Gutiérrez 1986). Commitment to the poor was seen as the very place for spiritual experience and interaction with the Divine (Smith 1991). The youthful clergy at Medellín argued that it was in the presence of the poor that the church would find and commune with God. Thus, the bishops conference called upon the church to transform itself, to be first and foremost a church of the poor, to carry out its mission as Christ did in poverty and under oppression (Levine 1990c; McGrath 1990; Neal 1990).

The Medellín documents suggest that solidarity with the poor was to be manifested in specific action in two important ways (Drury 1970; Gutiérrez 1986). First, the new presence of the

17

Many murals depict the people's struggle and are testament to the history of the Nicaraguan Revolution. The painting shown in this photograph is in the parish of San Pablo and is approximately eight feet high.

church was to be lived out through the prophetic denunciation of social injustice in Latin America. This prophetic denunciation demanded a new stance against all those practices and institutions that exploited human beings and demeaned the human spirit. The church was called on not only to denounce social injustice but also to break its historical alliance with repressive persons and institutions. For the Latin American church denouncing social injustice implied a commitment to side with the oppressed against the oppressor, to "enter into conflict with those who wield power" (Gutiérrez 1986: 115).

Second, the Latin American church was mandated to engage the laity in a consciousness-raising evangelization (Lernoux 1982). *Conscientization* and *participation* are key words that appear throughout the Medellín texts. (The word *conscientization* is frequently used in Latin America and is understood as a maturation of awareness. In its fullest sense, conscientization refers to a gradual awakening, an awareness of the present moment from the standpoint of one's Christian faith.) The documents also speak often of the need for involving the masses in participation with their own liberation. The church was challenged to live out the liberation commitment by enlisting the faithful in that process (Berryman 1987; Smith 1991). The goal was defined as awakening the minds of the oppressed so that by developing a critical consciousness the poor could work with the church in becoming active agents in their own liberation (Gutiérrez 1990).

Because the clergy recognized the development of a critical consciousness as the link between social and personal conversion, the bishops recommended promotion of these goals through a clerical identification with the poor (Berryman 1987; Levine 1990c). At Medellín the bishops had recognized the church's historical neglect of the poor and spoke of the need for outreach programs to areas traditionally neglected by the clergy (Mulligan 1991: 75). Up until the 1960s the religious had been concentrated in colleges, schools, and in wealthy parishes within the urban centers of Latin America. After Medellín, this reality underwent a radical transformation. The region witnessed a mass exodus of priests and nuns to the rural areas and poor barrios of Latin America. There the clergy sought to engage the laity in a more intimate awareness of their faith. The challenge for the church was to build solidarity with the poor and to promote a religious consciousness that could liberate the oppressed from the forces of ignorance, poverty, and sin.

This clerical engagement mandated a means for addressing the historical—and critical—problem of mass illiteracy. Here, the bishops looked to the work of Brazil's educational philosopher, Paulo Freire, the architect of popular conscientization (Lernoux 1982; Berryman 1987).

Paulo Freire had developed a pedagogy that linked the skills of critical thinking with popular discourse among the rural poor. The Socratic method he employed invited people to question their problems and experiences and to explore explanations and solutions. One of the most important innovations of Medellín was the linking of Freire's popular method with a new way of using the Bible (Berryman 1987). Priests and nuns who reached out to the poor utilized the Scriptures as the primary tool for engaging the laity. The Medellín method encouraged the reading of key Christian doctrines from the experiences and deliberations of the poor (Lernoux 1979; Mulligan 1991; Berryman 1987).

This new method departed dramatically from the traditional practice of Catholicism (Smith 1991). It reversed the original practice of the church as the sole interpreter of the sacred word of God. Scriptural understanding was no longer the sole domain of the Catholic hierarchy. It became a living and meaningful part of the Latin experience. Thus, Medellín set in motion a process whereby the word of God took life from the experiences of a forgotten and neglected constituency.

The new method had monumental consequences for many poor Latin Americans. It gave an invisible and silenced people a new sense of personhood. According to Father Joseph Mulligan, a Jesuit priest who works with many of the Christian base communities in Nicaragua, "it gave to the poor the necessary resources for combating traditional fears, and it challenged their own sense of inferiority." Reading the Scriptures for themselves, poor Latin Americans began finding many of their own experiences reflected in the Bible (Berryman 1987). They also discovered in the gospel an emphasis on God's preferential love for the poor. In the process they were finding their dignity and self-worth affirmed (Dodson and O'Shaughnessy 1990).

Liberation theology began challenging the old ways of thinking about the Scriptures. As the poor were encouraged to discuss the Bible from their own point of view, they began challenging the conventional wisdom that understood social injustice and human exploitation as the expressed will of God. In reading the Bible with their own eyes, poor Latin Americans were encountering a different kind of Jesus, one whose life and struggle was taking on a whole new meaning for them (Berryman 1987; Mulligan 1991; Lernoux 1979). This new Christology had profound meaning for them. Jesus Christ was coming to be understood as the great liberator of the poor. His life and work came to be interpreted as the inauguration of a kingdom of God on Earth.

The Medellín conference initiated a theological awareness that evolved into a highly politicized consciousness. The movement for liberation was indeed spawned by the theology of liberation. But the two activities are different endeavors: One remains theological while the other remains political. For many poor Latin Americans, however, the two have become interwined and inseparable. Understanding their role as cocreators with God, cocreators of a more humane social order, many Nicaraguan Christians could not help but become deeply involved in a highly politicized movement.

THE CHURCH IN NICARAGUA

In Nicaragua as elsewhere in Latin America, the environment arising from the Second Vatican Council fostered a climate of change and liberation. "The period between Vatican II and the Latin American Bishops Conference awakened the religious community to the conditions and plight of the poor," suggested Miguel Vigil, Catholic priest and president of the Board of Trustees of the University of Central America in Managua. "The awakening gave the Latin American church a much needed frame of reference in defining the role it would play in the process of social transformation."

In Nicaragua the historical context in which the evangelization effort grew was characterized by vast poverty and human deprivation. The Nicaraguan reality was firmly rooted in the pattern of economic development of the preceding decades. It was no less a consequence of the official corruption of the Somoza dynasty that had ruled the country since the 1930s (Gilbert 1986; Cockcroft 1989; Booth 1985; Christian 1986).

The Somoza dynasty had come to power in the 1930s with the promotion of Anastasio Somoza García, a general in the newly created Nicaraguan National Guard forces. The infamous Guard had been created by the United States in the interest of protecting American land and business ventures in the country.

The United States had become intimately involved in Nicaragua as early as the 1840s (Cockcroft 1989; Booth 1985). Groups in the United States looked favorably at Central America as an opportunity for self-aggrandizement. Men looked to the region for interests as diverse as the expansion of slavery, the right to control water facilities, banking opportunities, and railroad speculation.

One such person was U.S. mercenary William Walker, who took advantage of conflicts among the country's elite. In 1855 Walker and a small mercenary army invaded the country. After seizing power, Walker declared himself the new president of Nicaragua. His short, unsuccessful tenure as president—he was killed in a countercoup the following year—did little to end U.S. involvement in the region.

From 1909 to 1933, Washington promoted its economic and strategic interests in Nicaragua by backing conservative and then liberal governments with repeated military interventions and occupations. The U.S. Marines spent "twenty years in Nicaragua, imposing or trying to impose U.S. policies" (Booth 1985: 27).

Before U.S. troops completely withdrew from the nation in 1933 they established the Nicaraguan National Guard under the leadership of Anastasio Somoza García. After the marines' departure, General Somoza staged a coup against the then newly elected Liberal President, Juan Bautista Sacasa. With the overthrow of Sacasa in June 1936, Somoza assumed power and Nicaragua thus entered into forty-five years of illegitimate and tyrannical rule (ibid.: 50–54).

Guided by the military dictatorship of the Somoza family, Nicaragua underwent a gradual economic transformation. The country evolved from a subsistence agricultural economy to one characterized by an expanding agro-export market (Gilbert 1986). This process set in motion a growing landless peasantry as campesino farmers were displaced from their traditional lands. The process also exacerbated social and economic inequities for a majority of Nicaraguans. Early in this evolution, however, members of the country's elite prospered, and they enjoyed an accommodating relationship with the Somoza dictatorship (Booth 1985).

As the economic might of the Somoza family grew alongside the development of the nation's industry, this relationship was gradually challenged.

The industrialization process of the post–World War II period contributed to the growing inequalities of Nicaraguan society. While the poor grew poorer, the expanding economic aggrandizement of the Somoza group began to threaten some sectors of the Nicaraguan bourgeoisie. Most elites attempted to find continued accommodation with the Somoza government. Most of their attempts, however, were no more successful than those of the poor. It was not uncommon for the National Guard to respond to criticism of the regime with swift and violent retaliation. In these conflicts the Nicaraguan church remained conspicuously allied with the ruling family.

The positive relationship that the Nicaraguan church enjoyed with the Somoza regime reflected the general historic dependence of the Latin church on the ruling elites (Serra 1985). The church's privileges and institutional well-being were largely predicated on the generosity and agreeability of those in positions of political power (Mulligan 1991). During periods when Liberal forces attacked the privileges of the clergy, the "bishops never tired of offering the church as an institution which would be useful to the state" (ibid.: 70). Indeed, the church used its influence to legitimize and perpetuate the authority of those in power, fighting against any changes that might threaten its own privileged status in Latin society. Thus, the Nicaraguan Catholic hierarchy played an important role in legitimizing the Somoza dictatorship (ibid.: 73).

The absence of any meaningful tie with the poor in Nicaragua was a reflection of the church's general historical neglect of the poorer segments of Latin society (Núñez 1985; Serra 1985; Planas 1986). Like elsewhere in Latin America, the Nicaraguan church suffered from a severe lack of religious personnel. Historically, however, little had been done to develop a national clergy. Recent studies have suggested that for every three thousand Nicaraguans there has been only one representative of the Catholic Church (Berryman 1994: 154). Of that presence the majority of the clergy were European or North American who exclusively served in wealthy parishes in the urban centers of the country. It was not uncommon for rural Nicaraguans to see a visiting priest just once or twice during their lifetimes, once at baptisms or marriages and then again following the death of a family or community member.

Following the Latin American Bishops Conference, however, clerical contact with the poor grew in frequency. Nevertheless by 1968 the Nicaraguan church was not yet prepared to embrace the radical challenge that Medellín advocated. In Nicaragua particularly, the church was not yet ready to sever its alliance with the rich and powerful. Nor was it ready to opt for the poor (Mulligan 1991: 79). Change, however, was inevitable.

In January and February 1969, the Nicaraguan bishops held the First Pastoral Congress in the capital city of Managua. Two hundred fifty-eight people, both clerical and secular, participated in the eight-week meeting (Foroohar 1989: 100–101). The congress had been called to examine the social and religious realities of Nicaragua and to recommend pastoral strategies for achieving the mandates of Medellín. In addition to discussions toward building a grass-roots church, the pastoral conference opened a watershed of criticism of the country's sociopolitical and religious structures (Serra 1985; Williams 1989; Mulligan 1991). The enthusiastic and progressive group of clergy who attended put Nicaragua's dictatorship under intense discussion and scrutiny. New Catholic periodicals, including *Testimonio,* vigorously denounced the military regime and took the unprecedented liberty of challenging many traditional values and practices of the Catholic hierarchy (Mulligan 1991).

As had been the case at the Medellín conference, conservative Catholics exhibited an uneasy tolerance toward criticism of the Nicaraguan church. And while the hierarchy was less than enthusiastic with the tone of the pastoral conference, the congress was successful in legitimizing the need for continued denunciation of social injustices (Mulligan 1991).

Most important, the conference set in motion new pastoral strategies for building outreach projects that were specifically targeted at the poor majority. Efforts for building a grass-roots church were complemented by the generational change of ecclesiastical leadership that occurred in Nicaragua between 1968 and 1972 (Booth 1985). The exit of the old guard and the entrance of the new included the appointment of Monsignor Miguel Obando y Bravo who was named archbishop in March 1970. The appointment of Obando to replace Archbishop Alejandro González y Robleto, a staunch supporter of the Somoza government, came as a surprise to many people in Nicaragua (Williams 1989). The young Nicaraguan priest clearly lacked the necessary experience demanded of formerly appointed archbishops. It is possible that Obando's appointment by the Vatican was clearly intended as a signal to the church's former allies. Previous studies have suggested that the Vatican's appointment of Miguel Obando clearly signified that the church no longer wished to cultivate its long-standing relationship with the Somoza dictatorship (Booth 1985; Williams 1989).

The appointment of Obando "altered sharply" the hierarchy's policy toward the Somoza government (Booth 1985: 134). Under the leadership of the new archbishop the Nicaraguan bishops began issuing a series of pastoral letters that criticized the existing political order. These criticisms raised hopeful expectations among the progressive clergy. The archbishop's antidictatorial attitude clearly raised expectations for structural change.

Despite such optimism, the church's criticism remained quite conservative in tone (Foroohar 1989; Williams 1989; Mulligan 1991). Archbishop Obando began calling for political reform, yet he conspicuously avoided any criticism of Nicaragua's socioeconomic structure. As early as 1970, it was already becoming clear that the Nicaraguan hierarchy would be at odds with the more radical camps developing in the country.

At the beginning of the decade the hierarchy's focus appeared fixed on the church's primary responsibility for promoting religious proselytizing. In line with Medellín's preferential option for the poor, evangelization became the center of the church's theological reflection and activity.

In reflecting back on those years, Father Joseph Mulligan suggested that "the bishops encouraged and legitimated pastoral activities that could contribute to the poor's growing religious awareness. These strategies centered around clerical efforts that could create opportunities for empowering poor people. The aim was to allow the poor to become subjects in their own spiritual liberation."

In an effort to establish an integrated pastoral plan, progressive elements within the church looked to the work of a Trappist monk, Father Ernesto Cardenal. In the mid-1960s, Ernesto Cardenal had begun the earliest effort toward religious conscientizing in the country. In 1966, the priest had established a contemplative community on the island of Solentiname in Lake Nicaragua (Sigmund 1990: 119).

"It was a miracle to have a man like Ernesto come to Solentiname," recalled Olivia Guevara, who was residing there when the priest arrived. At that time the islanders had been living in dire poverty, suffering the effects of a traditional Catholicism that demanded unquestioned submission.

Like elsewhere in rural Nicaragua, the church had only a tentative relationship with the poor islanders of Solentiname before Father Cardenal's decision to reside with them. According to former residents, it was typical for them to receive a visiting priest only once every six or seven months.

"With great difficulty we would collect the little money we had and give it to him to say mass," Olivia Guevara explained. "Then he would scold us for drinking *guaro* and smoking, and in our fear of him, we would run around looking for the best chicken to cook to present to him." In time, community members said, they recognized this great contradiction. "Can you imagine a priest coming to scold a few hungry people without shoes? He should have come to Solentiname to help!"

Recognizing this situation, Father Ernesto made a historic decision to alter his pastoral strategy. Although he had envisioned a contemplative community, he worked instead in promoting the parish as a more participatory community (CEPAD 1991: 1).

Olivia Guevara remembered that early in the community's formation residents would meet in the morning for a worship ser-

26

vice. Then they would gather for a communal meal that took place under a thatched pavilion next to the church. Contributions of food were made by each of the residents, including Father Ernesto, who brought cooking oil, rice, and beans.

Miriam Guevara, Olivia's daughter, remembered that the weekend was also a time for organizing service projects: "On Saturdays a group of twenty-five young people would meet to work for the whole community. For example, if a campesino's house fell down or was burned, we would build it back."

Father Cardenal's method was deliberately inclusive. Instead of preaching to his parishioners he selected passages from the gospel and invited the community to discuss them with him. The lively discourses that ensued were eventually captured on tape and edited into a world-famous book, *The Gospel in Solentiname* (ibid.: 2).

This religious experiment was a profound experience for the islanders. They suggested that a different world was suddenly opening to them. Residents began understanding the conditions that had led to their great impoverishment. Their understanding of God was transforming, too. Olivia Guevara recalled that "we began discovering a God of love, one who has worked actively in human history for the rights of all people to be free from hunger and want."

Out of a deep appreciation for the island's culture, Father Cardenal created Nicaragua's first successful consciousness-raising experiment (Foroohar 1989). Indeed, the project was so successful that it did not escape the attention of participants at Nicaragua's First Pastoral Congress. The Solentiname project thus became the blueprint for other Christian base communities in the country.

The expectation for a second pastoral conference that intended to develop Cardenal's strategy further was, however, never realized. It has been speculated that the earthquake that struck Managua in December 1972 was responsible for the failure of the church to convene a second congress. Despite this speculation it also appears that some of the Nicaraguan bishops were already opposed to the idea of initiating a national pastoral plan

(Williams 1989). After all, the pastoral strategy called for the leadership of progressive clergy in initiating the plans for building CEBs like that of the Solentiname model. It is quite possible that the Catholic hierarchy recognized the difficulties involved in controlling such events and chose instead to work toward frustrating the creation of a concerted, nationalized strategy. As a consequence of this failure, the construction of a grass-roots church in Nicaragua began in a limited and ad hoc fashion.

The hierarchy's general lack of support, however, could not derail the enthusiastic intentions of the progressive clergy. Initial efforts were already under way following Father Cardenal's example in Solentiname. In fact, by the beginning of the 1970s the bishops had lost their ability to control events. The dynamics of Medellín had begun to unfold and, despite the opponents of a greater democratized church, a Pandora's box had been opened.

CHAPTER THREE

The Rise of the Popular Church

IN 1966, Nicaragua witnessed the birth of the first Christian base community in Managua. The San Pablo community came on the heels of the successful Solentiname model and was founded by a Spanish priest, Father José de la Jara.

Father de la Jara entered a residential area of the city that included a large, economically mixed neighborhood whose residents were less destitute than the families on the island of Solentiname. San Pablo is in the heart of the capital city and its residents had not endured the same geographic and cultural isolation that the Solentiname islanders had suffered. Despite this fact, the families of the community had experienced years of economic and social hardship. The majority had suffered generations of poverty, irregular employment, and the lack of health care services, sanitation, and education.

Immediately, Father de la Jara began working with the poorest families in the barrio. From its beginning the base community attracted attention. Today the large, original community has been broken down by district into four smaller base communities. Each of the CEBs has a membership of around thirty to forty members, including both women and men, although women represent the majority of the membership.

Most CEB members in the San Pablo parish are middle aged (thirties to fifties) but there are also young people as well as a mi-

Catholic church in San Pablo. Catholics typically worship in such small churches built by the hands of community members.

nority of women over the age of sixty. Members of the CEBs are predominately mestizo, generationally descended from "Spanish and Indian blood."

Most of the members of San Pablo's community make their living in the informal economy, although some hold public service jobs. San Pablo's youth group includes seventeen secondary school members and is an extension of the base community movement.

Early in the formation of the San Pablo community Father de la Jara focused his activities around religious concerns. Rafael Valdéz was an early participant in this endeavor. He is a very articulate man in his early fifties who continues his work with the grass-roots church. In reflecting back on the origins of the community, he remembered that they did not start with the theology of liberation but with the teachings of the Second Vatican Council. He recalled that Father de la Jara organized Bible courses and encouraged popular discussions of the Scriptures. He explained that the early focus of these activities was exploration of faith and a renewal of Catholic commitment.

Bible study and reflection in these small worship groups, however, began transforming the traditional, individualistic practice of Catholicism. Father Joseph Mulligan, a North American priest who services many of the Managuan communities, explained that what was unique about the theology arising from the Vatican II climate was the fact that it was departing from an individualistic and spiritually directed faith.

Since 1986, Father Mulligan has been working at the Central American Historical Institute in Managua. His own research and experience have helped him see that as families gathered together to study and discuss the Bible, they began developing a greater awareness and appreciation of their faith and their community. Within a short period of time this practice took on a highly collective and political character.

San Pablo residents who joined together for a discussion of their early experiences explained that within this context Catholic peoples were coming to recognize a personal, liberating God. They explained that the traditional Catholic conception of the Divine had always been that of a far removed, heavenly deity. The Vatican texts, however, had begun introducing a God understood in the secular, as one residing within the human community. Father Mulligan suggested that this new conception of God was collapsing the church's historical distinction between the sacred world and the profane. A crucial objective of the CEB effort was to build and nurture this new understanding of the Divine as expressed in the resurrected spirit of Christ. Part of the aim was to work together to provide an environment where people could come together to worship as a collective family and to recognize a liberating spirit within the community. Members of San Pablo joined the pastoral team to discuss the life, work, and resurrection of Jesus, who promised to be with the human family: "for lo, I am with you always, to the close of the age" (Matt. 16:20).

Rafael Valdéz suggested that after two years of basic community work the focus of discussions and activities began to change.

Gradually the pastoral team began dealing with the issues of human dignity and the Christian position on the political reality of Nicaragua (see also Foroohar 1989). Together community members began exploring how their own hardships might be expressed from this liberating, highly focused Christology.

The Bible *cursillos* (short courses) soon took on the name "*cursillos* of conscientization" or *cursillos de concienciación*. Rafael Valdéz explained that for Christians the means of becoming conscious required of them the practice of a method that could connect biblical themes to the questioning of their own sociopolitical reality.

This method is often referred to in the liberation literature as the hermeneutic circle (Berryman 1987: 60–62). As parishioners in San Pablo explained, Christians are asked to see their reality and to judge it by connecting the conditions of their world with reflections from the holy gospel. From their reflections and judgments about their reality, they are then guided to act in a Christian way to alleviate the suffering they witness around them. For example, members frequently cited the book of Matthew (25:35) as a blueprint for their action. Members pointed out their shared reflection on the sacred words of Jesus, "for I was hungry and you gave me food, I was thirsty and you gave me drink, I was a stranger and you welcomed me." On reflection and discussion, CEB members suggested that their Christian obligation asks them to see this reality in their own lives and communities. Where hunger and thirst are witnessed they are then commanded to respond as Jesus taught, "Truly, I say to you, as you did it to one of the least of my brethren, you did it to me" (Matt. 25:40).

This witnessing, reflecting, and resulting praxis are a synthesis of seeing, judging, and acting. For CEB members the method is cyclical. The hermeneutic method asks Christians to reflect continuously on their praxis, to reincorporate the lessons of their experiences, and to allow the lessons of their experiences to inform the process again and again. This technique, adopted in San Pablo, is the same strategy used in all of the Christian base communities in Latin America. It is a striking feature, and it is the practiced methodology of liberation theology.

In the early years of the formation of the San Pablo parish, the Nicaraguan hierarchy maintained a largely indifferent attitude toward it. They viewed it "as a pilot project and a unique phenomenon" (Williams 1989: 45). The liberating climate of the post–Vatican II environment thus provided Father de la Jara with opportunities to reach beyond his community. Within a few years San Pablo's pastoral team extended its work and established at least twelve other projects, including the Christian base communities of Adolfo Reyes and San Judas.

Adolfo Reyes was founded with the help of a former Spanish priest, Father Antonio Esqueba. The community of Adolfo Reyes began with sixty members and became independent from San Pablo a year before the 1979 insurrection. Like its mentor CEB, Adolfo Reyes was and continues to be a community of mixed economic status. Like the majority in San Pablo, most of its residents suffer from poverty and a lack of essential services. Whereas some of the neighborhood enjoy electrical services, many homes are without running water or sanitation facilities.

Julita Soza is one of the oldest members of the Christian base community of Adolfo Reyes. She is a small, slender, soft-spoken woman who lives in one of the poorest homes in the barrio. She is mestiza; her dark features suggest a strong indigenous ancestry.

The cement structure she shares with her son and grandchildren encloses a dirt floor and houses a few bare pieces of wood furniture. Julita is now in her seventies. A founding member of the community, she recalled that a "very special priest, Antonio Esqueba, had come to the neighborhood to speak to them about their faith. Father Esqueba showed us a new way to read and think about the Scriptures."

Julita remembered that at that time the community faced many problems. For one thing, there was no neighborhood church, so the residents met in a darkened dance club. "We kept the lights off," she explained, "because at that time the Somoza government considered our community subversive." Some of the residents' sons had left the barrio to join the rebels who were fighting in the mountains. As a consequence, the neighborhood of Adolfo Reyes was often the target of unannounced, random searches by the National Guard. "We had to meet in secret to read and study the Bible," Julita remembered. "But as more priests came to work in our neighborhood our fear receded." Membership in the community grew.

Today, Adolfo Reyes continues to boast a large membership (about thirty-five to forty members). It is also considered to be among the most independent of the Christian base communities and is the leader in many social justice projects in the capital city.

As in San Pablo, most of the members are poor mestizos and are middle aged, and as in many other CEBs, most of the participants are women. Throughout Managua women represent the numerical majority both in neighborhood churches and in communities. Indeed, one striking feature of the church of the poor is its growing feminization.

The fact that the church of the poor is a predominantly female institution reflects the fact that women have been traditionally responsible for the religious life of their children. This fact remains true today. It is women who see that their children attend Sunday services and it is they who play an active role in preparing the children for their First Holy Communion and their Catholic Confirmation.

The feminized aspect of the popular church also reflects the fact that many poor men have been forced to leave their communities to find employment elsewhere; their leisure time, as a consequence, is limited for both religious and community projects. Scarcity of men, coupled with the lack of trained religious clergy, has forced the Catholic hierarchy to look increasingly (albeit reluctantly) to women to assist in the neighborhood's pastoral needs.

There is another explanation for the highly feminized face of the church of the poor. Over the last two decades the libera-

This shanty settlement in the periphery of the community of San Judas is a typical site in Managua.

tion church, increasingly at odds with the established Catholic Church, has been one of the most accessible and legitimate outlets for women. Traditionally excluded from public life by the norms of their society, Latin American women have found their neighborhood churches a convenient and safe place to try out new leadership skills.

As the grass-roots church developed in Nicaragua, women's responsibilities in less traditional roles have grown. Today, for example, it is not atypical to see laywomen leading Bible discussions. They are involved in planning and conducting paraliturgical ceremonies, prebaptismal talks for parents, and prematrimonial instruction for couples, and often they are the leaders in development of new base community activities. This phenomenon can be observed elsewhere not far from the Adolfo Reyes community.

The CEB of San Judas is a kindred community of Adolfo Reyes and it, too, is the product of the early outreach effort of San Pablo. The community of San Judas is twenty-five years old and today includes two adult and two youth group CEBs. There are more than 50,000 residents in San Judas, most of whom are very poor. Surrounding the heart of the barrio are nineteen poorer neighborhoods and seventeen peripheral settlements. The settlements are characterized by metal and cardboard shanties with dirt floors and wood-burning fireplaces. There are few paved roads. It is not uncommon to find children playing in sanitation runoffs.

Indiana Larios, a strikingly attractive woman in her forties, is an active member of the San Judas community. In fact, her service to the community spans well over twenty years. Indiana remembered the founding of San Judas, dating to the early 1970s when the Sisters of the Assumption paid a visit to the barrio. Like their colleagues in San Pablo and Adolfo Reyes, the sisters invited the residents to share in Bible studies and discussions.

"We began reading the Bible for ourselves for the very first time," Indiana recalled. "The sisters encouraged us to discuss the Scriptures and to relate them to God's presence in the world." The residents began discerning the active intervention of God in human history. Indiana Larios noted a favorite community discussion that focused around the story of Exodus (3:7–8), in which God leads his people out of captivity. "We began seeing a God that was concerned about human suffering."

Raquel López, another active member in San Judas, also recalled the sisters' visits. "They would come to the barrio and speak to us about our needs." Until that time the needs of the community had been neglected by the church. "The sisters were here to help guide us, to give us support. But they also gave us the autonomy to solve our own problems in our own way." Their presence was reassuring, and the community found strength in the growing number of residents.

Thus, as in San Pablo and Adolfo Reyes, San Judas's formation was focused around religious questions and concerns, a focus that was true of the base community movement throughout Nicaragua. What was different about this new evangelical strategy was the church's promotion of popular study of the Scriptures. As CEB members were encouraged to read the Bible and to analyze their problems through the study of the gospel, the experimentation fostered a sense of dignity and self-worth. At the same time it created within the community a climate of growing fellowship. Not only were people coming together to discuss their problems, but they were also being encouraged to participate together in solving them.

Today, integrated development continues to be a major goal of the CEBs in San Judas. For example, its experiment with grassroots democracy in addressing the problems of the community has been very successful. Each of the CEBs has committees with representatives from each of the nineteen neighborhoods. The delegates spend a great deal of time visiting with their neighbors to learn more about their needs. These concerns are then represented at weekly council meetings where the communities make decisions on how best to address their neighborhood problems. The strategy has produced remarkable successes.

THE PROLIFERATION OF THE BASE COMMUNITY MOVEMENT

Following the establishment of San Pablo, Father de la Jara's pastoral team moved beyond Managua. The community sent representatives to a shanty town outside the city. The Christian community of OPEN 3 (Operacion Permanente de las Emergencia Nacional) had been established by the Somoza government as a solution to the plight of some 300 families who had been displaced by the overflowing of Lake Managua in 1969 (Williams 1989: 45). Like elsewhere, progressive clergy and Christian lay workers assisted the community in religious instruction and conscientization. Like the experiences of Adolfo Reyes and San Judas, the outreach effort contributed to a growing community solidarity. Together, members of the community set out to improve the deplorable living and working conditions of the neighborhood. These same efforts were later replicated elsewhere in Nicaragua.

While initial efforts for building a grass-roots church were

Nicaraguan children pose for the camera near Lake Managua, close to the original site of OPEN 3 (Operacion Permanente de las Emergencia Nacional).

blossoming in Managua, by the late 1960s two rural programs were also being established in the Nicaraguan countryside. The Delegates of the Word program was developed in the Atlantic region of the country, and the Evangelical Committee for Agrarian Advancement (CEPA) was established in the Pacific region. Like the communities in Managua, both projects were dedicated to socioreligious conscientization of the peasant communities.

Under the supervision of the Capuchin friars in the Atlantic regions of Zelaya and Nueva Segovia, the Delegate of the Word program was created in 1968 and provided lay leadership in rural areas not regularly serviced by a priest. Delegates of the Word were trained to provide worship services as well as literacy training and health programs. As in Christian communities growing up throughout Latin America, religious services held by the delegates employed dialogues and Scripture to address the immediate problems of community members. The program was so successful that within ten years it had greatly expanded beyond the Atlantic coast. By 1979 it was estimated that approximately

5,000 delegates were spread throughout Nicaragua (Williams 1989: 52).

The CEPA program that was created on the Pacific coast was established in 1969 by Jesuit priests. This project sought to provide a religious presence in areas previously ignored by the Catholic Church. Like the Delegate of the Word program, CEPA provided worship training for peasant leaders as well as agricultural education and training. Originally based in the cities of Carazo and Masaya, the program was so successful that it spread northward to the cities of León and Estelí.

With the success of the San Pablo experiment and the rural programs outside the capital city, other CEBs took root in Nicaragua during the 1970s. All of these communities share a number of characteristics despite their vast geographical differences. For example, Luis Serra's work (1985) found that all of the communities link biblical study with critical reflection. The frame of reference for this reflection always begins with the experiences of the poor.

The Nicaraguan popular mass has grown out of these shared reflections and is another common characteristic of these communities. San Pablo was the first of the CEBs to establish this particular type of mass, a religious ceremony that is highly inclusive. For example, the popular mass encourages the reading of Scriptures by volunteers from the community. The audience is then invited to discuss the readings and to offer how their own experiences might be related to the biblical story.

This simplified liturgy not only embraces popular language but also includes the people's music. For instance, Nicaraguans' favored instruments (such as guitars and woodwinds) are typically introduced to the ceremony. The music is distinctively Latin American; with its discernible Spanish rhythm it can be full of joyful enthusiasm or soulful sorrow.

Another common characteristic of CEBs is the collective experience. All of the CEBs organize their projects around the expressed needs of their neighborhoods. Most of the projects are tackled by small groups composed of the community's members. It is not uncommon for others in the barrio, those who are not formal members of the base community, also to assist with these projects.

Finally, responsibility for the CEB projects and for further evangelization efforts has been gradually assumed by the laity. In nearly all of the communities the clergy remain outside the informal structures of the CEBs. The clergy are largely available for providing training, guidance, and, when necessary, resource support.

REACHING OUT BEYOND THE POOR

While the CEBs remained rooted in the poor barrios of the country (very few were established in middle-class neighborhoods), representatives of the Nicaraguan church sought to facilitate a growing religious consciousness among wealthier classes of the faithful. Short *cursillos* on Christianity were adopted by parish churches and were predominantly taught by members of the progressive clergy. Additionally, Catholic radio programs, periodicals, and religious pamphlets raised consciousness among a growing audience. The work of Catholic outreach organizations, such as the Center for Agrarian Education and Promotion, and the Nicaraguan Institute for the Promotion of Human Rights also assisted these efforts. These organizations trained new Christian leaders, supported Christian organizational efforts, and promoted further community development.

All of these Catholic programs and initiatives were understood to be the fulfillment of Rome's directives for resurrecting the spirit of the church in the lives of the faithful. Following Medellín's lead, these initiatives revolved around the theology of liberation, which placed a special emphasis on the preferential option for the poor.

The political consequences of this preferential option were not the effects intended by the Nicaraguan hierarchy. The bishops' support for many consciousness-raising programs was for religious purposes, not political ones. Still, many Catholics—affluent as well as poor—could not help but be affected by the liberating climate.

Juan and Piada Tijerino were among the wealthy elite who were influenced by the early work of the Nicaraguan church. Piada and Juan spoke from their beautiful, Spanish-style home in the foothills of the city of Boaco. They are a striking couple. Eloquent and passionate speakers, they are third-generation Nicaraguans whose families came to Nicaragua from Spain and made their fortunes in cattle ranching.

Piada Tijerino remembered her socioreligious awakening. She explained that as a couple they were called to conversion in 1972 when she and Juan were still quite young. "We had everything: We had money; our five children were all healthy. Everything Juan touched turned to gold. But something was missing from our lives."

Raised as a devout Catholic, she did not find it unusual to attend weekend retreats for deepening her faith. She remembered that in spring 1972 she attended a *cursillo* that changed her life. It was sponsored by the parish church in Boaco, and she was so inspired by what she learned during the course that she brought her husband with her when she returned for another retreat.

Piada explained that "Vatican II was alive at this time and the parish was promoting religious proselytizing that was structured around the preferential option for the poor." She said that she had never considered the Bible from this point of view. "Suddenly my eyes opened. We discovered that we had to commit ourselves to those who were suffering the most, the poor in our society."

Piada's husband Juan explained that they began understanding their obligation as Catholics in a totally new way. He suggested that until that time their obligation to the church included baptizing their children, attending confession and Sunday services, and making a significant financial contribution once a year. But after their retreat they began to understand that their faith required a "living Christian conscience."

Juan suggested that the couple came to understand that their wealth and privilege offered opportunities for them to live out their faith in a new way. They began to see that they had resources to use toward the alleviation of the suffering around them. In many respects the Catholic retreat was an epiphany for them.

Piada and Juan were so moved by their experience that they invited Juan's brother to the next session. Flavio Tijerino was also deeply affected by the Bible *cursillo*.

Flavio is older than his brother, an attractive man in his early sixties. "I had been a rancher and a Christian for thirty years, but I came to see that I had lived in contradiction," he explained. He said that he came to this realization when he began reading the Bible for himself and reflecting on his life. "I came to understand that I had not lived a just life. I had gotten lost in my wealth and the things that I could buy, so I opted to be poor." Flavio decided to give the land he owned to the church so that it could be used for community development. Flavio proudly extended his hands and displayed the dirt under his fingernails. "Today," he said, "the only land I own is what is left on my body at the end of the day."

The work of Zwerling and Martin (1985) documents the growing consciousness among privileged families in Nicaragua. Rafael Solís, who had been raised as a traditional Catholic in a wealthy family in Managua, was also affected by progressive elements within the Nicaraguan church. Like so many other privileged youths in the country, he was educated at the Colegio Central America.

He recalled that in the late 1960s a progressive priest from Spain introduced the students to some of the harsh realities in the country. The priest engaged his students experientially by taking them to the poorest barrios in Managua. In the northern part of the city the students worked in neighborhoods where residents lived in houses of paper and cardboard. There they helped to construct a health center and a latrine. "For me, coming from a wealthy family and background, it was a new and awakening experience" (ibid.: 35–36). Rafael Solís believed that the experience enabled the students to link the theoretical discussions of the dictatorship's repression to its concrete manifestations. The experience changed many of them both spiritually and politically.

After 1968 and following Medellín's lead in focusing on the preferential option for the poor, Christian focus grew beyond religious matters to include discussions regarding the social, economic, and political reality of Nicaragua. Father Antonio Castro, a progressive priest in Managua, explained that Catholics were being asked to reflect upon their reality en masse. At this time injustices in Nicaragua were well known. Many Christians were well aware of Somoza's despotic rule, the cruelty of the National Guard, the regime's administrative corruption, and the use of power for private privilege. Father Joseph Mulligan suggested that as Catholics matured, religious consciousness gave way to a greater awareness of the need for taking social and political responsibility. "Poor Christians throughout Nicaragua were coming to discover the structural causes of their poverty and oppression. With the practice of liberation theology, people both rich and poor were coming to understand the importance of community, collective action, fellowship, and solidarity."

Father Mulligan suggested that Jesus was coming to be identified with the poor and the exploited. "In the liberating climate of Vatican II, people began to hear that the human being was not only spirit but matter and as such had a right to food, clothing, land, and health care." From their faith the poor were finding the personal confidence to question practices that continued to oppress them. Father Castro said that from their community solidarity, Christians were also finding the courage to work with others in pressing for reform.

Sister Cecilia García, a member of the community of Adolfo Reyes, explained that "for many Christians, participation in the transformation for a more just society came to be regarded as a logical (and necessary) extension of the demands of their faith." Booth's work (1985: 134–36) suggests that the move toward political mobilization seemed to be a logical outgrowth of religious proselytizing and the themes of liberation theology. This was certainly the case in San Pablo where CEB member Rafael Valdéz claimed that "the community progressed with the Catholic practice of liberation theology." Valdéz recalled that as the practice gained momentum the community of San Pablo "was flourishing in two directions." The community flourished spiritually with biblical studies, and "as we learned more, we realized that there were political aspects to our situation. As a consequence we began to grow in a political direction."

As the community of San Pablo matured it grew in its responsibilities both socially and politically. Between 1967 and 1979 the community took part in protests of many social injustices, including protests against the increase in bus fare and against discriminatory practices in state-funded education.

"When we started participating in strikes to denounce the treatment of prisoners, our motivation was basically political," recalled Valdéz. The community had grown sick of death and of the corruption of the Somoza family. "We took inspiration from our biblical outlook, which believes that God is a freedom fighter. We used that as our backbone."

Like Valdéz, Julita Soza in Adolfo Reyes explained that her decision to become involved in the protest movement was a consequence of her growing faith. "As our community grew and as our reflection deepened, our eyes opened to the corruption of the government."

In San Judas, Indiana Larios credited her growing political consciousness to the work of the Sisters of the Assumption: "As our discussions grew and as we reflected on our political and social situation here in Nicaragua, our eyes opened to the sins of the Somoza government. As a consequence, the community made the collective decision to become involved in government protests." Raquel López agreed with her neighbor and explained that their faith taught them to question their reality and to mobilize in support of change.

Father Antonio Castro, who services the community of Larreynaga, expanded on this theme: "In many barrios in Managua, people were coming together to discuss their problems, but the pastoral teams also encouraged them to participate together in solving them. In time this could not help but take a political form."

By the early 1970s Medellín's preferential option for the poor was having important consequences not just at the grass-roots level but among the Nicaraguan hierarchy as well. The dynamics unleashed by elements of the progressive clergy were having effect. Paralleling the development of the Christian base communities was the bishops' growing opposition to the Somoza regime (Williams 1989: 43). Shaw (1989: 4–5) suggests that increased criticism of Somoza reflected this fact. "For the majority of the hierarchy, and especially for Archbishop Obando y Bravo, fulfilling the church's prophetic ministry meant undertaking a concerted but restrained effort to remove the apparent root of social injustice. . . . This meant the personal dictatorship of Anastasio Somoza Debayle" (ibid.).

While the liberation movement gained momentum at the grass-roots level, the conservative sociopolitical role of the Catholic Church was incrementally evolving in a more liberating direction. Father Mulligan suggested that by promoting consciousness-raising activities, the liberation movement provided an environment in which popular demands for rights were justified by Medellín's religious principles. Once the Vatican had defined sin in terms of social injustice, the church in Nicaragua was left with some very difficult choices. The hierarchy could continue to side with Latin American elites, or it could take the road of revolution or reform (Cockcroft 1989: 24). The Nicaraguan bishops chose the road of reform.

In 1968 the Nicaraguan bishops made their first formal effort to join with the voices of the base communities. In a public letter the bishops called on the Somoza government to "halt repression and torture, to free political prisoners, and to promote a more just and equitable order" ("Declaracion" 1968).

THE STUDENT CONNECTION

In the spirit of Medellín, the Nicaraguan church became the focal point for much of the protest activity that grew against the Somoza government. Unlike other Latin American countries—where liberation priests had encountered resistance from their conservative superiors—in Nicaragua social activism was actually encouraged (Booth 1985: 135). One manifestation of this activism was the growing involvement of priests in student youth

45

movements. The student movement grew up alongside the CEBs and supported many community base efforts. The most famous student organizations included the Revolutionary Christian Movement, the Catholic Workers' Youth, the Movement of Young Christians, and the Christian Student Movement.

These student organizations gained attention and grew in influence as a result of their combative mobilizations. They worked with members of the base communities and together they participated in church takeovers, strikes, and propaganda efforts that denounced the regime's social injustices (Serra 1985: 153). One of these students was Patricia Mulligan. Today, Patricia is a forty-nine-year-old woman who was willing to share the story of her role in the popular insurrection.

Patricia Mulligan was raised in an upper-middle-class family in the city of Granada. Her mother was Nicaraguan and her father North American; Patricia was born in the United States but was raised in her mother's country. Today she owns a comfortable home in the city of Managua in an upper-income neighborhood.

Like many of her privileged contemporaries, Patricia was raised as a traditional Catholic and was educated in parochial schools. Her involvement in political protests against the Somoza government began in the 1970s when she was studying at the National University. She remembered that from 1969 on a gradual fervor was building in Nicaragua. She explained that it was as though Nicaraguans were suddenly awakening from a long, deep sleep. She believed that while most people were conscious of the brutality and corruption of the Somoza regime, almost everyone avoided discussion of it.

By the early 1970s, however, students began to be challenged by their professors to think about the national reality. Outside the classroom students began to speak more openly and critically of the regime. Patricia Mulligan remembered that at the beginning of the 1970s huge arguments and debates took place on campus, as did many protests against the abuses of President Somoza. For example, students began participating in church takeovers to protest the treatment of political prisoners. Patricia remembered that one of these takeovers was the 1970 occupation of the large cathedral in downtown Managua. "Toward the end of the 1970s the National Guard would invade the campus grounds and use tear gas to break up the political discussions and student demonstrations," she said.

The student movement that Patricia remembered was organized by two progressive priests, Father Uriel Molina and Jesuit Father Fernando Cardenal. Father Molina, a Franciscan priest, became involved in the liberation movement shortly after the Second Vatican Council. He explained that the pronouncements of the council had deeply affected him and he felt moved to organize a base community in the barrio of Riguero (Randall 1983). Here students and community members met to discuss their faith and to ask themselves what it demanded of them in light of the times (Foroohar 1989). With Molina's leadership the students and community worked together to form the first university common in November 1971 (Williams 1989). From that point on, barrio Riguero became an important meeting place for student activists.

From this experience many university students chose to live with the poor, and they took leadership roles in directing study groups in other communities. The students' focus with the communities grew beyond religious proselytizing to discussion of the socioeconomic problems of Nicaragua. Under their guidance, people within the communities worked to organize a neighborhood association that could voice grievances and work for reform (ibid.: 47).

Father Molina's work in Riguero introduced him to another priest, Father Fernando Cardenal, who was at that time the vice-rector at the University of Central America. Cardenal credits his activism with his own clerical training with the poor in Medellín, Colombia, in 1969. Following his return to Nicaragua, Cardenal participated with his students in hunger strikes, public demonstrations, and church sit-ins (Zwerling and Martin 1985: 75). His involvement in these activities eventually led to his dismissal as vice-rector of the university and opened more opportunities for

47

him to work with Father Molina. Together the two priests created the Christian Revolutionary Movement (MCR). The movement gradually extended its work into communities beyond Riguero. Adolfo Reyes was one of those communities.

Mercedes Ortega is a small woman in her fifties who explained that her involvement in the revolution grew out of her contact with the student movement. Today, Mercedes is an active member of the Christian base community of Adolfo Reyes. Her membership came out of the student contact of those years. In reflecting back, she remembered that in the mid-1970s she began listening to the students who were coming to the barrio to speak of government injustices. "I listened intensely to the things they were saying. They spoke not only of the political reality here but also about our social situation. From these discussions my consciousness grew," she said.

Daysi Quiutauilla Rocha, a neighbor of Mercedes, also remembered those years. She explained that the university students had come to speak to the community about the treatment of political prisoners and about their impoverished condition. "You see, we had for so many years resigned ourselves to a life of poverty and hard work. This was just the way things were, and no one really believed that life in this country could be any different."

Daysi Rocha is a large, round woman. Her dark eyes and skin, like Mercedes', suggest a mixed heritage of indigenous roots. Her dark brown eyes fought back tears as she recalled that more than anything else, "the students and priests brought the community hope, and a vision for a new Nicaragua."

Student activism grew in those years. Archbishop Obando y Bravo several times endorsed the student protests (Booth 1985: 135). When student leaders and priests were arrested by the regime, the bishops came to their defense. Still, despite this show of solidarity, important distinctions divided the Nicaraguan church. While priests like Father Molina and Father Cardenal became intellectual defenders of the liberation movement, members of the Catholic hierarchy, like Archbishop Obando, remained reluctant to condone efforts that called for the dictator's removal. While the thrust of the traditional church had been to criticize President Somoza, the archbishop continued to seek peaceful means for bringing political reform, not revolution.

Revolutionary fervor in Nicaragua nevertheless continued to build. With or without the church, it appeared that the liberation process was taking on a life of its own. For many Nicaraguans there could be no turning back.

CHAPTER FOUR

Radicalization of the Popular Church

UNDER THE GUIDANCE of the progressive clergy, the Christian base communities in Nicaragua flourished. As we have seen, the liberation movement grew out of base community formation and by the early 1970s was furthered by student involvement and solidarity. For the communities of San Pablo, Adolfo Reyes, and San Judas this activism often took the form of protests to obtain things like electricity, a cemetery, or fair water prices (see also Williams 1989). For most Nicaraguans these activities were their first experiences in organized political struggle.

President Somoza was not patient with these challenges to his authority. In the 1970s Christians increasingly became the target of government resistance and, in many cases, violent repression. Somoza's decision to repress Christian agitation had unintended consequences for the regime. One consequence of this terror was that many members of the Christian base communities shifted their support from political reform to advocacy for insurrection.

While the relationship between the Somoza regime and the grass-roots church deteriorated, the affinity between the regime and elite sectors of Nicaraguan society was also strained. Luz Elena Mejía, a member of Nicaragua's bourgeoisie, remembered that despite the fact that she and her family were living well, they were not blind to the abuses of the Somoza family.

Sitting in the garden of her beautiful Spanish-style home, she recalled the abuses of his authority: "Somoza ruled as an autocrat. He did not tolerate challenges to his power. In fact, it was not uncommon for political opponents to be jailed here. Before the earthquake most people knew better than to get involved in politics."

Luz Mejía was referring to a devastating earthquake that struck the capital city of Managua in December 1972. Luz believed that after the crisis, however, things started to change. She remembered that in the wake of the disaster people were less willing to remain silent over the abuses they saw. During the international relief effort, the overt greed of the Somoza group reached shocking levels even for Nicaraguan standards. She recalled that it was not uncommon for the National Guard to divert food and medicine deliveries so that the supplies could be sold for profit. Help for poor neighborhoods was ignored. Somoza himself looted international funds and his companies seized control over reconstruction projects (see also Booth 1985 and Gilbert 1986).

In the community of Adolfo Reyes, Daysi Rocha recalled the terrible suffering of the city where thousands of people had died and thousands more remained homeless. She also remembered the shocking behavior of National Guard forces, who neglected the earthquake's victims. She and her neighbors recalled that everything one needed to survive had a price, "even blood." The experience was radicalizing for her community. She suggested that in this climate, worship services turned into politicized discussions denouncing the regime. Even the Catholic hierarchy began to speak out publicly against the abuses of the government.

Luz Mejía remembered that in both religious and political circles there were discussions about the need for reform: "Everywhere you went people were talking about social justice." These discussions paralleled a growing defiance among Nicaraguans. Luz Mejía recalled that it was in this climate that churches were taken over by students and clergy and that worker demonstrations and protests spread. All these actions occurred in the context of tremendous suffering, the effects of which unified many sectors of society against the dictator.

51

Among the poor and especially among progressive sectors of the church, the appalling behavior of some in the relief effort exacerbated grass-roots radicalization. At the same time the excessive behaviors by the state officials formally ended elite cooperation with the dictatorship (Gilbert 1986; Booth 1985). The growing alienation between the government and the Nicaraguan people did not mean there was unanimity over the proper solution to the crisis. By the mid-1970s, the majority of Nicaraguans were divided over a proper course for dealing with the dictator. Conservative camps in the country argued for a peaceful transfer of power through political succession. More liberal forces argued for the peaceful transfer of power through democratic elections. The radical opposition that was developing in Nicaragua argued for Somoza's removal through nonpeaceful means (if necessary) and went further in demanding major economic and social reform. These public demands for removing President Somoza ultimately led to a monumental and historic fusion. The decade of Nicaraguan political history that began in 1972 reveals the story of how these diverse currents finally came together, but it was the beginning of an uneasy and suspicious alliance.

THE ENTRANCE OF THE FSLN

Around the time of the earthquake a small guerrilla group, the Sandinista National Liberation Front (FSLN), increased its agitation in the rural areas of the country. Patricia Mulligan was a student at the National University at that time, and she remembered that in the city they knew very little of the guerrilla movement. Of those who knew of the movement, "most perceived the Sandinistas as communists," she said.

Apparently little collaboration existed between most Nicaraguans and the rebel forces. "No one in the country had taken them very seriously," Patricia explained. In time, however, many Nicaraguans, including Patricia Mulligan, came to be active supporters of the guerrilla group.

Patricia's remarks offer a brief glance into the differences that later developed within the Christian liberation movement. As early as 1971, some Catholics were awakening to an option for a more radicalized kind of thinking, one that ultimately transcended religious faith. Patricia Mulligan believed that the catalyst for this change in consciousness grew out of the agitation caused by the Sandinista National Liberation Front.

The guerrilla movement was founded in 1961 by three young Nicaraguans who had been active in leftist student movements during the 1950s (Christian 1986: 31). Carlos Fonseca, Tomás Borge, and Silvio Mayorga chose the name for their organization from Nicaragua's early nationalist hero, Augusto César Sandino.

In the late 1920s Augusto Sandino had lived as a poor campesino and had dedicated his life to expelling U.S. occupation forces from Nicaragua. Sandino's prolonged engagement in a guerrilla war against the U.S. Marines earned him great respect among many sectors of society. His subsequent death at the hands of the rising National Guard general, Anastasio Somoza, earned him the title of Nicaragua's greatest liberation hero.

It has been written that Augusto Sandino was staunchly anti-imperialist but that his ideology was also strongly populist in character (Booth 1985). Despite the accusations of many of his critics, Sandino was not a Marxist. In fact, he had apparently distinguished himself from the Marxist intellectuals of his time. Sandino etched out this difference by disagreeing with Marxist thinkers who were at that time advocating the overthrow of the capitalist system (Booth 1985; Berryman in Girardi 1989). Sandino argued that it was far more important for Nicaragua to attain national sovereignty than to concern itself with the country's capitalist structure.

Sandino was not a Marxist nor was he a Christian. His biographers have argued that at heart he was both a nationalist and a Theosophist (O'Brien 1986; Mulligan 1991). Apparently he was not a religious man, but spiritual issues—and his belief in God—played a formative role in his thinking. Berryman (in Girardi 1989) argues that Augusto Sandino was an early visionary. His spiritual thinking enabled him to bridge eschatological themes with his arguments about the liberation of oppressed people. In the struggle for Nicaragua's liberation he also apparently understood the need for broad alliances.

The group of young men who took Sandino's name for their cause had been—unlike their hero—greatly inspired by Marxist ideology (Christian 1986: 31–32). The three men found Marxist theory useful for analyzing their country's reality, and they employed its intellectual tools to clarify their own objectives and strategies. Carlos Fonseca, the FSLN's most outstanding intellectual, was a serious student of Sandino's life and had written extensively about the leader's struggle against Yankee imperialism (Girardi 1989). Early in the group's formation, Carlos Fonseca had urged FSLN members to study Sandino's writings. In fact, it was on Fonseca's advice that one of the group's members, Tomás Borge, sought out Esteban Pavletich, the man who had served as Sandino's personal secretary (Vanden and Prevost 1993: 6, 36).

After involvement in revolutionary activity in Nicaragua, Tomás Borge had been exiled to South America in the 1960s. While in exile he located Pavletich in Peru. After the two men met, Borge clandestinely returned to Nicaragua. Back in the mountains of his homeland, he and Fonseca began laying the groundwork for a highly nationalistic and strongly populist ideology. Together the two men used Sandino's populist ideas to argue for a revolutionary, proletarian struggle. Indeed, Fonseca's legacy was his genius in merging the class-oriented arguments of Marx with Sandino's nationalistic thought (see Girardi 1989; O'Brien 1986).

There was another unique element in the thinking and strategy of the Sandinista leaders. Despite their Marxist leanings and despite the fact that the group openly identified itself as Marxist-Leninist, the FSLN's ideology largely represented a departure from orthodox Marxism (Girardi 1989). O'Brien (1986: 66) suggests that what grew up in Nicaragua was a "homespun variety of Marxism recognized in the country as Sandinismo." This new ideology was a native response to the alien domination of capitalist countries. In fact, one of the most remarkable features of Sandinista Marxism was its radical departure from the Marxism that had developed in the Soviet Union and Eastern Europe.

Vanden and Prevost (1993) suggest that the leaders of the

FSLN developed a non-Stalinist Marxism, one that broke with the old authoritarianism of the past. Not only did it depart from the "stolid, bureaucratic state socialism that Stalin and his followers had developed in the Soviet Union and Eastern Europe," but it was also "much more in touch with the democratic, popular dimension of Marxism" (ibid.: 6). In this respect, Vanden and Prevost have argued that Sandinismo was much more compatible with Nicaragua's contemporary reality.

The Sandinistas thus evolved their own theory of mass struggle using a mix of Marxist theory and Sandino's populist thought. Because Sandinismo was seeking a liberation of the oppressed and exploited of Nicaragua, it resonated well with the new aspect of social Christian thinking exhibited in liberation theology. Despite the fact that the leaders of the FSLN were not Christian in the traditional sense of the word, Sandinismo offered an unusual blend of Christian precepts with the notions of class struggle. Tomás Borge articulated this view when he argued that the "revolution was on behalf of all human beings, but—as with Christ—above all for the poor" (Randall 1983: 77).

This ideological fusion of class struggle with the common theme of love for the poor attracted the growing attention of the progressive clergy. Girardi (1989) suggests that it was this very commitment to further the interests of the poor that was at the root of the collaboration between many Nicaraguan Christians and the Sandinistas.

CHRISTIAN RADICALIZATION

For Christians, and particularly for Father Uriel Molina, it was not inconsequential that the founding of the Sandinista Front in 1961 coincided with the opening of the Second Vatican Council in 1962 (Randall 1983: 130). The climate arising from Vatican II helped to foster the conditions favorable for a future relationship between members of the popular church and the Sandinista guerrillas.

Progressive leaders within the grass-roots church found intellectual accommodation with the Marxist thinking of the Sandinista leaders. Father Molina explained that this accommodation was encouraged by the church's preferential option for the poor: "The Medellín conference had legitimized the right for Christian intellectuals to seek analytical tools capable for understanding the Latin American reality. In Nicaragua, Christian leaders were also seeking a strategic perspective that could nurture spiritual love as a transforming historical force." According to Father Molina, it was precisely this option for love and for the poor that attracted them to Marxist theory.

Historically the Catholic Church had long recognized social injustices in the world. Pre–Vatican II doctrine, however, had largely expected transformation of the world to come about through an individualized conversion process (Gibellini 1987: 48–50). In contrast to the church's thinking, Karl Marx's work had recognized worldly injustices as structural in nature and, as a consequence, he advocated class struggle in bringing revolutionary change. Contrary to the church's thinking, Marx understood change as a product of the clash between man and his social environment (Macridis 1992: 105–09). Marx theorized that the inevitable tension between the beneficiaries of the system, and the increasing exploitation and dehumanization of the worker, would eventually foster a revolutionary conscience on the part of the proletariat.

Marx saw little value in religion for developing a revolutionary consciousness. He had argued that social institutions like the church were tools used by the state to legitimize and maintain its social order. He argued that religion served as a means for reinforcing passivity and resignation among the lower classes. Indeed, Marxists have always understood religion as essentially reactionary. Believers will never be revolutionary in the full sense, so the conventional wisdom goes, because their loyalty is to another logic, namely that of the church. Indeed, Marxists have believed that religious faith jeopardized—even undermined—the quality of revolutionary commitment (Engels 1964: 99). The struggle against the church, therefore, had always been seen as an essential task of traditional Marxist theory. In Nicaragua such assumptions were being challenged. In the case of many Christians it appears that participation in the revolution was not despite their faith but rather a consequence of it (Gutiérrez 1986).

It is important to recall that in the post–Vatican II climate poverty was being acknowledged among progressive elements in the church as more than just a historical accident. Christian intellectuals were acknowledging the fact that poverty was a product of faulty societal and economic structures. At the same time, Medellín's advocacy for consciousness-raising activities was providing Nicaraguans with a means for "linking how the needs of the many were relating to the wants of the few" (Serra 1985: 154).

It has been argued that progressive elements within the grass-roots church wanted to impart a reformist—even a revolutionary—consciousness to the poor to undertake the same task theorized by Marx's proletariat (Macridis 1992: 227–28). Many leaders of the people's church began advocating radical economic reforms in the direction of socialism (ibid.). Thus, in Nicaragua cooperation grew between many people, both among the religious and among those of the guerrilla movement. Father Molina suggested that this cooperation was facilitated in the country by the special convergence between Christianity and Sandinista Marxism (see also Girardi 1989).

Alberto Morales, a coordinator of theological work at the Antonio Valdivieso Center in Managua, suggested that during the revolutionary experience the two camps—the Sandinistas and members of the progressive clergy—joined in a marriage of ideals and goals. This union was facilitated by the church's preferential option for the poor and the Sandinistas' class option that sought to defend the interests of the majority. The home-grown variety of Sandinismo was apparently instrumental in this fusion. Of course, not every member of the popular church embraced the stated goals of the Sandinista party. Nor would all progressive Catholics support Sandinista demands for a new economic order. Clearly, the grass-roots church did attract Nicaraguans who were actively committed to the FSLN. Yet while some members of the popular church were obviously sympathetic to the Marxist ideology that evolved in Nicaragua, most had never been exposed to nor had formally studied Marxism. The ideological differences and political implications of these realities grew more glaring as events unfolded in the country.

For the Sandinistas the early relationship that developed with Christians was made possible by the pronouncements of the Second Vatican Council and by the grass-roots work of the liberation clergy. Father Ernesto Cardenal was the first of the clergy to attract their attention (Foroohar 1989: 117).

Father Cardenal's Solentiname community had grown more political after the priest had returned from a visit to Cuba in 1973 (Sigmund 1990: 119). Cardenal had been impressed by what he had seen in Havana, where clergy had begun bridging the principles of Marxism with the precepts of social Christianity. His work captured the imagination of the Sandinista leadership.

The early contacts between the Sandinistas and the liberation clergy in the 1970s were primarily tactical (Girardi 1989: 32–33). Christian leaders explained that the Sandinistas were very conscious of the fact that they needed a strong, broad-based movement to carry out their struggle. They recognized the usefulness of the Christian movement for this purpose (see also Randall 1983: 166).

It was obvious that the Sandinista Front could not work openly in Nicaragua. On the other hand, the Christian movement had the freedom to do so. It was not lost on the Sandinista leadership that CEB leaders could advocate the need for radical change yet still be protected by the power of the Cross.

The popular church was also extraordinarily special because its leaders could move beyond the poor to include contact with members of the elite. For the Sandinistas this, too, would be an invaluable channel for propagating their revolutionary ideology.

Tomás Borge was the first Sandinista leader to make contact with Father Ernesto Cardenal. In summer 1968 he invited the Trappist monk to a meeting to discuss the mutual interests of the Sandinistas and the progressive clergy (Foroohar 1989: 117). This early contact suggested that an intellectual appreciation of each other's goals existed between the guerrilla forces and some members of the grass-roots church.

Carlos Fonseca, who joined the discussions, wrote of the possibility of working with the religious. He equated the tradition of the early Christians with the commitment of the Sandinistas who were also willing to give their lives for the poor and oppressed (Randall 1983; Foroohar 1989).

Initial meetings between the Sandinistas and the progressive clergy led to further and broader contact in the months to come. Father Miguel d'Escoto, a Nicaraguan Maryknoll missionary, was among these early contacts. Father d'Escoto was already involved in housing projects for the poor. He argued that the church's commitment to the oppressed opened the door to dialogue with the guerrillas. He also suggested that he found the Sandinistas capable of accepting Christians into their armed struggle (Lernoux 1982: 102)

Father d'Escoto was joined in his revolutionary work with the Sandinistas by both Father Uriel Molina and Father Fernando Cardenal. The founders of the Christian Revolutionary Movement (MCR) had by that time extended their student group's work outside barrio Riguero. Father Molina explained that by the early 1970s the student movement had begun using Marxism as a method of analysis (Sigmund 1990: 122). This method had been inspired by his own visit to the Christians for Socialism Conference that had met three months earlier (in 1972) in the country of Chile. Having recently returned from the conference, Molina explained that he had become convinced of the importance of Marxist-Christian cooperation against the Somoza dictatorship. Prior to the conference, he had apparently been incapable of accepting the idea of armed struggle (Christian 1986: 246). While in Chile, however, a leading member of the FSLN, Víctor Tirado, made contact with him, and the two men developed strong and lasting ties.

Father Molina recalled that Tirado was interested in uniting the Christian experience with that of the Sandinista struggle. After several important contacts, Molina returned to Nicaragua a changed man (Foroohar 1989: 79).

59

For the next several years Father Molina maintained clandestine contact with the Sandinistas, and his grass-roots church served as a gathering place for them (Christian 1986: 246–47). Father Fernando Cardenal, who assisted Molina in this endeavor, believed that his own clerical training with the poor in Colombia had influenced his choice to work with the Sandinistas. Having returned to Nicaragua in 1970, he had begun working with the guerrillas because he was convinced that revolution was the only hope for the poor. His work in Colombia had convinced him of the church's limitations in its ability to address the poor's material and spiritual needs. He said that he had come to recognize the larger system of oppression under which the poor struggled. Like others in the revolutionary movement, he became convinced that the entire structure had to be transformed (Zwerling and Martin 1985: 74–75). In 1972 Father Cardenal declared himself a Marxist Christian and began advocating the need for class struggle against the Somoza regime (Christian 1986: 246).

Similar convictions came gradually to other members of the Christian movement. For Father Edgar Parrales the commitment to join the revolution began with his involvement in the student movement. Because he was both a priest and a lawyer, he had represented some of the university students who had been arrested by the Somoza government. He said that the experience for him was radicalizing. He, too, became convinced of the need for revolutionary change and, as a consequence, he participated in demonstrations, gave national and international press interviews, and used the pulpit to speak out against the dictatorship (Zwerling and Martin 1985).

Father Ernesto Cardenal represented the Sandinistas internationally, arguing the legitimacy of the underground movement. In 1976 he appeared before the Russell Tribunal in Rome as a spokesperson for the Sandinistas and denounced the violations of human rights in Latin America. A year later he left the Solentiname community to solicit support for the Sandinista cause from solidarity groups in different countries of the world (CEPAD 1991: 3).

After the initial contacts between members of the progressive clergy and the Sandinistas, the student movement became more radicalized. Incrementally, students and priests began collaborating with the underground movement. According to Sigmund (1990: 122), the MCR played an instrumental role in the integration of Nicaraguan Christians in the revolutionary process. By the mid 1970s, student organizations adopted Marxist theory to deepen the tenets of liberation theology. According to Christians in the grass-roots church, Sandinista Marxism enhanced their growing political commitment (ibid.).

By no means was this revolutionary commitment inclusive of all CEB members. Not all progressive Christians were willing to accept the total dismantling of Nicaraguan society. In fact, the tenacious marriage between members of the liberation camp and the Sandinista guerrillas eventually divided the popular church in Nicaragua. Disagreement grew over the social aspirations and objectives of the Sandinistas and of some liberation Christians. While many revolutionary members of the grass-roots church dedicated themselves to constructing a new Marxist society, others sought a Nicaragua that could more authentically internalize the values of social Christianity. For these progressive Catholics this new society did not necessarily demand a classless society. In time these contradictions grew more apparent. However, in the immediate aftermath of the earthquake crisis, these differences were submerged for a larger, more immediate objective: the removal of the dictator, Somoza.

CHRISTIANS IN REVOLUTION

The priests' decision to join the struggle and to provide a means for student participation had important consequences for many other Christians. For instance, Mercedes Ortega in Adolfo Reyes remembered that she was moved by discussions concerning the place of women in Nicaragua. The students who came to her barrio spoke of many forms of oppression, including the subordinate place of women. Mercedes explained that she began to recognize the need for a radical restructuring of society if the issue of women's oppression was ever to be addressed. She said that, as a consequence, she gradually came to believe that revolution

61

was a good way not only to end the Somoza dictatorship but also to liberate women from machismo culture.

Not all members of the base community joined the underground movement. Some Christians remained apprehensive and continued to look to the Catholic hierarchy for guidance. While some progressive priests were becoming intellectual defenders of the FSLN, members of the Catholic hierarchy remained reluctant to condone revolutionary efforts. Archbishop Obando's hesitancy in supporting insurrection reflected the church's deep-seated fears of revolution. After all, the church had little practical experience with social and political revolution. Indeed, the cases of Mexico, Cuba, and Chile seemed to suggest that revolution was inherently threatening to the institution's power. It appeared that in Nicaragua similar fears existed that revolution would swallow the church's identity (Williams 1989: 230–35; Mulligan 1991).

While progressive priests were agitating for revolution, members of the Catholic hierarchy sought to encourage reform. They discouraged the active involvement of priests and religious lay leaders in politicized organizations. When it was necessary, the bishops defended publicly those priests accused of revolutionary activities, but at the same time they maintained strong pressure on the clergy to abstain from such tasks.

The hierarchy's opposition to revolution worked to confuse, frustrate, and alienate many Catholics. It took several years to discern clearly the consequences of the hierarchy's position, but its effects are well pronounced in Nicaraguan society today. In 1972, however, the bishops' pressure did little to discourage a small percentage of priests from joining the Sandinistas' armed struggle. One such clergyman was Father Gaspár García Laviana, a Spanish priest who had been serving the poor in the Nicaraguan parish of San Juan del Sur. Father Gaspár was disappointed over the hierarchy's lack of involvement in the struggles of the poor, and he eventually lost hope in the legal channels for change (Mulligan 1991: 99–112). In time, Father Gaspár concluded that armed struggle was his only available option. In a letter explaining his decision to join the Sandinistas, Gaspár wrote: "The hunger . . . for justice of the crushed people whom I serve as a priest demands more than the consolation of words—it requires action" (ibid.: 112).

Gaspár's decision to join the guerrilla movement appeared to have been a difficult one. Father Fernando Cardenal remembered that he and Gaspár had spent time discussing the pros and cons of joining the Sandinistas. His decision rested on the conviction that his participation as a priest would discredit Somoza's campaign to convince Catholics that armed struggle could never be an option (ibid.: 105).

Father Gaspár fought alongside the Sandinistas and was killed in battle on December 11, 1978. His example and death inspired others to join the insurrection. Rafael Solís, who fought on the southern front with Father Gaspár, remembered him as such an inspiration. Solís explained that growing revolutionary consciousness led Catholics like himself to search for an adequate political ideology (in Zwerling and Martin 1985: 36–37). He believed that priests like Father Gaspár had grown to recognize their lack of political analysis. He also has suggested that the value of Sandinismo was that it provided Christians both with analysis and with concrete strategies in bringing social change (ibid.).

For other Catholics, like Piada and Juan Tijerino, the entrance of priests into the armed struggle was radicalizing. The clergy's commitment to the insurrection and Somoza's increasing oppression against the CEBs convinced them to join the struggle. Their participation, however, took a different form. Piada explained that she and Juan decided to use their energy and their wealth to buy arms for the popular movement. They also decided to work with consciousness-raising activities, particularly among Nicaraguan youths.

Piada emphatically explained that their motivation for joining the insurrection was a Christian—not a political—one. She argued that their conversion was religious in origin and that it had much to do with the recognition that without an insurrection the Somoza regime would not allow a peaceful transfer of power or steps toward democratization. When asked about Marxism, Piada laughed: "I have never read Marx! My husband, Juan, might have been exposed to some in his university training, but I believe his motivation was the same as mine. We believed, as Christians, that we had to chip away at this evil structure."

She adamantly denied any suggestion that the priests at her church had convinced her or her husband to become politicized members of the underground movement. Piada explained that in the climate of growing public dissension they simply felt moved to opt for insurrection. "The priests didn't direct us to be political," she explained. "To be political was to be true to our faith. It grew out of our faith in the liberating model of Christ."

Piada's comments offer early glimpses into the subtle differences that developed and ultimately fragmented the popular Christian movement. Her commitment to the insurrection grew less from her attraction to Sandinista Marxism than it did from the demands of her faith. Like that of so many other progressive Catholics, Piada's and Juan's devotion to the anti-Somoza movement eventually came into conflict with those who believed that they were fighting a revolution for a radical transformation of Nicaraguan society.

These tensions were also apparent in rural parts of Nicaragua. Uli Schmidtt, a theologian and former member of the Antonio Valdivieso Center, discussed his study of the campesino movement in Nicaragua. Professor Schmidtt explained that the Delegate of the Word program had become very strong in the late 1960s. "But peasant leaders who advocated change were not coming from a revolutionary perspective. Rather, they were oriented around a mystical one," he explained.

According to Schmidtt's work, Vatican II and Medellín were important influences in Nicaragua but the lay movements that arose from them were very traditional in nature. For example, he argued that in the rural areas of the country "the communities were strongly oriented around prayer, singing, and devotional practice. The program grew into a revolutionary movement as a consequence of the campesino effort in Honduras. But this movement in Honduras in the early 1960s centered around agrarian reform as well and labor rights."

At the end of the 1960s, the Latin American church had recognized that the campesino movement in Honduras shared similar goals and objectives for improving the life of the poor throughout the region. Professor Schmidtt explained that this was an important influence in contributing to the social and political awareness of Nicaraguan lay leaders. "With this influence the Delegate of the Word program became more radicalized, particularly with the growth and strength of the Sandinistas," Schmidtt said. In the 1960s and early 1970s, the guerrillas had begun making contact with leaders of the program.

Schmidtt's study suggests that the Sandinistas used the delegates to do their political work within a religious structure. For instance, "the campesino church participated with the Sandinistas in passive ways, by allowing them to hold meetings and by providing the guerrillas with food and other supplies," Schmidtt explained.

As a consequence of this cooperation, delegate leaders became frequent targets of National Guard terror. In the city of Estelí, peasants still recall the terror. When asked about their experiences, residents were willing to recount stories of the attacks against church people, to discuss the murder of priests and lay leaders, and to share their memories of the arbitrary arrests and torture of members of their communities.

Such memories were also mentioned by CEB members in San Pablo and Adolfo Reyes. In the latter community, CEB member Dominga Urbina remembered how the National Guard would raid their neighborhoods. "The Guardia would come unexpectedly and loot our homes and terrorize our neighbors. Innocent people were arrested and never seen again," she said.

Indiscriminate atrocities committed by the National Guard worked to radicalize many progressive Christians who otherwise might not have joined the insurrection. The persecution of the faithful presented many Catholics with a clear dilemma: They could remain silent and in their silence be accomplices, or they could raise their voices in defiance. Many Christians in Nicaragua chose the latter course of action.

In San Pablo, Catholics came together to participate in student strikes and the takeover of churches in Managua. CEB member Rafael Valdéz remembered that by the mid-1970s the community became increasingly aggressive. He explained that as they continued to use the methods of liberation theology—to see, to judge, and to act—the grass-roots church took on political acts of defiance.

For example, the grass-roots church decided to protest the treatment of Somoza's political prisoners. One act included the takeover of the national cathedral. Rafael Valdéz remembered that those not involved in the takeover stayed outside in self-constructed booths, which were used as barricades to help protect the protesters inside and which served as points of warning and as food stations.

These protests inspired greater National Guard violence. Residents in San Pablo recalled that the National Guard made random incursions into the community, beating and arresting innocent people. Rafael Valdéz explained that as a result of these visits the community created a Commission for Civil Defense to safeguard the barrio. In time, the commission began making more formal contacts with the Sandinista guerrillas. "We would use our homes for the shelter of arms and as safe-houses for the guerrillas when they came to the community to speak to us," he said.

The commission took responsibility for sheltering and feeding the guerrillas during these underground visits. Members of the commission also erected buildings that appeared to be legitimate businesses rather than the Sandinista headquarters that they were. Rafael Valdéz explained that this activity was a big risk for the families who were involved: "If you got caught you could be shot on the spot."

Despite the dangers, the community's participation in these activities continued to grow. Rafael believed that participation grew as their religious faith deepened. "Our worship services were no longer theoretical. We had evolved from reflection and discussion to taking action. We became devoted to the revolutionary movement because we believed self-defense was both right and necessary," he said.

Julio and Amélida Sequeira shared the stories of their own involvement in the insurrection. They explained that their home in San Pablo was a safe-house for the Sandinistas during the struggle. As a consequence, both were on the infamous Somoza "hit list."

The Sequeiras were forced to flee to the city of Chontales where the church helped them take their children to relatives in Costa Rica. Once the children had been sent to safety, the Sequeiras returned to Chontales and organized a resistance group based on faith. Using the method they had been taught in the community of San Pablo, they read the Bible with their new neighbors and sought guidance together. Like other Catholics, Julio and Amélida argued that their motivation was religious, not political. "We never picked up arms to fight the dictatorship, but we picked up the Bible to pass on the good news of liberation," Julio explained. This news apparently convinced others to raise their voices against the dictatorship.

Julita Soza believed that the community of Adolfo Reyes was influenced by the radicalization of San Pablo. She credited the work of the student movement for her own involvement in insurrection activities. She explained that her neighbors used to meet with students who distributed pamphlets about the FSLN. The pamphlets were passed around with instructions that people were to read them carefully and then destroy them. Julita remembered that the pamphlets offered a new vision for Nicaragua, one that would guarantee social justice.

She committed herself to the struggle. "I would dress as a street vendor and wear two aprons. Hidden under the first apron I would place the students' pamphlets. Then I would go house to house and distribute the material," she said. It was dangerous work. When the National Guard learned of this activity, guardsmen began to follow many of the residents, including Julita. Julita and her neighbors joined together to protect one another. They quickly learned to walk in groups and never alone. When the students staged a public protest, the community would circle them with torches to protect them. Julita remembered that their courage for these activities was intensified by their solidarity and by the sense of liberation generated by their revolutionary chants and songs.

Julita Soza also recalled that the students taught the community how to give medical aid, and she, like others, used this knowledge to teach other people in their neighborhood. Medical supplies were often hidden underground in her home. One day the box was taken to the local school where it was found and destroyed by the National Guard.

During the struggle the community of Adolfo Reyes created a commission that stood watch at night. Some CEB members like Angela Ortega assisted in hiding the guerrillas in her home. Her neighbor, Daysi Rocha, explained the danger that these decisions always implied. The community was not immune from the terror of Somoza's National Guard. The soldiers came unannounced and randomly searched the neighborhood. No one felt safe, not even in their own homes.

Like Julita, Daysi Rocha distributed propaganda for the FSLN. Her assignment to distribute the pamphlets in the marketplace and to talk to people on the buses was the beginning of her involvement in the insurrection. She explained that her commitment to the Sandinistas was a result of the work of liberation priests. One of the clergy in her community had asked her to allow use of her home as a safe-house. Daysi explained that she trusted the priest and so her home became a security house for students and guerrillas. "It was a safe-house for boys and girls and we eventually made explosives there. I also sewed red and black flags that were used to distinguish Sandinista sympathizers," she said. Daysi explained that the red color of the flags stood for blood and the color black for death. "The community was committed to fighting to the death in order to bring a new way of life to the people of Nicaragua," she remarked.

In San Judas, Indiana Larios explained the radicalization of her community. She remembered that many people died because of the National Guard's indiscriminate raids on their homes. Indiana said that because the government thought all young people were the enemy, in San Judas young people were rounded up, taken to the mountains, and killed. Many others simply disappeared. "I remember that many people were afraid to leave their houses. During one base community meeting the soldiers came and took ten of our men. Three of them never returned," Indiana said.

As a consequence of the terror, many residents in San Judas gave their homes to the guerrillas. As in other barrios, their homes served as safe-houses. It was all done very quietly. Indiana Larios recalled that at this time she, too, was on Somoza's enemy list; the National Guard had discovered her involvement in the safe-house effort. She recounted that one evening the soldiers came to San Judas carrying a picture of her. "At that time there were two Indiana Larioses living in the barrio and by chance they went to the wrong house. Before they could arrive to my home I was warned of their search by my neighbors and I fled with my children to the church," she said. Father Rafael Aragón took Indiana and her children immediately to Sandino City, where they were hidden for several days. A week later she went into hiding and began clandestine work for the Sandinistas.

Indiana Larios, Rafael Valdéz, the Sequeira family, Julita Soza, and Daysi Rocha represent a segment of Nicaraguan Catholics who became involved with the underground out of religious conviction. For many of these progressive Christians, revolutionary activity was predicated on their faith in a loving and merciful God. Rafael Valdéz articulated a common and repeated assertion: "that the God of liberation is one of justice, and love, one who struggles against all that oppresses."

Like many of her contemporaries, Indiana Larios explained that as she came to understand the Bible she believed that she had to help the movement in some way. She believed that she was being commanded to love her neighbors. She remembered reading in the Bible that "the greatest love is the love for our brothers. So while my first motivation was my faith, my second motivation was the witness of the death of so many innocent people. I thought to myself that if I was going to die it might as well be for a cause."

On the island of Solentiname, Miriam Guevara recalled that

the violence exhibited by the National Guard convinced many within her community to join the Sandinistas. "It was through the gospel that we became aware that the human family should live in more humane conditions," she said. Miriam explained that members of the community were witnesses to the oppression in her country. "The community wanted to do something—not simply go to mass. We wanted to do more than discuss the gospel; we wanted to carry it out," she remarked. Miriam said that the community chose to side with the guerrillas because many of their members were convinced that the Sandinistas shared many of the same concerns.

The year 1974 appears to have been a major turning point in the history of the revolution. In the winter of that year, the Sandinistas staged an impressive and successful kidnapping. The spectacle was planned to coincide with Somoza's reelection as president (Booth 1985: 142).

On the night of December 27, the Sandinistas assaulted the home of José María Castillo Quant, a wealthy cotton exporter and former minister of agriculture. On that night, Quant was hosting a party in honor of a number of influential figures. At 10:50 P.M., thirteen Sandinistas attacked the house and took the entire party hostage. Included among the hostages was President Somoza's brother-in-law (ibid.).

The kidnapping incident was a significant success for the guerrilla movement. Not only did the Sandinistas secure the release of a number of political prisoners (including Daniel Ortega) but the Somoza government also permitted the release of two Sandinista communiqués issued to the people of Nicaragua. Patricia Mulligan recalled the historic event.

"Students in Managua were wild with excitement, and I remember that it was in that moment that people were beginning to accord the guerrilla movement with a greater seriousness," she said. Shortly after the incident there was a constant denouncing of both press censorship and National Guard abuses. Patricia explained that by this time she herself had become involved with a revolutionary musical group. "Our mission was to sing protest songs in the barrios as a means for raising greater consciousness," she recalled.

Music was just one of many student-initiated activities. Patricia Mulligan remembered other student-led activities including those that assisted people to resist National Guard offensives. For example, students worked in building neighborhood barricades. The students dug up paving bricks from the streets and used them to erect walls for shelter and protection. Students also served as neighborhood watchdogs and helped with underground communication by serving as couriers for the Sandinista guerrillas.

By 1974, in the community of Adolfo Reyes, Mercedes Ortega decided to become involved with the resistance. "At the time I realized that I could make a contribution," she said. "You see, I was a dressmaker, so I had been asked to make black and red scarves that could be used to designate supporters of the FSLN." Mercedes spent nights making the scarves and in the morning would take them to a place for distribution. "In time I also made cloths to cover the coffins of the boys who were dying in the mountains," she recalled.

All the death and terror of those years influenced many Christians to join the insurrectionary struggle. Mercedes said that during the struggle she also underwent a personal conversion of religious faith. She left her Protestant church and became a practicing Catholic. "You see, Protestantism was very strict and there were always many rules you had to follow. My greatest conflict, however, came about as a result of my interest in the guerrilla activity. I wanted to be a Sandinista and my church said this was sinful. So I left the Protestant faith," she explained.

Mercedes Ortega said that after this decision her courage grew. She found support within the base community and she offered her home as a haven for the guerrillas. She recalled how the Sandinistas would clandestinely enter her home to discuss their strategies and goals. They also used her house to hide their weapons. "We buried them under the floorboards," she recalled, laughing at the memory.

Mercedes also began speaking to her neighbors about governmental injustices, and she served as a Sandinista courier. In reflecting back, Mercedes said that people were beginning to open their eyes to the Nicaraguan reality and that by the time of the final offensive the people were in solidarity with each other.

Patricia Mulligan remembered that after the successful kidnapping episode of December 27, Somoza imposed three years of martial law and that a "tense calm descended over the country." It was a time of greater violence and fear. Most civil liberties were suspended and all real and suspected opponents of the regime were terrorized by the National Guard (see also Booth 1985: 157).

During the imposition of martial law, Yamileth Ortega Sequeira, Mercedes Ortega's granddaughter, witnessed some of the raids in Adolfo Reyes. "I was just a child during the insurrection, and what I remember most is always being afraid," she said. Yamileth was living in her grandmother's home and she recalled that the house had constant activity. "Guerrillas came in and out all hours of the day. One day I remember that one of them was making explosives in the house. He threw it outside to test the device and the bomb went off," she exclaimed. The National Guard arrived shortly thereafter. "They rounded everyone up, including the neighbors, and they threatened us. They said that if we didn't tell them who had done this they would not hesitate in killing all of us," Yamileth said.

Apparently, as Yamileth remembered it, no one in the barrio was willing to speak. Yamileth's mother, who was among those detained, stepped forward and challenged the young soldiers. Yamileth recalled that she had never seen her mother so angry: "My mother demanded that the soldiers leave. She commanded that they kill everyone because she assured them that no one was going to say anything! I was scared to death, but my mother's bravery convinced the soldiers to turn away and they left us."

Yamileth remembered another occasion when an airplane bombed the neighborhood. "We called them the dread planes because we would hear them coming and we would run to the bedroom and lay on the floor with the mattresses over our heads," she said. This was the reality of Nicaragua in the mid-1970s.

Many scholars (Booth 1985; Walker 1981; Black 1981; Millet 1982) have argued that Somoza's state of siege intensified citizen hostility toward the government. The campaign of mass terror spread antiregime sentiment over wide sectors of Nicaraguan society. For Patricia Mulligan the mass jailings and grand disappearances encouraged her own radicalization. She became more involved with guerrilla logistics and agitation in the barrios. By this time, however, something also as radicalizing was occurring in her life: She was no longer practicing her faith. "What was happening here had a profound effect on me," she said.

Patricia explained that she had been raised as a traditional Catholic and had been educated in Catholic schools by nuns. Despite this socialization, she said that she could not help but be influenced by the staunch antidemocratic posture of the Catholic Church. "Young priests at the university where I studied were very critical of the church's relationship with the Somoza regime," Patricia explained. "I came to recognize the traditional church as a defender of the status quo. It was obvious that while the church spoke with a moral voice its history throughout Latin America was blemished. In time I came to see religion as a false spiritual movement."

Patricia's disillusionment with her faith was not completely atypical of other Catholics who were at this time reexamining their religious convictions. Like Patricia Mulligan, many Christians in the base communities were disappointed by the bishops' unwillingness to support the revolutionary effort publicly. While many Christians were seriously answering the call to arms, the Catholic hierarchy remained neutral among the differences between Sandinista sympathizers, opposition political parties, and anti-Somoza business groups.

Patricia Mulligan represents an important segment of Nicaraguans who found themselves renouncing their faith to embrace a new ideology: Sandinista Marxism. Patricia stated that her collaboration with Christians in revolutionary activity continued, but she also explained that her motivation became political, not religious. Members of her family, traditional Catholics, were also among this group.

"Perhaps religion continued to be of some motivation for my mother, who also became involved in revolutionary activities," Patricia recalled. She remembered that her mother's involvement began in February 1978. Patricia remembered the date because it was a time when a large Sandinista offensive was planned to take over the city of Granada.

At the National University, Patricia had been contacted by some of the students to see if her family would allow the guerrillas to use their home in Granada as a safe-house for the planned offensive. When she went to her father with the idea, Patricia recalled, he was very resistant, believing that it would be much too dangerous. Because her father was unwilling to get the family involved, Patricia appealed to her mother. "It was my mother who told him that it was the right thing to do," she said. Thus, a few days before the offensive, the Mulligan family took a number of the guerrillas into their home.

Patricia recalled that her family spent long nights with the guerrillas discussing the Sandinista motivation. Apparently as a consequence of these discussions, close ideological and political ties developed between the Sandinistas and the Mulligan family.

The Granada offensive began at eleven o'clock a few nights later. Patricia remembered tremendous resistance by the National Guard and considerable loss of life. She recalled that during the height of the attack four badly wounded guerrillas made their way back safely to her family's home. "We hid them from the Guard and my mother went out in the middle of the night to appeal to my uncle, who was a doctor," she said. "My mother convinced him to come to the house and administer first aid."

Patricia Mulligan credited the survival of those young men to her mother's bravery. Upon reflection she believed that her mother's motivation was a Christian one: "My mother believed in the need for change. But the events of the times had also convinced her that if we waited for the church to lead, social justice would never be achieved." The Mulligan family was thus committed to the revolution.

Other Catholics were influenced by the climate of the times. Alvaro Baltodano, a former member of the Riguero Christian community, explained that the question of whether or not there was a God became immaterial. "What was of pivotal importance was how one was living out his faith," he said. Alvaro recalled that in those difficult times during the 1970s he believed that his Christian faith demanded that he work with the poorest. He said the Sandinista Front provided Christians with a plan for liberating the poor and for working toward a more socially just world (Foroohar 1989: 132–33).

The Sandinista offensive against Granada and other cities resulted in largely symbolic victories. Although the guerrillas did not take control of the cities, the offensive further galvanized diplomatic and civic pressure for a resolution to the national crisis. In both conservative and social Christian circles, leaders were demanding political reform (Booth 1985: 159).

Among those speaking out in favor of the Sandinistas were twelve prominent professionals. The "Los Doce" group included both Father Fernando Cardenal and Father Miguel d'Escoto.

In 1977, Father Cardenal had been invited to join Los Doce by Daniel Ortega. This was a year after he had returned from the United States where he had been invited to testify before a congressional committee on sending U.S. aid to the Somoza dictatorship. Father Cardenal's acceptance of Ortega's offer to serve in the group was an important victory for the guerrillas. Patricia Mulligan recalled that Los Doce enjoyed strong student and community support after that. "We saw Cardenal's acceptance into the group as legitimizing the Sandinistas, and this had important consequences throughout Nicaragua and the international community," she said.

In the latter part of 1977 Los Doce issued a declaration to the people of Nicaragua that called for a national dialogue. Most important, the Los Doce declaration coincided with the formal break of the Catholic hierarchy with the Somoza regime.

The hierarchy's decision to collaborate with the moderate opposition was very much in response to the growing popular support of the Sandinistas. Many scholars have argued that the formal break came only as the hierarchy realized that the church's disassociation with Somoza was necessary for preserving its own influence with the faithful (Williams 1989; O'Shaughnessy and Serra 1986; Harris and Vilas 1985; Foroohar 1989). Because the church's traditional alliance with the Somoza government no longer seemed sustainable, the hierarchy apparently looked to moderate members of the bourgeoisie as a means for continuing its influence in society. After all, "the moderate opposition neither questioned the political-economic system as such, but rather called for a reform of the system to avoid its radical overthrow" (Williams 1989: 41). This was a political position the bishops could support.

The church's decision to support the moderate opposition (and not the more radical camp that demanded revolution) had important implications for Christians in the postrevolutionary years. The hierarchy's continued unwillingness to embrace the Sandinista alternative profoundly divided the progressive Catholic sector.

THE FINAL OFFENSIVE

In the months following the Los Doce declaration, Archbishop Obando took the lead in mediation efforts between opposition parties, Sandinista sympathizers, and private business groups. Among those involved with the initiative was a prominent businessman, Pedro Joaquín Chamorro.

Pedro Chamorro had been a longtime critic of the Somoza family. He had used his newspaper, La Prensa, to report opposition activities, governmental corruption, and human rights abuses (Crawley 1979; Tijerino 1979; Millet 1982). Chamorro's denunciation of and active opposition to the Somoza family had earned him great admiration among many sectors of Nicaraguan society. In fact, not only was Chamorro a vocal critic of the Somoza government but he also had stood as a political threat to the military dictatorship.

In the later part of the 1970s, Chamorro had played an active role in negotiating the way for democratic elections in Nicaragua. It was commonly known that he himself had aspirations for running for public office in a free and fair election. Patricia Mulligan recalled that Chamorro's assassination by Somoza National Guardsmen on January 10, 1978, "sent a shock wave through the nation." Pedro Joaquín was murdered in his car on the way to his newspaper office. His murder not only shocked the nation but also unleashed throughout the country a wave of riots, mass mobilizations, and armed resistance. Shortly thereafter, a series of strikes was called and the city of Managua came to a tense, explosive standstill.

Despite the shock of Chamorro's murder, the Catholic hierarchy and other elites were not yet ready to sanction the use of violence to overthrow the regime. Rather, the two groups continued to seek alternative means for resolving the national crisis. In the days that followed Chamorro's death, the church's pastoral letters encouraged Nicaraguans to remain calm. Nevertheless, the popular mobilization took on a greater militancy (Booth 1985; Weber 1981). Violence continued between National Guard forces and Nicaraguans both in the cities and in the countryside. In the barrio of Monimbo, on the outskirts of the city of Masaya, a memorial service for the slain Chamorro erupted into a full-scale revolt, which in turn ignited other barrio uprisings. The Sandinistas took advantage of the climate by planning another kidnapping, and Patricia Mulligan remembered how these events incited greater involvement by her own family.

"During the planning stage of the next Sandinista offensive, Camilo Ortega was hidden in my sister's house in Managua," she said. "At that time both my sister and I became more actively involved in the Sandinistas' plans for a final offensive. The guerrillas intended an attack on the National Palace."

A few weeks later Camilo Ortega was killed in battle. Despite the great personal loss of his brother, Daniel Ortega ordered the Sandinista attack against the National Palace. The offensive was launched August 23, 1978. Patricia Mulligan later recounted how the Sandinistas had stormed the building and had taken hostage many government officials. "The operation was a success and the

Sandinistas earned the freedom of more political prisoners and the release of a public statement calling on the people of Nicaragua to rise up against the dictatorship," she recalled.

At that time both Patricia and her sister, June, were arrested for antigovernment activities. She remembered that they were imprisoned for ten days, but because of their U.S. citizenship they were deported to Miami. Patricia explained that she took advantage of her great luck and quickly returned to Central America, to Costa Rica, to work in the solidarity movement there. "Then I simply waited," she remarked.

The guerrilla attack on the National Palace gave new life to the popular struggle. Throughout the countryside the incident ignited spontaneous armed rebellions and in the cities it encouraged massive strikes. The vast number of insurrections through the month of September was crucial in solidifying support within the ranks of the FSLN. It also consolidated elite and religious support for Somoza's resignation. Tenaciously, the two groups—the Nicaraguan bourgeoisie and the Sandinista guerrillas—came together in a marriage of convenience. A provisional government was agreed to, one that was headed by members of Los Doce.

At that moment in Nicaragua's history, Archbishop Obando made a final attempt to negotiate with the dictator. By this time the government's newspaper, *Novedades,* had launched its own attack against the Catholic hierarchy. It was apparent that President Somoza now perceived Archbishop Obando and the bishops as among his most formidable enemies. Somoza refused to cooperate with any efforts that called for his resignation, and the mediation talks with Archbishop Obando broke down. It was the last domino to fall. Finally, on June 2, 1979, in a pastoral letter to the people of Nicaragua, the bishops of the Catholic Church justified armed resistance.

On July 19, 1979, the Somoza dynasty fell to a popular revolution. As we have seen, many progressive Catholics became committed to the revolution as a result of their religious faith. They took the call to arms as soldiers of Christ, working on behalf of a more socially just society. Others became involved out of their disgust with corruption of the Somoza government and with Na-

This monument in downtown Managua represents the victory of
the guerrilla movement over the Somoza dictatorship.

tional Guard abuses. Still others devoted themselves to the revolution for philosophical reasons, that is, they embraced the ideology of Sandinismo.

Yamileth Sequeira later remembered the day the guerrillas
marched into the city of Managua. Her family and neighbors
were jubilant. "On the day of the triumph many guerrillas came

to the barrio. My family ran out to greet them, but I remained inside the house and began to cry," she recalled. Yamileth explained that the sight of so many young men with guns frightened her. "My mother brought one of the guerrillas to the house and I remember that he put me on his knee and told me that his gun was just a toy. Then he let me touch it and I was no longer afraid," she said as she smiled at the memory.

Yamileth's memory of the Sandinista guerrillas as friends and heroes of the people is affirmed by many Nicaraguans who remember those years and the excitement surrounding the final days of the Somoza dictatorship. But the sense of solidarity and goodwill among all sectors of society was to be short-lived.

CHAPTER FIVE

Shattering of the Christian Coalition

FOLLOWING THE SANDINISTA triumph, there appeared to be great hopes for the construction of democracy in Nicaragua. At first it appeared that the Sandinistas sought to keep their promise to create institutions that could provide channels for mass participation and for expressions of the popular will (Vanden and Prevost 1993: 19). The political honeymoon that the Sandinistas enjoyed, however, was short-lived. The acrimony that had developed between sectors of society reflected the fact that the coalition that had come together to oppose the Somoza regime remained divergent in its vision for a new Nicaragua.

The events of the time had brought together an eclectic group of Nicaraguans: Christians and non-Christians, poor and rich, politicians and housewives. The early fragmentation of this vast and divergent coalition probably was to be expected. Despite their consensus on the need for peace, they agreed on little else. It appears that the vast majority of poor Nicaraguans expected the Sandinistas to deliver a more equitable system of power and social justice. Among the bourgeoisie—those who had chosen to remain in Nicaragua—there existed expectations for a new capitalistic and pluralistic order. Among elders of the church there existed hopes for both political and religious stability.

"Immediately following the triumph, these competing visions and hopes clashed," explained Alejandro Bendana, secretary general of the Sandinista Foreign Ministry. "Sectors of the poor demanded political and economic reform. Sectors of the bourgeoisie demanded autonomy and authority. Within a few months of the Sandinista triumph, elites grew suspicious that a socialist state was developing—one that would continue to deny them the power and privilege that they had once enjoyed under the Somoza government."

These tensions were aggravated when the Sandinistas concentrated on converting many of the popular organizations of the Christian communities into organized and politically aware bodies (Foroohar 1989: 201). Working from the bottom up, the FSLN concentrated on channeling the people's participation into institutional structures, such as the new representative assembly. In addition, the Sandinistas set about empowering the people through the development of mass organizations, including the Sandinista Workers' Central, the Rural Workers Association, and the Nicaraguan Association of Women (see also Walker 1982: 9–11).

Soon after the establishment of the first junta, the Sandinistas proposed an increase in the number of seats in the Council of State. According to Bendana, "this proposal was intended to give the newly formed mass organizations a proper representation in the new government." For the Nicaraguan bourgeoisie, however, this decision was perceived as evidence that their own power and interests might be thwarted (Booth 1985: 185–86; Foroohar 1989: 201).

The crisis within the state developed immediately after Christians began assimilating themselves into organs of the Sandinista state. Among the liberation clergy, four priests accepted high positions in the executive branch of the new government, including Father Ernesto Cardenal who was appointed minister of culture and Father Edgar Parrales who served as minister of social welfare and as ambassador to the Organization of American States. Many Christian base communities also sent representatives to the new Sandinista Congress. In addition to a high profile of Christians in governmental organs, other religious people were highly active in ongoing mass mobilizations (Foroohar

1989: 201). This involvement included participation of thousands of young people from religious schools and more than 200 members of the clergy in the National Literacy Crusade (Serra 1985: 155).

The early prominent role and activity by progressive Christians, however, was not without its critics. Criticism emerged both within and outside the Christian base communities. It was not long before such criticism fragmented the popular coalition.

A HOUSE DIVIDED

The proliferation of CEBs in Nicaragua had developed alongside that of the revolution. During this process, overwhelming religious factors (and not class or political ideology) had brought the popular sector together. But just as the form and substance of the popular church were conditioned by the social, political, and economic forces that helped to nurture this religious inspiration, changes in these same factors worked to fragment the popular coalition. Solidarity unraveled and contradiction and conflict soon emerged. Indeed, following the insurrection, dissensus rather than consensus characterized the climate within the Christian base communities. With the overthrow of President Somoza, the social and spiritual cement that unified the popular sector dissolved.

In the CEBs fundamental disagreement apparently centered around the means for actualizing the popular church's preferential option for the poor. With different and competing spiritual and political convictions, members of the popular church had difficulty agreeing on the proper role the church should play in this new revolutionary process. As a consequence, the popular response was multidimensional and marked by conflict.

Outside the CEBs and at the macrolevel, Nicaraguans disagreed over the proper direction of the political economy. Despite promises for respect of private property, the Sandinista government expropriated Somoza properties and created a new agency for land reform. Banks and insurance and mining companies were nationalized and foreign trade was taken over by the state (Christian 1986: 146–47).

The socialist direction of the economy appeared to be a crucial and divisive issue. Patricia Mulligan had now returned to Nicaragua and she remembered that shortly after the insurrection business leaders began voicing their concerns. "When I returned to Nicaragua I was invited to work with the Foreign Ministry and I did a great deal of translating for the Sandinista government," she explained. Patricia used her language skills to do summaries for the government and she worked as a translator for North American diplomats who came to Nicaragua during the 1980s. "At that time I also did a lot of translating work between COSEP [the Superior Council of Private Enterprise] and Archbishop Obando. The men came to discuss their differences with the Sandinista project."

Patricia suggested that Archbishop Obando and the COSEP group both came to be early enemies of the Sandinista government. "I believe the business sector was threatened by the Marxist ideas of the FSLN, and the church perceived the new regime as a threat to its interests, too," she explained.

Gilberto Cuadra, a former president of COSEP (an umbrella organization of six different associations with a membership of about 150,000 people), also recalled the early discord: "We had a unique opportunity to allow change. But the Sandinistas did not dialogue in good faith. From the beginning decisions were made that were never discussed. Things just started to happen."

Cuadra charged that personal freedoms like the right to own private property were abridged. "The freedom to travel, the right to associate, to think, and the right to free speech were all compromised in those early years." Cuadra argued that members of his organization began to see the Sandinistas as a formidable threat to their interests and to their way of life. He suggested that the FSLN was intent on bringing an end to their dreams for a productive, privatized state.

"COSEP has always fought for the prosperity of Nicaragua and the preservation of private enterprise," Cuadra remarked. "We have always believed in a free market economy and free enterprise. But as farmers, businessmen, and professionals we began to endure harassment by the government and our land and businesses were slowly confiscated."

Within months of taking power a sharp conflict began both inside and outside the Sandinista government (Booth 1985; Christian 1986). Bourgeois members of the first junta resigned, including Pedro Joaquín's widow, Violeta Chamorro, and prominent business leader Alfonso Robelo. Upon their resignation, elites within the country began uniting to devise means for denouncing the revolutionary regime. By fall 1980, Nicaraguan elites began devising plans for free elections. At the same time they began denouncing the Sandinistas as communists (Serra 1985: 160).

The direction of the economy was an issue that continued to be used by opponents of the Sandinistas. In a later discussion of the revolutionary regime, Virgilio Godoy, vice-president of the new Chamorro government, suggested that "the road to hell is always paved with good intentions."

"The Sandinista economic programs were well meaning but they were a recipe for disaster," charged Godoy. "The cooperatives that were created by the state were a huge failure. Production went to an all-time low. The system could not produce half of what it consumed."

Vice-President Godoy argued that despite the abuses of the Somoza regime, Nicaraguan land had at least remained privatized and productive. But the business community's objections to the economic plans of the Sandinista government "fell on deaf ears."

Reflecting back on the 1980s, Julio García, general secretary of the Social Christian Party, also suggested that the Sandinista model had ultimately failed the Nicaraguan people: "In the 1970s Nicaragua was able to produce basic food stuffs for consumption as well as export. After the insurrection we began importing basics. This was a failure. The contra war that began in 1981 continued to hurt production. This situation was complicated by the Sandinista policy that attempted to make Nicaragua into an agrarian-industrial country rather than an agrarian-export one."

Dr. Francisco Mayorga, a leading expert on Nicaragua's economy who served as director of the Central American Institute of Business Administration, agreed with this analysis. He accused the FSLN of being "Soviet stooges." Mayorga explained that between 1975 and 1980 Nicaragua experienced a major drop in the country's gross national product. "By 1980 economic growth in Nicaragua had fallen to just 3 percent and the new Sandinista government began to impose price restrictions on basic foods," Mayorga explained. "Consequently, farmers ended up earning a meager wage. As farming became unprofitable, crops were no longer tended to."

Dr. Mayorga, a leading critic of the FSLN, charged that the Sandinistas' strategy was to impose on the country a centralized economic model—"the kind of model that had been used in Eastern Europe. It was a disaster. Many resources went into the hands of the state and production continued to fall."

Mayorga contended that by 1988 the Sandinista government realized its mistakes and began relying on more private enterprise. Despite the shift in policy, however, the majority of the resources remained in the hands of the state. "As a consequence," Dr. Mayorga charged, "production kept falling. By that year inflation in Nicaragua was the highest in Latin America! By 1989 our country had regressed fifty years by this revolutionary experiment," he said with disgust.

In a plan to overthrow the revolutionary government, some of the Nicaraguan elite joined Somocista forces who had fled the country and had assembled in Miami. With the assistance and guidance of the U.S. Central Intelligence Agency (CIA) they began organizing in neighboring Latin American countries and arming themselves for war. Many of those who remained in Nicaragua joined internal opposition groups.

Joseph Mulligan has argued (1991: 218) that many of these anti-Sandinista groups looked to the Catholic Church as their traditional ally. Many bishops and priests had personal relationships with wealthy Nicaraguan families, and apparently they shared many of the same fears that their property might be confiscated (ibid.).

Despite the fact that the Catholic hierarchy had finally con-
doned the popular insurrection, continued support for the revolution had been in question as early as November 1979. Immediately following the Sandinista truimph, a pastoral letter had been
issued to the people of Nicaragua. The letter forewarned of future conflict with the government, for it acknowledged the right
of the Catholic hierarchy to reserve judgment about the future
of the state (Lernoux 1989; Christian 1986).

The church's fear of losing its power and prestige has been
among the suggested reasons for the hierarchy's conflict with
the developing Sandinista project (Lernoux 1989; O'Shaughnessy and Serra 1986;). Father Joseph Mulligan, who has written on the subject, argued that the Sandinistas' arrival to power
provoked fear that the FSLN might reduce the political, religious, ideological, and social space traditionally occupied by the
church. This fear was substantiated when the Sandinista government began assuming responsibility for such social service projects as health care, housing, and education (Mulligan 1991: 237).
Thus, while it appeared that the socialist direction of the new
government was fundamentally at the root of the Nicaraguan crisis, other factors furthered the conflict.

The hierarchy's traditional fear of a Marxist revolution was
exacerbated by a government position paper that was leaked during fall 1979. According to critics of the Sandinistas, the paper
had been prepared by a member of the FSLN and had been presented for discussion at a policy planning conference. The paper
argued the need for discouraging organized religion and suggested that all religious practices should eventually be abolished.
The paper's contents were leaked to the Chamorro family, who
published it in their newspaper, *La Prensa* (see also Dodson and
O'Shaughnessy 1990: 149–52). The consequences for the regime
were dramatic.

Immediately, the hierarchy challenged the Sandinistas about
the proposition. The government's leaders explained that the position paper was simply a working document that "never had the
approval of the FSLN" (Mulligan 1991: 219). In spite of the gov-

ernment's disclaimer, the damage had been done. Neither the bishops nor other conservative Catholics were ever convinced by the Sandinista explanation.

In an attempt to reassure the church about the position of the party, the Sandinistas shortly thereafter published an official statement on the sanctity of religion. It reaffirmed the party's commitment to respect the freedom of religious practice in Nicaragua. Despite the public announcement, the bishops' response "strongly intimated that the good intentions would not be carried out" (ibid.: 176).

The furor over the leaked document exacerbated tensions on another controversial issue. Early in the 1980s the Catholic Church began raising grave concerns over the infiltration of Marxist thinking into Nicaragua's educational system. The Sandinista literacy program that had used Bibles as reading tools received little recognition by the hierarchy. Rather than applauding the effort of the campaign, as many supporters of the regime had done, the bishops seemed alarmed by the way many Christians had picked up the language of Marxism and of liberation theology (Dodson and Montgomery 1992: 175).

According to Mulligan (1991: 230–35), the Nicaraguan bishops perceived the literacy campaign as "too secular" and "too political." He has suggested that the Catholic hierarchy perceived the entire campaign as a threat to their own historic monopolization of the educational process. Thus, a certain rivalry for moral leadership developed between the Sandinistas and the church (ibid.).

Penny Lernoux's work (1989: 367) resonates with Mulligan's assessment. Lernoux suggests that the church "feared that the [religious] approval [of the revolution] would not be needed in the future." Hence, this fear "was at the root of the conflict between the government and the churches." By the early 1980s the Catholic hierarchy became convinced that Nicaragua was headed toward a Marxist dictatorship.

The falling out between the traditional church and the Sandinistas had important consequences for some members of the base communities. Less than a month after the resignation of

Violeta Chamorro and Alfonso Robelo, the bishops unexpectedly called for the resignation of priests holding public office (Mulligan 1991: 171). On July 14, 1980, Archbishop Obando declared the leaders of the FSLN "Marxists" and asserted that "Christian faith and Marxism could not coexist."

Father Mulligan explained that there appeared to be two dimensions to the conflict in Nicaragua. The first appeared to be secular in nature. Ideological, political, and economic differences worked to divide Nicaraguan society and aggravated the church-state conflict. The second dimension was theological in nature and concerned such questions as the place of religion in politics, church unity, and ultimately the church's moral authority. Underlying the crisis were questions of doctrinal purity and concern for Catholic unity. "At the root of the crisis were competing theological interpretations as well as competing visions of the function and purposes of Christian faith" (Mulligan 1991: 171).

Intensifying these fears was a growing concern among conservative sectors of the Nicaragua hierarchy that a separate Catholic Church was being established among the grass roots. These fears were exacerbated by the fact that shortly after the Sandinista triumph in September 1979, forty liberation theologians from eight countries had come to Managua to reflect on ways that could assist in the revolutionary process. Participants of "The Encounter of Theology" used the term *iglesia popular* (popular church) in their working papers and used the label in their speeches to describe the movement they were supporting.

The conference criticized the Catholic hierarchy for hesitating to confront the bourgeoisie and for failing to support the work of the revolutionary government. In the summary documents the conference members affirmed the need to push conscientization among the faithful and to use the base communities to promote Christian participation in Sandinista activities. The summary included an emphasis on continuing research and writing on the study of Marxism and Christianity. The theologians at the conference also advocated the need for converting nonbelievers of the Sandinista Front (Christian 1986: 251).

It appears likely that the conference reinforced the conservative sector's judgment that a new church was coming to life in Nicaragua. Many Catholic critics, such as Monsignor Bismark Carballo, believed that the popular church actually represented a foreign invasion. Speaking later on this point, he suggested that the popular church was initiated by foreigners from Eastern Europe, Cuba, and Haiti.

It is important to note that the theological debate was not isolated to the case of Nicaragua. The growing acrimony between the progressive clergy and the Catholic hierarchy reflected a larger division within the Latin American church. Among conservative sectors of the region, suspicions had been mounting that a religious "parallelism" was taking place within Latin America, a movement that ultimately threatened doctrinal purity and Catholic unity (Lernoux 1986; Smith 1991; Núñez 1985; Christian 1986).

The Third General Conference of Latin American Bishops that met at Puebla, Mexico, in January 1979 sought to address this concern. According to Christian (1986: 245), there was growing fear among some bishops that the movement for social justice had become the justification for some in the church to embrace Marxism and to become directly involved in partisan politics. The pope himself arrived to address the conference on what he considered to be "serious doctrinal errors of the liberation movement" (Schall 1982: 83–101).

In his address, Pope John Paul II admonished the clergy for confusing their religious role "with a political one." He rejected the notion of a people's church, declaring but one universal Catholic Church. In a challenge to the liberation clergy, the pope warned against efforts to encourage the development of a parallel church. He also defended the social teachings of the church against attacks that had been made upon it (Sigmund 1990: 100; Schall 1982: 90–97).

O'Brien (1986: 55) suggests that the pope's main aim at Puebla was to reassert the magisterium: the teaching authority and discipline of the universal church. Perhaps it should not have been surprising, then, that the pope had come to the aid of his archbishop in Nicaragua. Pope John Paul II's concept of papal authority was simply not compatible with the versions of liberation theology (ibid.).

From the beginning, liberation theology had been questioning the essence of what it meant to be a church. Liberation theologians thus were questioning those very practices that sought to reinforce a spiritual understanding divorced from the people's reality. Within this context, harmony and hopes for Catholic unity in Nicaragua could at best be elusive.

MARXISTS IN CHRISTIAN CLOTHING?

In Nicaragua, the issues raised at Puebla played themselves out in the clash between liberation priests and the Catholic bishops. It began with the revolutionary priests' refusal to step down from their governmental posts. The hierarchy's demand for their resignation hardened the clergy's resolve to remain in their positions of authority.

In July 1981 the bishops met with four key priests to discuss their resistance to resign their government jobs. The meeting included Ernesto Cardenal and Edgar Parrales. According to Parrales, the hierarchy's pressure concerned the issue of unity. While the church needed to look consistent and united in its criticism of the Sandinistas, it could not do so if popular priests remained in service to the revolutionary process (in Zwerling and Martin 1985: 32–33).

Parrales explained that the priests' refusal to step down reflected their conviction that religion and politics could not be separated into divergent ways of life. For the liberation priests, serving in the Sandinista government was a way to live out their religious commitment. The priests' refusal to resign thus led to an uneasy compromise with the bishops. The hierarchy reluctantly agreed to allow the clergy to remain in their governmental posts so long as they agreed to abstain from carrying out priestly functions. According to Father Parrales, the compromise was the hierarchy's way of separating the priests from their Christian followers (ibid.).

The compromise did little to settle the points of contention.

91

In fact, it had unintentional consequences. The uneasy agreement between the Catholic bishops and their subordinates only deepened the liberation priests' commitment to the unfolding revolutionary process. After all, the affinity in ideals between the Sandinistas and some progressive Christians had originally led priests like Father Cardenal to defend the Christian commitment to the revolution. Criticized for his continued support of the Sandinistas, Father Cardenal argued that his religious responsibility obligated him to live out his love of the people through his political role. "In my whole life nothing but the Revolution has given me the opportunity to live out this love" (in ibid.: 77).

Father Cardenal's theme of the revolution as the expression of love was embraced by many at the grass-roots level of the Nicaraguan church. The revolutionary experience had changed many Catholics' understanding of faith and the role of Christians in living out that faith. But the assimiliation of this experience came to erode the unity enjoyed by the popular sector. The consequences were divisive. As tensions grew in Nicaragua, some members of the base communities chose to renounce religion altogether. Others eventually felt compelled to divorce themselves from the practice of Catholicism. Among these Nicaraguans, the conviction of the revolution as an expression of love for the poor continued to be defended. While their devotion to the Sandinistas was originally inspired by religious faith, this motivation turned political as tensions grew. In spite of the developing church-state conflict, they continued to remain committed to the base communities.

In the case of Miriam Lazo, a middle-aged Nicaraguan who grew up in the time of Somoza, commitment to the revolutionary experiment came with her growing sociopolitical consciousness. Born to a wealthy family, Miriam was raised as a devout Catholic and was educated in a parochial boarding school at the Colegio María Auxiliadora in the city of Granada. Miriam recalled that at that time the school had been run by the Salesian sisters. She remembered a particular occasion when one of the poorer girls at the school dropped a flowerpot. The child had been severely reprimanded by the sisters who saw that the vase was broken. "When any of the wealthier students made mistakes, however, nothing was ever said" (Heyck 1990: 218–20). The difference in such treatment was startling. Miriam Lazo explained that at that moment she began recognizing the preferential treatment of those girls, like herself, whose parents could afford to pay for their education.

Miriam's social consciousness grew after she left school. Working as a teacher, she came to recognize fully the different grades of poverty that existed in Nicaragua and the vast differences that economic power and the lack of it could make in a person's life. Like other progressive Christians, Miriam Lazo explained that she began extending this understanding to the goals of the Sandinista leadership. Following the insurrection she became a dedicated worker for the Sandinistas, working with the government to create rural day care centers throughout the country. She continued this commitment in spite of criticism by the Catholic bishops (ibid.).

Charges against the Sandinista government grew and were legitimized by reference to the regime as a Marxist dictatorship. Despite the attempt by many religious Nicaraguans to justify their revolutionary commitment, the condemnation of their activity by the Catholic hierarchy grew more intense. The bishops also attacked the popular church, accusing it of being a breakaway church and a tool of the Sandinistas. The Catholic hierarchy accused the communities of being instruments of the party and a Sandinista device for attacking the traditional church (Christian 1986: 255).

Cardinal Obando's press secretary, Monsignor Bismark Carballo, argued this very case. In an interview in his office in Managua, he suggested that during the Sandinista years ideological manipulation had occurred within the communities. He suggested that this manipulation had ultimately resulted in a "parallel magistrate" in Nicaragua.

The monsignor credited the early work of the Latin American church for establishing the Christian base communities, but he also suggested that politics in Nicaragua had eventually polarized the communities and divided the Catholic Church. Another

bishop, Monsignor Bosco Vivas, agreed, accusing the CEBs of being an enemy of the church. He suggested that members of the
communities had used their religious motivations to develop a
Marxist political ideology.

Upon reflection of these accusations, some members of the
CEBs were willing to acknowledge the monsignor's interpretation. The majority, however, were offended by this view and
eagerly challenged it. Despite the differences of opinion, however, all camps seemed to agree that the fear of Marxism fueled
the early discord between the Nicaraguan church and the Sandinista state.

This discord was further exacerbated by U.S. involvement in
the counterrevolutionary activities of the Nicaraguan opposition. Lernoux (1989: 370) has argued that the contra war aggravated tensions between the traditional church and the Sandinista
government. Her research suggests that the two camps would
probably have found accommodation had it not been for the
ascension of Ronald Reagan to the U.S. presidency. Reagan's
promise to "roll back" the revolution counted on the Catholic
Church as an important ally, and he used it for that purpose.

Mulligan (1991: 177) has argued that the U.S. government
recognized the revolutionary potential of progressive Christianity as early as 1980. Under the direction of Henry Kissinger, the
Council for Inter-American Security drafted a paper known as
the Santa Fe Report that urged the incoming U.S. administration to take the offensive against progressive theology (see also
Nelson-Pallmeyer 1990: 15). At the University of Central America, Jesuit Father Alvaro Argüello explained what this offensive
meant to some sectors of the Catholic Church: "We were trying
to help achieve the transformation of our society, to promote
love, unselfishness, and justice. But in trying to live out this faith
we were labeled as communists." As a consequence, many progressive CEB members suffered great physical loss.

Javier Talavera, director of the Interchurch for Theological
Studies in Managua, offered a similar opinion. He remembered
that during the contra war many innocent Christians died for
professing and living a liberating faith. In the rural areas of Nica-

ragua, many progressive Christians were the targets of contra aggression.

Darwin López, a director of CEPAD (the Council of Evangelical Churches of Nicaragua), also remembered the effects that the U.S. campaign had on the progressive churches in Nicaragua: "The time of Reagan was a time of diabolical death."

López charged that with the help of Humberto Belli (minister of education for the Chamorro government) and a wealthy Nicaraguan who had been hired by the Institute for Democracy in the United States, "the U.S. government helped to promote us as communists. As a consequence, our organization lost a lot of private funding and some of our churches pulled out of CEPAD."

The Reagan team keenly manipulated the contra war by playing on the church's traditional fear of communism. The alliance between the United States, the bourgeoisie, and the traditional church, however, played badly upon the historically strong anti-imperialist sentiments in Nicaragua (Foroohar 1989: 202–03). The alliance eventually transformed the discord into a powerful class conflict. While the bourgeoisie worked with the traditional church to undermine the unity and cohesion of the revolutionary government, many people of the lower classes threw their support behind the Sandinistas. The consequences were divisive for the grass-roots church.

CHAPTER SIX

The Marxist Type

FOR NICARAGUANS WHO were struggling to maintain their Catholic identity, the effects of the contra war were alienating. In the case of Patricia Mulligan, the conflict simply reaffirmed her decision to leave the practice of her faith: "I knew many Christians in Nicaragua who remained dedicated to the church despite the fact that their participation in the revolution had been condemned by the bishops. I knew that they had a way to rationalize their commitment to the Sandinistas and that they had a sincere desire to remain devout Catholics. But there have been other Christians in Nicaragua who became disgusted with the hypocrisy of the church and, like me, they have left the practice of their faith."

Patricia Mulligan said she believed that for many Christians religious faith had been a handicap to the development of a new and more liberating consciousness. "For me, since I am no longer a practicing Catholic, working with the Sandinistas was not a personal dilemma. My motivation was political. It was a moral choice based on the Sandinistas' revolutionary program that aimed toward building in Nicaragua a truly democratic society."

Patricia Mulligan typifies those Nicaraguans who accepted Marxism as their political ideology. Former Catholics like her constitute the first of our ideal types, the Marxist type.

The paradoxical juxtaposition of Marxism and Christianity is the framework for this position. Nicaraguans who make up this type have two characteristics that differentiate them from the other three types that have been developed for this study.

First, these individuals accept Marxism as their political ideology. Second, although some still consider themselves members of the base communities, they no longer consider themselves Catholics or, in the traditional sense, Christian.

Throughout the revolutionary process of the 1980s, these Nicaraguans remained staunch supporters of the Sandinistas and today still identify themselves with the party's reforms. Nicaraguans who occupy this position cite one of two motivations for joining the revolution.

For some, like Patricia Mulligan, the motivation was purely political. These are people who today reject out of hand any type of religion. Indeed, in the truly Marxist sense they understand religion as an alienating influence in human society.

The second motivation within the Marxist type was spiritual but not authentically religious. These are Nicaraguans who no longer identify with the precepts of established Catholicism. Their divorce from the Catholic Church came gradually through conflict with the hierarchy during the 1980s. Their inner searching for the meaning for living a Christian life typifies a new kind of person evolving in Nicaragua—one who brings a new and different understanding to what it means to be a spiritual person. Despite their conflict with established religion, these Marxist-Christians have struggled to maintain their ties with sectors of the popular church and they speak in highly spiritual terms.

MARXISTS WITHIN THE BASE COMMUNITIES

At one of the weekly CEB meetings several members gathered together to offer their religious experiences and to reflect on their own evolution of faith. One of them, Ramón Gutiérrez, is a former member of the Catholic Church. Like many other Christians he explained that in the 1970s he had worked with the Sandinista guerrillas, but he suggested that for him this involvement was inspired by a growing political consciousness. "I had been an irregular member of the Christian community during the 1970s, but my commitment to the insurrection really came out of my own personal disgust for Somoza," Gutiérrez explained. "Foreigners often don't realize how bad things really were in this country. There was no personal or political liberty. Innocent people were harassed and murdered. The Guard was unaccountable."

Typical of this subset within the Marxist type, Gutiérrez explained that his commitment to the revolutionary process came from his conviction that the new Sandinista government was intent on bringing democracy to Nicaragua: "I believed in the revolutionary vision of the Sandinista leadership. They were offering an alternative for Nicaragua, another chance for the poor, a new chance for women and youths, a real chance for true representation. For me, being involved in the revolutionary project meant working toward a classless society."

Like other Christian base community members, Ramón Gutiérrez argued that democracy could only be achieved in his country if the poorest members in society were given resources and opportunities. Like other members of this type, he argued the inadequacy of traditional liberal models of democracy: "Political participation and the right to vote are not enough to ensure poor people's equality. They also have a right to a decent standard of living, and that doesn't come through a ballot box."

He recalled how money had always bought power and political access in Nicaragua: "It did not surprise me that the Catholic Church came out against the Sandinistas following the insurrection. This is to be expected of those who sit at the table to feast with the wealthy. Today, Obando blesses the very same people who worked to destroy the hopes and revolutionary visions of our heroes and martyrs."

Ramón Gutiérrez is disgusted when he speaks of the church. He suggested that Cardinal Obando has always acted to protect his own power and privilege. When asked about the church's alliance with the United States in the contra war, Ramón grew cynical: "Obando smelled change in the political wind and he knew how to take advantage of it. It was all hypocrisy! He was using religion for political purposes."

98

Unlike Patricia Mulligan who left her faith early in the insurrectionary period, Ramón finally decided to leave the church as the contra war became more destructive to Nicaraguan society. "I was raised as a Catholic and I suppose I will die as a Catholic, but, frankly, it means nothing to me. I have walked out of the church without turning my back, and this decision has not bothered my conscience."

Today, Ramón considers himself a Marxist. He suggested that the great value of Marxist ideology is its vision for a more equitable society where wealth and property are redistributed. Like Patricia Mulligan, Ramón also suggested that today he is no longer practicing any religious faith. In the traditional Marxist sense he sees religion as superstition, a tool used by people to help them cope with their daily hardships. Others like him also reject the notion that they are religious people. They argued that their motivation to work with the Sandinistas grew out of the belief that the revolution was advancing the process of democracy and the development of a new, more socially just person. Yet while these Marxists no longer belong to any church, most of them continue to find time for base community projects.

MARXIST-CHRISTIANS

For other Nicaraguans of the Marxist type, like Miriam Lazo and Horacio Lacayo, working for the Sandinista project did not rule out belief in God but meant a new awareness and understanding of what it means to practice spirituality. This awareness is what differentiates them from Nicaraguans who have chosen to remain areligious.

Horacio Lacayo explained that one of the truly original aspects of the Sandinista revolution was its appreciation of popular religion. Miriam Lazo argued that to her the people's religion—the kind that is lived daily in a community—is the basis of a genuine Christianity. "You know, the person who has the greatest social conscience of all is the campesino," she said. Miriam explained that when she visited the rural areas of the country she experienced a generosity of spirit that one seldom finds in the urban centers: "When the campesinos saw us coming they would bring their chickens, eggs, whatever they had, and offered them to us. And it was not only us but to anyone who came" (in Heyck 1990: 222–24).

For Miriam Lazo this generosity was recognized and nurtured by the Sandinista party, which attempted not only to meet the needs of the poor but also to empower the poor. She, like others, credited the revolutionary government with advancing the interests of the poor.

Devotion to the revolutionary experiment was also expressed by Horacio Lacayo, a member of the Christian base community in San Pablo. "I joined the insurrectionary forces when the community became involved," he said. "That was my formal entry into the struggle. During that time I had not been involved in politics. No one in Nicaragua had a right to be involved in questions of the state, especially poor people. But the revolution offered us a chance to become involved in the political process. This was a powerful experience for me. Out of the insurrectionary struggle I came to appreciate the power of the people." As a consequence, Horacio Lacayo became a supporter of the Sandinista government.

"In many ways you might say that my Christian faith brought me to this awareness," Horacio said. "It was the work of the community that gave me the inspiration to involve myself in the struggle. People can learn and grow from such experiences."

Like Miriam Lazo, Horacio explained that his devotion to the Sandinista government came from his conviction of the righteousness of the revolutionary struggle. "That is what motivated my work," he said. "After the Sandinistas came under attack by the Catholic Church, I continued to defend the historic project of the Sandinistas."

Horacio suggested that the Sandinista years were difficult ones for people of faith—"not because the Sandinistas disallowed religious practice, but because the Catholic Church declared war on the government and the Christian communities." But his decision to remain dedicated to the revolutionary cause alienated him from other Catholic Christians. "There were some who saw us as communists and sinners against God," Horacio explained.

"The conflict forced me to make a personal choice: to remain a dedicated Sandinista or to obey the bishops. I chose to remain a Sandinista. This was a political choice based on the necessity of the times. I felt that I had to support the historic program; otherwise for me the struggle for change would have been in vain."

Throughout the 1980s, Horacio Lacayo remained dedicated to the work of the community, but he explained that such activity was no longer in concert with the Catholic Church: "Our work became political but it remained spiritual at the heart. We were seeking to live out the gospel values of fellowship and generosity. But this activity remained in direct defiance of the bishops here."

Horacio Lacayo and others like him explained that their alienation from the Catholic Church did not preclude them from living out a spiritual life; they suggested that theirs was simply a new kind of spirituality. Thus these members of the Marxist type defended the revolution (and their participation in it) by insisting that the project incorporated the spiritual themes of justice and equality. Edgar Parrales explained that "for us [the aims of the revolution] signified a combination of religious and historical ideals" (in Zwerling and Martin 1985: 35).

Despite their early intent to remain good Catholics, it appears that the bellicose charges of the hierarchy eventually hardened the attitudes of Marxist-Christians toward the traditional church. Indeed, they were offended by the bishops' charges that Christianity and Marxism could not coexist. For example, Mercedes Ortega argued that her revolutionary work in the CEB of Adolfo Reyes had a lot to do with her belief that the principles of the Sandinista government were closer to the ideal of God than were the bishops' attitudes. "Obando said that Christianity and Marxism could not coexist," Mercedes explained. "But I came to believe that it was simply more to the truth that it was Catholicism and Marxism that could not coexist."

Unlike Patricia Mulligan and Ramón Gutiérrez who left the practice of their faith and today consider themselves areligious, Nicaraguans like Horacio Lacayo and Mercedes Ortega prefer to think of themselves as religious people who have simply divorced themselves from Catholicism. Mercedes said that on holidays she

101

may attend the parish church but that when she attends the Sunday services she does so to be close to God, not to practice the Catholic creed. "I do not believe in the traditional practice of Catholicism and I no longer believe in the morality of our cardinal," she explained.

Horacio Lacayo offered a similar point of view. He denounced the Catholic hierarchy and acknowledged that his faith no longer finds expression in an institutional framework—instead, he explained, his worship finds expression within the community. Like Mercedes Ortega, he also no longer observes Catholic practices. Asked whether this decision involved a personal conflict for either of them, Mercedes explained that her conscience was not troubled: "My identity is as a Sandinista and a Christian, not a Catholic."

Horacio Lacayo argued that the "rightness of action took precedence over religious obedience." Mercedes Ortega suggested that serving other people has become the way for her to serve God. "I think it is necessary to pray but I have also come to believe it is just as necessary to help others," she remarked. For example, Mercedes said that during the 1980s she devoted her time and energy to helping the sick. "I served in the Sandinista health brigade for ten years and applied much of what I learned to help others here in the community." In Adolfo Reyes she helped to promote a preventive health course and worked with her neighbors in teaching others about nutrition and sanitation.

Mercedes recalled that in 1981 at the start of the contra war she went to the mountains with a special military brigade: "It was the first brigade of women and it was there that I received army training. I spent four years in the mountains, and when I returned to Managua I helped to organize Nicaragua's Women's Association. Through my work with this organization I counseled battered women, I worked with the group to assist them from being evicted from their homes, and I helped to teach them about birth control choices. The church would not have allowed me to do this, especially my work with birth control counseling. But I saw my participation with the government's projects as a way for me to live out my commitment to God."

Horacio Lacayo recalled that during the 1980s the community of San Pablo came to be at odds with the Catholic Church: "Our work was under constant attack by traditional clergy. During this time I came to acknowledge my own participation in the community as a matter of faith to a higher law, one that seeks justice and brotherhood. It is at odds with the law of the cardinal who used his religion and his lofty position to denounce the true word of God."

For Marxist-Christians like Mercedes Ortega, Horacio Lacayo, Edgar Parrales, Miriam Lazo, and others, the support of the Sandinista revolution was all about living a more spiritual life. Like their more traditional Marxist counterparts within the base communities, their support for a classless society and their work toward the redistribution of wealth and power eventually led them to turn their backs on the religion of their birth.

ALIENATION, SEPARATION, AND DIVORCE

Seated together and reflecting on their experiences, members of the base communities recalled the tensions that increased between the Catholic hierarchy and the Sandinista government. Several of them remembered that by the middle of 1981, Sandinista groups were accused of periodically sending *turbas* (mobs) to taunt the archbishop and to attack conservative priests. These gangs also targeted religious meetinghouses and disrupted religious services. Despite the fact that the Sandinista party was accused of inciting these acts, the government disclaimed any responsibility. Nevertheless, the government censored the archbishop's pastoral letters and restricted his religious television services.

Speaking to members of the Catholic hierarchy, Monsignor Eduardo Montenegro argued that during this time the Sandinistas also encouraged the media to harass and mock some of the clergy. A well-known case was an incident with Monsignor Bismark Carballo, who was photographed in the nude when police arrested him in a controversial sex scandal.

Despite such infamous incidents, Nicaraguans who occupied the Marxist position defended the actions of the Sandinista govern-

103

ment. Mercedes Ortega explained that much of the controversy was "exaggerated," and others denied that there was persecution against the church. Horacio Lacayo suggested that "the church wasn't being persecuted, it simply wasn't enjoying any longer its privileges of the past."

Relations between the CEBs and the traditional church reached their lowest point during the pope's visit to Nicaragua in March 1983. Tensions began when news of the visit was initially censored by the Sandinista government. Marxists within the base communities recalled that in his public homily in downtown Managua, Pope John Paul II criticized the popular church and called for Catholic unity. According to CEB members, the crowd became agitated and Sandinista militants interrupted the homily with cheers of "people's power." CEB members smiled bitterly when they remembered that the pope was enraged by this behavior. He responded angrily and admonished the crowd. Apparently this reaction only made many Nicaraguans even more angry.

Horacio Lacayo said that the pope's visit to Nicaragua was an alienating experience for many people within the communities. Their sense of estrangement was furthered when reports circulated that the pontiff had insulted Father Ernesto Cardenal, who had fallen to his feet to greet the pope and to receive his blessing. Mercedes Ortega explained that instead of giving the blessing, "the pope wagged a finger in Father Cardenal's face and admonished him for being political." The event left the priest in tears and the communities in shock (see also O'Brien 1986).

Discussion of these events in the CEBs raised voices of indignation and humiliation. Marxist-Christians argued that the pope's behavior was "inexcusable" and that his condemnation of Father Cardenal and the popular church was the breaking point for them.

For people like Father Edgar Parrales the effect was radicalizing; for him personally it meant renouncing the priesthood. In doing so he argued that it was the institutional church that was guilty of driving him and other revolutionary leaders out. Identifying himself as a Sandinista and a member of the FSLN, he

argued that his government service had given him great opportunities to serve out his faith. His dedication to this service took
precedence over his lifelong commitment to a church of contradictions (in Zwerling & Martin 1985: 33–34).

Other revolutionary leaders and Sandinista workers apparently made similar decisions to leave the practice of their faith.
Sandinista leader Rafael Solís explained that he no longer considered himself a Christian and he no longer attended church.
Nevertheless he has continued his relations and his work with
several Christian communities (in ibid.: 37).

Miriam Lazo also condemned the actions of the Catholic hierarchy and accused the church of abandoning the faithful. She
suggested that the division within the church was the fault of the
bishops who had been incapable of allowing freedom of conscience for some Catholics to practice their faith in their own way
(in Heyck 1990: 224).

In the base community of Adolfo Reyes, Yamileth Sequeira discussed the effect all of this conflict has had on her religious faith:
"I don't know what to believe anymore. But a year ago I joined
the Christian community because I felt a need to be closer to
God." Yamileth explained that she had never agreed with the
Catholic practice of praying to saints or even to the Virgin Mary.
"But my grandmother told me about the work of the community
and its many projects and programs. When I went to see these
activities, I decided that they were worthwhile projects and I
wanted to contribute to them."

Yamileth explained that within the community she found a
deep sense of fellowship that transcends religious differences.
"People are always trying to help others in need. To me this seems
like the work of God. It seemed that I could be a part of this and
be closer to God. It doesn't mean that I have to be a member of
a church."

The opinions of those in the Marxist type are minority ones
but ones that can be discerned in all three Christian base communities of Adolfo Reyes, San Judas, and San Pablo. Today, it is
not uncommon to hear such members of the Christian communities speak of the hierarchy and the pope as "Judases."

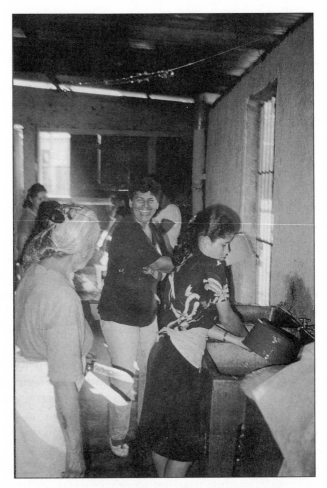

In the community of Adolfo Reyes women work in the Oya de la
Soya project six days a week, offering a free, hot, nutritional meal
to their neighbors.

As the challenge to ecclesiastical authority heightened in the
1980s, these communities responded by taking on greater autonomy in direct defiance of the cardinal. When asked about their
disaffection with the Catholic Church—and whether it troubled
their conscience—those in the Marxist type suggested that it had
not. They also all agreed that the well-being of the community

takes priority: When the well-being of their neighbors comes into conflict with decisions or demands made by the bishops, members of the Marxist type take sides. For example, Mercedes Ortega noted that, despite the church's disapproval, she supported workers who recently challenged the government for fairer wages. "Many of us in the community also supported the students when they went on strike to protest the legislature's attempt to deny them financial assistance for school."

Mercedes explained that during the last hurricane community members went from house to house leading people to safety. "We took some of them to the church and others came to stay with me in my home. When the tidal wave hit the coast of Nicaragua a few months ago, we were the first of the communities in Managua to collect relief supplies for the victims. These things we do out of a growing consciousness, not because the church tells us to. My motivation comes from the heart. I do not need a priest to tell me what my responsibility is to my neighbor. I feel it within my heart," she remarked.

Another example of the growing independence of the CEBs is the soya project in the barrio of Las Torres. The soya program is one of several CEB projects aimed at addressing the problem of malnourishment. Six days a week the program feeds a hot meal to malnourished children who live in the community. Soya programs have come under attack by Cardinal Obando, who accuses them of "encouraging dependency and parental irresponsibility." In October 1991, the *alcaldia* (mayorality) of Managua attempted to evict the soya project from the Las Torres neighborhood. The residents came together to fight the eviction and (for the time being) saved the project.

Raquel López, a member of the community of San Judas, spoke of similar pressures by the hierarchy in her CEB: "We don't feel bound by the hierarchy. Yet the bishops come with great authority, with great publicity, to denounce us. It is tiring and exhausting for members of our community."

CEB members within the Marxist type contended that one of the greatest errors of the church has been its incapability of permitting dialogue. They accused the hierarchy of an authoritari-

The soya program in Adolfo Reyes provides food for more than
100 children. Because the program was so successful it was used
as a pilot for similar programs during the Sandinista years.

anism that has no place in a country that speaks of working for
democracy.

Members of the Marxist type also have suggested that people
in Nicaragua continue to believe that the Sandinistas and their
organizations set out to undermine religion. They are familiar
with the accusations of some that Christians who had served in

those organizations were really Marxists whose real agenda was to destroy the religious fabric of Nicaraguan society. This kind of talk angers them, and they deny any notion that their own choice to leave organized religion was a mandate for others to follow. Insistently they argue that they—and the Sandinistas—continue to believe in the right of all Nicaraguans to practice any religious faith.

These members of the CEBs also suggested that throughout the 1980s, and despite the popular support behind the Sandinistas, the beginning of the contra effort helped to unravel support for the government. As the country was plundered by war, the Sandinista government declared a national state of emergency. The measure suspended a number of personal and political liberties and led opposition groups within the country to challenge the Sandinistas' commitment to political pluralism and democratic values. Opponents of the FSLN charged the government with abuses of human rights and repression. Jaime Chamorro, senior editor of *La Prensa,* accused the Sandinistas of censorship and harassment during those years. He explained that his paper has been shut down three times during its existence. The first time was in 1934 when President Somoza forced the newspaper to close down its operation during an earthquake. The second incident occurred in 1972, following Managua's second earthquake. In 1985, it was the Sandinista government that forced the paper's closure.

"We never suffered the amount of censorship under the Somoza government as we had under the FSLN," suggested Chamorro. "It was an outright attempt to limit political opposition and criticism. Somoza was a dictator, a gangster, but the FSLN was an ideological dictatorship."

Even among FSLN supporters there were increasing charges of the "vertical authoritarianism" of Sandinista rule. Flavio Tijerino, who served as a vice-minister of culture, said that he perceived a contradiction between the FSLN's objectives and its strategies. "I believe that in time people recognized the vertical and authoritarian nature of the regime," he explained. "As a minister of culture, I came to oppose the party's vertical form of control. It seemed a contradiction to democratization. Absolute liberty to question the revolutionary program was promised; frank, honest dialogue was assured. But this was not always the case."

Similar charges were levied at the church of the poor. Julio Sequeira, a member of the Christian community in San Pablo, explained that people viewed the CEBs as tied to the Sandinista government: "People saw us as an extension, a political organization that took orders from the top down without question, without reflection. In truth, many of our leaders isolated themselves from the more urgent problems of our communities. Communication broke down between the party and our neighborhoods. At the base level we failed to recognize this erosion of support. In time, we found ourselves in greater isolation with less ability to reach out to other sectors of society."

During the course of the contra war the Nicaraguan bishops denounced human rights violations, including those of the Miskito Indians who had been forcibly transferred from militarized zones along Nicaragua's northern border. The forced move was resisted by many of the Miskito Indians and there was a loss of life and the destruction of property.

The hierarchy also severely criticized the government's compulsory military service policy. At the height of the contra conflict, young men were drafted. Those who tried to evade the draft were picked up by the Sandinista army against their will.

Other opponents of the Sandinistas charged the government with failing to issue land titles to peasant farmers and with using the land reform program for propaganda purposes. Peasants who had been given land for the first time became disgruntled when the government insisted that prices for their crops would be fixed by the state. Peasant support for the government was also undermined when rural campesinos became the innocent victims of the contra terror.

Members of the Marxist type acknowledge some of these decisions as errors, but they continue to maintain their support for the party. Ramón Gutiérrez defended the highly unpopular policy of conscription, explaining that the "contra aggression against the Nicaraguan homeland warranted it." In the words of Roberto Flores, a Delegate of the Word in the city of Estelí: "A true Christian will defend his home and does not think only of himself, because if one sees that they come to kill children as the contras did, Christians were forced to fight back. Just like Jesus, we had to feel the pain of those who suffered" (in Serra 1985: 156).

Despite the peace accords and the demobilization of the contra in 1991, terrorist acts by disgruntled forces have continued in the country. Patricia Mulligan, Ramón Gutiérrez, Mercedes Ortega, and Horacio Lacayo spoke of their concern over continued violence in Nicaragua. They expressed hope that peace can be maintained, but they did not rule out the right of citizens to arm themselves again. In fact, all of these Nicaraguans expressed concern over efforts by the new Chamorro government to disband the Sandinista army. Members of the Marxist type expressed belief that "citizens should have the right to defend their revolutionary gains." This point of view is in conflict with other Christians in the base communities, and it differentiates the Marxist type from the other ideal types.

Continued faith in the classless objective of Marxism is another distinguishing element among members of this type. Insistently they argue that democracy can only be achieved with a radical redistribution of wealth. These CEB members express the idea that democracy will remain impossible so long as material inequality remains a reality in their country.

Despite the Sandinistas' loss in the national elections of 1990, Marxists and Marxist-Christians continue to applaud the efforts of the Sandinista party. In reflecting on the past they acknowledge the mistakes made by the regime. Patricia Mulligan suggested that the FSLN lost touch with the people. In this respect, she argued, the revolutionary government had ultimately failed in its most important mission: "Many ministers were living very comfortable lives and many people in my generation lost faith in them. I think it was a good thing that the party lost the election. It opened the eyes of the FSLN to its own corruption. But it also opened the eyes of many people who voted for UNO [the oppo-

111

sition party], who see now that they are losing what they gained under the revolution."

Patricia explained that during the 1980s people complained about waiting in long lines to buy milk or toys for their children. "But while people were frustrated by these things they at least had the right to buy. Now many people can't buy because there is no money, there are no jobs, or because today prices are much too high." Asked whether she would do it all over again, Patricia smiled. "Would I do it again? Would I participate in the insurrection and the revolutionary project if I could relive those times? You bet I would! I'm only sorry that I didn't do more. When my son is older I will teach him about social justice. I will explain to him that during the revolutionary process you didn't see children in the streets selling chewing gum. This is the reality today; we have taken a big step backwards."

Patricia said that she has no faith in the new Chamorro government. "There has been a rise of crime and drugs. Women are being attacked in the streets. Cars are being vandalized. It's the desperation of our social situation. In the 1980s, as difficult as things were, this was not the case."

Yamileth Sequeira agreed with others in the community that some members of the Sandinista party were corrupt, but she suggested that the Sandinistas intended to do many good things for the people of Nicaragua. "Yes, there was corruption among some of them, but isn't there corruption in every government? I really believe that the majority in the party were honest people and I also believe that the majority of the Nicaraguan people were in support of them." Asked about the Sandinistas' electoral defeat in 1990, Yamileth suggested that the loss was a consequence of the contra war. "People were so worried for their sons. And there were economic problems, too. Many people believed that the economy would improve with international aid and the lifting of the U.S. embargo. For these reasons I think many people voted against the Sandinistas."

Mercedes Ortega also believed that the contra war and the compulsory military draft contributed to the Sandinistas' defeat. She suggested that the large amounts of money spent by the U.S.

government in the electoral campaign against the FSLN also had effect: "The United States bought this election. Their money was used to buy people's votes."

Today, members of the Marxist type still have confidence in the Sandinista leadership. This belief also differentiates them from other types within the Christian base communities. Mercedes Ortega said that if she could be assured that Daniel Ortega would be president again, she would be just as active in Sandinista projects. "Daniel suffered a lot; he knows how things are. He was in jail for seven years; he hid in the mountains for many years. He knows what it is to suffer. I still have confidence in the party, but I am afraid that they will never hold power again."

When asked about her participation in the insurrection, Mercedes Ortega said that when her great-grandchildren are older, she intends to tell them everything she did to contribute to the revolution. "It is possible that the revolution will only remain a memory for future generations. But I will explain to my great-grandchildren why I participated in the revolutionary process and what I did in it. The revolution did many good things and it would have done greater things if people would have simply allowed it."

It is not uncommon to hear these Nicaraguans express concern over the new government's dismantling of Sandinista projects and cooperatives. They are also well aware of the government's plans for renewing a capitalist economy. Despite these concerns they continue to look to the Sandinista leadership to protect the interests of the workers and the poor. They believe that the party will defend the gains of the revolution.

In line with this hope and this expectation, CEB members of the Marxist type argued the need for continuing their work toward a classless society. Mercedes Ortega contended that the Sandinistas "were genuinely intent on bringing about this transformation. They took into consideration all members of society—not just the poor, but all people—and they opened my own world to grow and develop as a person."

Today these CEB members continue to identify themselves as Sandinistas. Mercedes Ortega proudly displayed her party identification card. Despite the fact that the FSLN is currently out of favor, these Nicaraguans remain devout and enthusiastic supporters.

For members of the Marxist type, the revolutionary experience had a radicalizing effect on their religiosity. Many of these Nicaraguans were persuaded to accept the value of Marxist theory and the legitimacy of class struggle. As a result, some members of the Marxist type renounced their faith in religion altogether. For others the struggle resulted in a divorce from the Catholic Church—if not from their spiritual search for a more "authentic" Christianity.

As former practitioners of Catholicism, they have turned away from the faith of their birth. Because they have lost confidence in the traditional church, many are struggling to define a new spirituality for themselves and their grass-roots church. For Edgar Parrales this search meant leaving the priesthood. For others like Patricia Mulligan and Ramón Gutiérrez, the search has led them to seek an areligious path, one that exists apart from any established religion or any organized church. Free from the restrictions of established religion, their worship finds expression in the community, in work for the common good. They are joined by others like Horacio Lacayo, Mercedes Ortega, and Yamileth Sequeira. Although their path appears secularized, it seems to remain spiritual in nature. This idea is probably best articulated by Father Ernesto Cardenal, who has written in *The Gospel in Solentiname* that "declared faith in a personal redeemer may no longer be indispensable to 'Christian' belief" (Shaw 1989: 30).

For Marxists and Marxist-Christians, the march forward for a new Nicaraguan society remains challenged by forces perhaps larger and more powerful than they. But the revolutionary experience has brought to members of this type confidence in their ability to chart a new way. For Marxists and Marxist-Christians, the revolution has been just the beginning. Their determination to break with the past, their devotion to a new way of being, and their commitment to the radical, democratic ideals of equality and justice encourage them to continue their journey forward.

CHAPTER SEVEN

The Revolutionary Christian Type

THE PREVIOUS CHAPTER suggests that one element of the popular church, members of the Marxist type, embraced the Sandinista project in Nicaragua and consequently renounced their Catholic identity. Another grouping within the popular church is similar to that of Marxist-Christians. Members who occupy this similar position accept the notion that there are structural obstacles to human development. As a consequence they, too, were won over by the idea of the need for class struggle.

In the 1980s, members of the Revolutionary Christian type gave broad support to the Sandinistas. Like their Marxist counterparts, these Nicaraguans still believe that the Sandinistas are the only party that has been—and continues to be—sincere about bringing social justice to Nicaraguan society.

What is strikingly different about the Revolutionary Christian type is the centrality of the spiritual dimension of their experience. Contrary to the Marxist position, Revolutionary Christians do not speak of having undergone a de-Christianizing process, either for themselves or for their grass-roots church. Revolutionary Christians speak of their political commitment to social justice as a consequence of their faith, a new Catholic faith, one that continues to motivate their political activity.

Revolutionary Christians claim that the rise of liberation theology provided the direct impetus for their sociopolitical activ-

115

ism. At the same time they have also suggested that Marxism provided them with a theoretical framework for reading social and historical events relevant to Nicaragua. More importantly, they believe Marxist theory to be compatible with liberation theology's evangelical inspiration. For members of this type, the move toward political mobilization and involvement in the revolutionary process seemed to be a logical outgrowth of three factors: (1) growing social conscientization, (2) the themes of liberation theology, and (3) the acceptance of the Sandinistas' historical project.

"The motivation for many Christians to become involved with the revolutionary process of the 1980s can perhaps be best understood if we think of Sandinismo as a faith rather than as an ideology," explained Father Antonio Castro, founding member of the Christian base community of Larreynaga. Sandinismo is a synthesis of Christian vocation with revolutionary consciousness, one that combines religious conviction with Nicaraguan nationalism (see also O'Brien 1986: 70).

According to Revolutionary Christians, commitment to Sandinismo helped them to legitimize their political activity. Unlike some members of the previous type who were greatly inspired by Marxist theory, members of the Revolutionary Christian type suggested that their motivation came from a revolutionary reading of the gospel. Their inspiration was based on a distinctly proletarian interpretation of the Scriptures. It is typical to hear them speak of God as the liberator of the poor and of the role of Christ as a political revolutionary. For many of these Nicaraguans, living a new Christian consciousness in the 1980s meant working with the Sandinistas to build the kingdom of God on Earth. In practice today it means continuing the work for social and political justice.

Today, however, Revolutionary Christians are less convinced than are members of the Marxist type that the revolutionary project should continue if that means working toward a classless society. They are not convinced that in the climate of the times such a project is possible or, more importantly, politically wise.

Unlike their Marxist counterparts, Revolutionary Christians

remain serious Catholic people. They argue that their faith requires them to continue their vanguard role in transforming Nicaraguan society toward a more socially just society. Faced with new social and political challenges, Revolutionary Christians are today asking themselves what this role requires in a climate of political crisis.

CREATING THE KINGDOM OF GOD: A NEW DEMOCRATIC PROJECT

After the triumph of the insurrection, a large number of Revolutionary Christians apparently left their religious work to offer themselves to the service of the Sandinista government. Many who became involved in the revolutionary experiment did so out of a commitment to democratic socialism. Many of these Nicaraguans argued that their service was an effective way of taking on the Christian commitment of Jesus' commandment to love their neighbor and to work for the community's well-being. Brazilian Bishop Pedro Casadaliga has called such Christians "revolutionaries for the gospel" (in Cabestrero 1986: vii).

María Del Socorro Gutiérrez exemplifies the Revolutionary Christian type. She and her husband were among the founders of the Christian Family Movement that did apostolic work in Nicaragua between 1963 and 1965. After the insurrection she became general secretary of the Ministry of Housing. She explained that her work with the Sandinistas in providing land and housing to very poor Nicaraguans was a way for her to actualize her faith: It was a concrete way of putting the preferential option for the poor into practice (Cabestrero 1986: 41–42).

In the community of San Pablo, Julio and Amélida Sequeira explained that after the popular insurrection they left Manauga to participate in Sandinista projects in the countryside. Julio remembered that during the 1980s he helped rural farm workers establish agricultural cooperatives. During this period he also taught reading, writing, and Bible studies to the families there. While he was in the mountains his wife, Amélida, was involved in the Commission for Civil Defense. Julio explained that the organization was involved in many things: taking a census, pro-

117

moting health care, distributing food ration cards, and providing for neighborhood protection.

Others members of CEBs remained in their barrios and became active participants in local Sandinista organizations. Julita Soza remained in Adolfo Reyes. "After the insurrection," she said, "the FSLN organized us into groups to help them distribute food. We also joined in teams to help rebuild the neighborhood."

Julita recalled that after the insurrection the neighborhood had no water because the National Guard had raided the barrio and had broken the pipes to look for weapons. After the insurrection the community came together to begin working on reconstruction projects. "We also created a revolutionary vigilance to guard the neighborhood against antirevolutionary activity. There were eight to ten of us in a team. I held guard from eight at night until three o'clock in the morning. We would walk the streets, guard against crime, and basically ensure the safety of the neighborhood."

These projects were not without their critics. In particular, the Civil Defense patrols came to be highly unpopular by the end of the decade. Critics accused the patrols of spying on their neighbors and using their authority to force others into compliance with political projects with which they disagreed. But that it not how Julita remembered her work.

"During the 1980s we were assisted by members of the clergy. Priests would come into the barrio to help in all of these projects," Julita explained. "The Sandinistas were trying to create a new way of life here in Nicaragua. We were trying to protect the neighborhood, and at the same time we were trying to promote sharing and a type of living as brothers and sisters."

Julita remembered that priests would call special meetings during these years to distribute information about the goals of the Sandinistas and to denounce the injustices of antirevolutionary activities. But she denied the accusations of some that people were spied on or forced into political compromises.

The Catholic hierarchy's public accusation of the Sandinistas as communists furthered this crisis. Revolutionary Christians explained that they were troubled by the hierarchy's position concerning the revolution. Many suggested that the bishops had grossly misunderstood the goals of the revolution and the Revolutionary Christians' motivation for working with the party. Yet unlike members of the Marxist type, Revolutionary Christians responded by holding on to their Catholic identity: For them, this identity had taught the necessity of living out their faith every day.

"This is why I enjoyed being a part of the community and why I made the choice to remain committed to the Sandinista revolution," explained Graciela García in Adolfo Reyes. "Throughout the 1980s we were always trying to find useful projects to assist those of our neighbors who were in need."

As the decade unfolded, the need for many such projects was evident. As the government's attention (and money) was increasingly diverted to the contra war, the communities faced mounting problems. Raquel López described one such problem that was confronted in the community of San Judas.

"In our community we saw the problem of malnourishment, and so the Common Pot was born," Raquel explained. "Our idea was to create a common dining room to offer neighborhood children, pregnant women, and nursing mothers a soybean snack. Our principle objective was to work against malnourishment and to educate young mothers on how to help their children. Our aim was also to teach students and mothers how to cook with soybeans, how to cook in a balanced way."

The San Judas soybean experiment was so successful that the Sandinista government used it as a pilot project for other community programs. Today, with San Judas's assistance, similar soybean projects have been established in Managua, which currently has eight *ollas* (pots) in the city; the cities of Matagalpa and Granada also have *olla* projects.

In San Pablo, community members directed their attention to the construction of a preschool for poor neighborhood children. Rafael Valdéz explained that during the 1980s the Sandinistas assisted these kinds of community efforts, but they are not supported by the current Chamorro government. The day care program continues to care for sixty children between the ages of three and five years with volunteers from the grass-roots church assisting with this program. Despite the fact that these activities were inspired by faith, involvement in them came to be increasingly criticized by other Christians.

The religious attack came from members of more conservative sectors of the Catholic Church who accused the CEB members of being communists. Revolutionary Christians said they were particularly offended by charges that they had turned their back on their faith. Unlike members of the Marxist type, Revolutionary Christians denied accusations that they are no longer religious people. Rafael Valdéz explained that whereas he was attracted to the ideology of the Sandinistas, he was different from others in his community because he clung to his faith. "Although my faith did not lessen in the Somoza struggle, I was influenced by Marxist-Leninists. I believed as the Sandinista leaders did that it was necessary to build a society that could take care of its people."

Other Revolutionary Christians suggested that the Sandinistas were atheists who were respectful of their faith. "Just because I worked with them did not mean that this service lessened my own religious beliefs," argued Julio Sequeira. "I believed in the party's ideology but not from a philosophical point of view. Unlike them, I am not an atheist; I am a Catholic."

Others agreed. Amélida Sequeira said their new way of thinking is different from traditional Catholic doctrine: "To me it is a way of thinking, of acting, a purity of mind that is more Christian than Catholic. Our new way of thinking suggests that if you act on behalf of the poorest, if you assist them with their social and political needs, you are fulfilling the obligations of being a Christian."

"There were people who didn't agree with us because the community was doing projects for the poorest," explained Graciela García. "They believed we were being political. But it seemed to me that if politics meant doing good things for poor people, then I suppose I was political. People accused me of being a Sandinista and they accused the soya project of being FSLN, but that wasn't true. We had members and supporters of other political parties involved in our programs," she said.

What Revolutionary Christians regarded as a natural evolution of religious commitment, the Nicaraguan Catholic hierarchy continued to judge as a politicization of religion that went far beyond the framework of the social doctrine of the Catholic Church (Serra 1985: 154). Revolutionary Christians argued that the bishops denounced their activity because they saw the work as promoting one class interest over another. Julio Sequeira remembered that they were often accused of taking sides: "We *were* taking sides with the poor. The truth is that in time we came to understand that the charitable work of the traditional church was an inadequate solution to the problems of our society." Julio explained that their gradual awakening to this reality motivated them to promote change at the structural level of society. This motivation is the reason so many Revolutionary Christians left their communities to offer themselves to the service of the Sandinista government.

Revolutionary Christians said that as they grew in their sophistication they came to believe that poverty had to be eradicated by working toward a classless society. The fact that they were finding accommodation with Marxists did not mean that they were forsaking their faith. If anything, it was only reaffirming it.

Such an understanding, however, was criticized by the Catholic hierarchy who continued to accuse the popular sector of manipulating official church doctrine and of dividing the Catholic community. In an interview in his office in Managua, Cardinal Obando suggested that about 80 percent of Catholic Nicaraguans remain faithful to the traditional church while the other 20 percent "are in contradiction" and remain Sandinista sympathizers. "They call themselves the popular church but the name in itself represents a failure of this sector because the word *popular* suggests a majority. . . . Twenty percent is not the majority of the Catholic community! The popular church has nothing to do with the traditional church here," he charged.

Throughout the 1980s, the conservative hierarchy of the

Catholic Church insistently identified the Christian communities as instruments of the Sandinistas. Monsignor Eduardo Montenegro acknowledged this view. "The Nicaraguan church is divided. One of these divisions is the traditional church. On the negative side, and in a more liberal sense, there exists a church of the base communities. Unfortunately, during the 1980s this second group took on a leftist character. Theirs has been a Marxist movement. In time, members of this church joined the Sandinistas. They considered themselves the religious arm of the FSLN and they used their organization to propagate the party's dogma," he contended.

Revolutionary Christians denied these charges. They were particularly sensitive to the accusation that they were responsible for having divided the Catholic community. Indeed, the subject of a separate popular church has been a contentious one ever since the insurrection. When asked about the allegations of their separation from the traditional church, Revolutionary Christians were more evasive. In fact, they were very careful in their use of language in discussing their work. Self-identification labels like *la iglesia popular* (the people's church) and conversations that used terms such as a *breakaway church* or a *parallel magisterium* appeared to be consciously avoided.

"They avoid such labels and discussions," explained Father Joseph Mulligan, "because being a member of a base community has been a very sensitive, corrosive subject here in Nicaragua."

While members of the Revolutionary Christian type acknowledged that they have departed from the traditional interpretations of the gospel, they also pointed out the fact that their communities observe and celebrate traditional Catholic sacraments. Although they defied the bishops by making a commitment to the revolutionary process, they suggested that the criticism of their political activity has been hypocritical. These Nicaraguans argue that historically Christians have always offered themselves to political service. What was different in Nicaragua in the 1980s was the fact that the Catholic hierarchy was unwilling to support the Sandinista leadership.

Despite charges from people like Monsignor Bosco Vivas, who

accused the popular church of being an enemy of the established church and of using a Marxist political ideology, Revolutionary Christians repeatedly contended that their motivation was religious and not Marxist.

Unlike their counterparts in the Marxist type and in spite of the acrimony between the grass-roots and the institutional church, Revolutionary Christians repeatedly reaffirmed their identity as Catholics. "We have been born and raised as Catholic Christians," explained Rafael Valdéz. "Our faith is deeply rooted and simply finds expression in our work with the poor. It would not be possible for me to renounce my faith."

Revolutionary Christians defended their participation in the revolutionary program as a means of preserving the principles of Christianity in the post-Somoza society. Julio Sequeira explained that many Catholics felt their participation was necessary to ensure that the revolutionary process remained true to its ideals. They suggested that their presence in the Sandinista program was a means for safeguarding the process, to prevent just the kind of totalitarian state that the Catholic hierarchy feared. "We saw our participation as a way to ensure a revolutionary program," argued Rafael Valdéz, "one that could be both humanitarian and pluralistic."

Monsignor Bismark Carballo rejected this argument. "All this talk of the poor—it sounds good—but once people like this get into power they forget about the poor! They used the poor to hide their leftist ideas and their communist ideology," he charged.

Community members were offended by this kind of perspective and pointed to what they considered to be the hypocritical behavior of the Catholic hierarchy. "They made a mockery of compassion," suggested Amélida Sequeira. "During the contra aggression, the cardinal never once condemned the atrocities. Even after he was ordained cardinal he didn't return here to be with his people to give his first mass. Instead he went to Miami to bless the wealthy and to be received by them."

Julio Sequeira agreed: "Cardinal Obando had been criticizing the liberation clergy for involving themselves in politics. But everyone could see that this was hypocritical. The cardinal had used his own office to be political. He used his office and his authority to denounce our matryrs and heroes; he used his office and authority to destabilize the Sandinista government. He used his position to advance his and the Vatican's own political views. Yet he condemned us for being political!"

ALIENATION AND SEPARATION

By summer 1985, Revolutionary Christians began fighting back. Their alienation was furthered after the pope's infamous visit to Managua, and tensions deepened when Archbishop Obando was ordained as Nicaragua's cardinal. The last straw for them came when Obando used his new position to support the contra forces openly. The Revolutionary Christians joined in support of Father Miguel d'Escoto, who used the occasion to denounce his superior publicly.

Father d'Escoto's personal participation in the Somoza struggle and his position in the Sandinista government as minister for foreign affairs had earned him tremendous respect and moral authority among Catholics. In summer 1985, he apparently used this influence to counter the hierarchy's propaganda campaign. The priest denounced the bishops' complicity in the contra aggression and personally criticized Obando, accusing the cardinal of using his power and influence against the people of Nicaragua (see also O'Brien 1986: 64).

Looking back, CEB members of the Revolutionary Christian type recalled that in July 1985 Father d'Escoto began a thirty-day *ayuno* (fast). The fast was followed a few months later by a march for peace. The three-hundred-kilometer demonstration involved hundreds of Catholics, including CEB members from Adolfo Reyes, San Pablo, and San Judas.

The purpose of the fast and march was to increase Christian solidarity and to support the Sandinista position that was seeking an end to the civil war. CEB members suggested that the demonstration was a crucial event in their increasing alienation from the Catholic Church. Father d'Escoto's attack on the hierarchy and his warnings that tensions with the bishops were coming to a breaking point were very radicalizing for them. Indeed, the demonstration was the first formal hint that a separate Catholic Church might be emerging in Nicaragua.

"We were not a separate church," explained Julio Sequeira in San Pablo, "but the possibilities were there. We could not ignore the fact that our values and beliefs were increasingly in conflict with those of the hierarchy."

In this climate, the alliance of the popular church with the Sandinista party continued to have its costs. Not only did their relationship with the Sandinistas alienate them from the Catholic hierarchy, but this position also weakened the communities' public support. This waning support for the popular church was particularly evident as the civil war dragged on and the Nicaraguan economy slipped into crisis.

Today, Revolutionary Christians speak freely of their disillusionment with the Sandinista government. As the contra war dragged on, many people in the communities came to believe that their problems were being ignored by the party leadership. As economic times grew more desperate, many Nicaraguans believed that the Sandinistas had lost touch with their harsh, daily reality. Many also believed that members of the grass-roots church had lost sight of their neighbors' problems. These critics accused CEB members of giving greater priority to national problems than to their own immediate struggles.

Revolutionary Christians admitted that many of these accusations were true. They suggested that the decision of so many Christian leaders to leave their communities and to enter into government service was a mistake. "The CEBs were very strong following the insurrection," explained Rafael Valdéz, "but gradually many of our members were lost to revolutionary projects." For example, the loss of CEB youth to revolutionary projects left the communities very weak. "The older people tried to keep the communities alive, but they only met periodically and this, too, sapped our strength," Valdéz explained.

Revolutionary Christians believed that, as many people left the communities to work with the new government, the grass-roots church began to lose touch with the larger community. "More importantly, we began to lose touch with our religious tradition," Rafael went on. "Some of us had become very militant in this process and far too involved in political work."

The defeat of the Sandinistas in the national elections of 1990 seems to have coincided with the severing of ties between the traditional church and members of the Revolutionary Christian group. The electoral defeat of the Sandinistas dealt a serious blow to the party faithful.

In the communities of Adolfo Reyes, San Judas, and San Pablo, the election results were said to have been unexpected, even shattering. It is clear that members were shocked and disoriented by the defeat of a party that they still believed maintained popular support.

The contra war and the economy are consistent explanations for the Sandinista defeat. Julio Sequeira suggested that the primary problem was the contra aggression: "Most people wanted their sons back. People believed that the United States would not stop the war if there was not a change in political leadership here. Many young people who did not want to serve in the war also voted against the Sandinistas."

Members in the CEBs also suggested the influence of CIA money in swinging public votes. They believed that a great deal of money went through the church to buy support for the opposition and that money was given to extreme right-wing groups to get them to support the opposing UNO coalition.

In the Christian base community of Adolfo Reyes, Father Arnoldo Santana offered his explanation of the electoral defeat: "Following the insurrection the Sandinistas did many good things: a literacy campaign, a vaccination program, land reform. Unfortunately the revolution was not magic. In the countryside the peasants became the pawns in the civil war. In the rural areas the revolution did not reach out far enough to provide the benefits the Sandinistas had promised, and many peasants became vulnerable to contra propaganda."

Father Santana suggested that a greater problem was the fact that Nicaragua had never developed beyond an export economy of bananas, corn, and sugar. "Lack of industry and development

126

complicated the economic situation," he explained. "This was a situation that the Sandinistas could not address under war conditions."

In San Judas some Revolutionary Christians placed the blame on Cardinal Obando for having used his influence to undermine support for the revolutionary government. Today at CEB meetings it is not unusual to hear more open and vocal criticism of Nicaragua's cardinal. He has been accused of aligning himself with the rich, and tensions have continued to build.

For example, in the community of San Pablo, relations with the cardinal have been just short of explosive. Tensions began shortly after the Sandinistas lost the election. "Obando attempted to hire two reactionary priests to service our community," explained resident Modesto Baltodano. "But our community refused to accept them."

"They have the keys to the parish house," explained Father Joseph Mulligan. "They raise their own money to pay a priest, so the cardinal was forced to back down on this one." But it was a short-lived success for the community. A year later the cardinal transferred another priest to service the San Pablo parishes.

"He has completely alienated us," explained Rafael Valdéz. "He refuses to recognize us and he tells us that we are not up to the standards of a church. He says that we should have an altar and statues. Imagine, he even called our church a barnyard!"

Rafael said the community was indignant: "We told him that if he wanted to service the community and supervise us, he was welcome here. So long as he didn't try to push his ideas on us, we would try not to push our ideas on him. But we warned him that if he persisted with this behavior we would kick him out!"

Community tension concerning this particular priest eventually erupted into a bitter conflict following the unexpected visit of Father José de la Jara's widow, who had traveled from Spain to visit the community carrying with her the former priest's ashes. Apparently Father de la Jara had requested that his ashes be buried in San Pablo, the community that he had founded twenty years before.

According to community members, the Obando priest refused

to acknowledge Mrs. de la Jara during her visit. This behavior was interpreted by members of the CEB as contemptuous. The incident typified the deepening alienation between Revolutionary Christians and the traditional clergy. The conflict, however, was more than one of personalities. It was and continues to be a reflection of the deeper conflict between the church models that have evolved in Nicaragua.

"The problem is that we have a different conception of the church," explained Julio Sequeira. "For many of us, our conception of the church is an informal one, one that ultimately serves God through service to others. Decisions are made by the community in the interest of the community."

This vision appears to be in conflict with their own perception of the traditional church's position. They accused the institutional church of remaining hierarchical and authoritarian. Revolutionary Christians understand the top-down model of the traditional church as one that seeks to control the laity. Such a model is in opposition to their own understanding of what it means to be a church of God. They argued that this traditional model wrongly seeks to be served by its followers.

"Another conflict here has to do with authority," explained Rafael Valdéz. "The priest comes here and tells us that he is going to organize us, and we tell him we are already organized! Despite this, he brings in other people to replace those of us doing community work."

Rafael used the example of the preschool program that is now coming under the traditional priest's direction and authority: "He has been trying to take control of a CEB program that has its own logic. His attempt is understood by many of us as subversive and alienating."

While Marxist-Christians divorced themselves from the Catholic faith, Revolutionary Christians spoke of living a new, more democratic form of Catholicism. The effects of liberation theology and the revolutionary experience have led them to challenge the hierarchical structure of the church. But unlike the Marxist type that has completely abandoned the practice of their religion, Revolutionary Christians are simply less willing to accept authority, particularly when it runs counter to their conceptions of faith.

Today this approach appears to be central to the conflict. Rafael Valdéz suggested that the priest in San Pablo continues to impose rules from the top, a practice that conflicts with the Revolutionary Christian conviction that the church should exercise a process of democratic participation and decision making.

"There is another problem, too," suggested Julio Sequeira. "Today there is no place for biblical analysis and discussion. The priest tells us that only he can do reflections and he silences us if we try to speak. This man is against all Vatican II and Medellín documents and he disregards all aspects of the poor."

According to Revolutionary Christians, the attempted return to more traditional Catholicism is more than just a religious challenge. They understand the conflict as a political one, too. Julio Sequeira said that he believes the church's inattention to the poor is deliberate: "What is happening here is that the cardinal is trying to convert us into Chamorro supporters. But the fact is we worship two different kinds of gods—one rich, one poor. For me, it's a sin to see my nation's cardinal disregarding the poor and favoring the party of the rich!"

Marta Castillo from the community of Villa Revolución shared her perspective: "We watched on television Cardinal Obando asking for relief for the homeless. He asked for millions of dollars when the hurricane hit the Atlantic coast. I asked myself the question, 'why?' "

Marta answered her own question: "He has to ask for help because he lacks the necessary funds. And he lacks the [necessary] funds so that he can build his palace of gold [the new Nicaraguan cathedral]."

The subject of the construction of the new Nicaraguan cathedral has been sensitive in the Christian base communities. Dominga Urbina, a CEB member from Adolfo Reyes, articulated a common point of view. She suggested that with the need for so many necessities in Nicaragua, the money being spent on the cathedral is further alienating Christians. "Sixty percent of our children here in Nicaragua are malnourished," Dominga explained.

"Yet I have heard the cardinal say that it is not good to be feeding children—it makes them very dependent. Imagine that!" she exclaimed.

Increasingly, Revolutionary Christians are coming to acknowledge openly major differences with the Catholic hierarchy. Luis Aguirre, a leader in the community of Adolfo Reyes, suggested that they are creating a new way of being a church: "This new way requires sacrifice. This new way is not accepted by the majority of Catholics because sacrifice is a difficult thing. Yes, we feel the split in the church. It is over many differences, both religious and political."

Sacrifice is a word repeatedly used when members are asked to describe their faith. Julita Soza suggested that as traditional Catholics the only thing that was asked of them was obedience, to go to church. "The new way requires sacrifice, and it is rejected by many who do not want to give what they have," she said.

Julita said that her faith continues to be strong, but she admitted sadness over the religious division. "The new preaching has turned many away. Today, more Catholics are with the Obando church. It is far easier to be a Catholic if it does not ask anything of you. But one of the things that I have learned is the art of sharing. I try to share all of my things."

Despite the fact that Julita lives in one of the poorest dwellings in Adolfo Reyes, she manages to share her meals of rice and beans with others in the neighborhood who are sick or in need. Such acts of generosity are abundant. Despite the evident goodwill of the communities, however, the criticism of the popular church by the Catholic hierarchy continues to erode neighborhood support. Julita Soza explained that community members are constantly accused of being political. She herself has been called a communist.

Revolutionary Christians are particularly concerned that the bishops will eventually break apart their communities. For example, Marta Castillo from Villa Revolución discussed the problem her community has had in its efforts to establish a medical clinic.

"Villa Revolución is an Obando barrio," Marta suggested. "This means that the cardinal has named a traditional priest to our parish. Our efforts therefore are constantly undermined. Promoting a medical clinic is seen as promoting the church of the poor. This presents political problems for the priests and bishops because they do not want to be in disagreement with the cardinal."

Luis Aguirre from Adolfo Reyes explained that the majority of priests today are no longer working with the communities: "Many supportive priests have been expelled or have been transferred from their local churches."

A recent study by Berryman (1994: 37) suggests that during the 1980s a clear majority of the clergy could be classified in some sense as anti-Sandinista, but most priests (60 to 65 percent) sought to avoid the extremes of active opposition. This appears to be a trend that continues today.

Father Arnoldo Santana still works with the CEBs, but he agreed that the grass-roots church is under tremendous pressure: "The cardinal has the power to bring new priests into the barrios. This has not happened in the past simply because there were no churches in the poor neighborhoods. During the 1970s and 1980s churches were built by the communities. Today in some of these neighborhoods new priests have come in to replace those who have been transferred out. In some cases they have allowed our work to continue, but in many other cases they have not."

Mark Lester, a former Catholic priest who served several CEBs in the city of Matagalpa, suggested that the Catholic hierarchy has made a concerted effort to undermine support for the Christian communities. "In order to gain control over the pastoral practice, revolutionary priests and Delegates of the Word have been relieved of their duties, and new traditional-thinking priests have been selected to serve," Lester explained. "These priests and delegates are trained under a very different orientation. Unlike the past, where training was done by local parish priests, training is now done by each diocese."

Lester explained that courses and seminars are now approved by the bishops. Apparently, priests are constrained to preach from preapproved guidebooks that are reissued each year. "It is a ministering divorced from the people's immediate reality. The

131

element of reflection on the reality in Nicaragua has simply been taken out," Lester said.

He also suggested that, for many clergy, identification with elite interests (rather than the poor) could be traced to the historical experience of the Catholic Church in Latin America: "Financial support has always depended upon the wealthy." In Latin America, priests are not paid a salary but rather are supported by the upper classes. "This has been one structural reason why many bishops and their priests have remained conservative," Lester said. "The structure simply works against their identification with the poor."

Mark Lester suggested that in Nicaragua the clergy who have direct daily contact with the poor are more likely to adopt a revolutionary commitment. "On the other hand, those members of the church who maintain frequent contact with the middle to upper middle classes remain conservative and, at best, cautious about revolutionary ideals."

The behavior of the Catholic hierarchy and the fact that many barrio churches are now served by conservative priests have had more than one impact on the CEBs. Not only is their work constantly challenged, but also fewer and fewer Revolutionary Christians are staying involved in the life of the local church. In many cases, they no longer attend the Sunday services; they also are less likely to participate in religious activities that are under the direction of a traditional priest. Increasingly, Revolutionary Christians commune with God in the circle of chairs where they pray together and engage in Bible study at their weekly CEB meetings.

Revolutionary Christians regard their active service to the community as taking priority over their devotion to the local church, a belief that is similar to that of their Marxist counterparts who remain devoted to the community but not to the Catholic Church. What is strikingly different is the fact that Revolutionary Christians still openly regard themselves as "Catholic peoples of God."

While the frequency of formal liturgical practices is down

among members of this type, autonomous projects are up. Incrementally, members of the CEBs are initiating programs that challenge conservative priests and Catholics alike. Two such projects surround the celebration of Santo Domingo and the Purísima.

The Santo Domingo celebration is an annual summer event in the city of Managua where Catholics pay homage to the patron saint. Much like North America's Saint Patrick's Day celebrations, the occasion includes parades, crowds, dancing, and drinking. Because the celebration often becomes disorderly, the event has been discouraged by the Catholic hierarchy. Despite this fact, the festival continues to be supported by members of the CEBs. They argued that dancing and singing are expressions of love for the Lord. Why should they try to repress that? they asked. Revolutionary Christians argued that such celebration is popular religiosity and has a right to be expressed.

This argument reflects a growing desire often articulated by Revolutionary Christians that the church should work toward recovering the people's indigenous faith. Many are becoming increasingly aware of their ancestral past. These individuals affirmed their support for encouraging popular religiosity, and they argued that it is an important part of the CEBs' continuing work.

This attitude was especially evident in the Purísima celebration, a December observance in which homage is paid to the Virgin Mother. During the 1980s, the Sandinistas held large festivals in the center of Managua to celebrate Purísima. At those celebrations, many organizations created huge altars in honor of the Virgin, and there were competitions and prizes. This activity was severely criticized by the Catholic hierarchy who accused the FSLN of using the event to politicize religion. As a consequence, the hierarchy discouraged the public celebration. Since the election of the new UNO government, the religious holiday is once again a private celebration and the hierarchy continues to ignore it.

The Purísima seems to be a uniquely Nicaraguan festivity and may have been part of the original harvest celebration of indigenous peoples. Because roots, produce, and fruits have always been part of the ceremony, it is possible the occasion was meant to give thanks for a bountiful harvest.

The communities continue to try to recover popular religiosity, but Revolutionary Christians accused the conservative hierarchy of undermining such efforts. Today, as the economic situation in Nicaragua becomes increasingly severe, they also have accused the hierarchy and the new government of undermining efforts that seek to empower the poor.

The dismantling of Sandinista projects and programs by the new Chamorro government led both Marxists and Revolutionary Christians to agree that the UNO party has done nothing to assist the poor. Both groups perceive the Chamorro government as anti-Christian. They are not convinced of its rhetoric about democracy, and they continue to accuse it of being a regime that favors the rich.

The recent spread of fundamentalist thought in Nicaragua is also of serious concern for the Christian base communities. Revolutionary Christians are likely to explain the infusion of fundamentalism by accusing the United States of sponsoring many well-financed, well-organized fundamentalist missions. Julita Soza explained that missionaries suddenly began appearing in their barrios in the 1980s, offering blankets, food, clothing, and toys. In the deprivation of the contra years, the charitable goods were enticing. Like others, Julita believed that the missionaries were deliberately attempting to undermine the solidarity of their communities, and in many cases they did. Julio Sequeira said they lost community members to the new evangelical churches that went up around the San Pablo barrio.

Others argued that the fundamentalist campaign was successful because young people who flocked to these churches in the 1980s could use their membership in them as an excuse for avoiding military service in the Sandinista army. Rafael Valdéz suggested that these campaigns not only sought to undermine the CEB movement but also were deliberately intended to undermine public support for the Sandinista government.

Revolutionary Christians also believe that the rise of fundamentalism was enhanced by the cardinal's constant criticism of the popular church. Apparently, many people left the CEBs as acrimony increased between the institutional church and the communities. By the end of the 1980s the communities had lost about half of their members.

In spite of the church-state crisis and the electoral defeat of the Sandinistas, Revolutionary Christians continue to have faith in the party and remain vocal supporters. Many were active in the party's reelection campaign in 1990. Some volunteered at local party offices, some volunteered their services to get out the vote, and others worked as staff support at the election centers. Despite the Sandinista defeat, Revolutionary Christians contend that the revolution furthered democratic practices in Nicaragua.

"The strikes that take place today would have been impossible before the revolution," argued Julio Sequeira. "The revolution brought with it a freedom of consciousness that gave Nicaraguans the courage to speak out against the things that they saw as social injustices."

Revolutionary Christians do not believe that the socialist experiment failed the people of Nicaragua. Yet they admit that policies that sought to redistribute wealth and resources frightened people who had something to lose. In retrospect, they believe that Nicaraguans were not yet ready for such a radical vision for a new society.

"Our communities still believe in this ideal," explained Julio Sequeira. "We struggle for greater equality because the majority of our people are so poor. It is for this reason that we supported laws that favored their interests. But what we have learned from this experiment is that we should have taken into account the wealth that does exist here."

Revolutionary Christians suggest that class divisions were exploited both by the enemies of the Sandinistas and by the bellicose rhetoric of the Catholic hierarchy that manipulated these insecurities. "What we failed to do was learn to coexist with those who ultimately had the power to destroy this revolution," suggested Rafael Valdéz.

Revolutionary Christians appear to typify a growing belief

135

that Nicaraguans still need to learn how to cooperate with one another. They suggest that their objective today is to continue the work for social justice. Still, they readily admit that this endeavor will be difficult. Despite the fact that they have hopes that the classes can learn to work together in eradicating poverty, they admit that they have lost faith in the viability of a classless project. They differ strikingly from their Marxist counterparts by suggesting that a classless society may never be possible in Nicaragua. The loss of such faith does not, however, suggest total abandonment of party support. Revolutionary Christians believe that the Sandinistas made a significant contribution to the process of democracy, a contribution that permitted them to participate in a political process that would have been impossible ten years before.

"Today, I take my twelve-year-old son to witness the people's struggle," explained Rafael Valdéz. "We attend strikes and protests together. During the election, I took him with me to help with the Sandinista campaign, and we gave out hats and pamphlets." The point of the exercise was to help his son understand the meaning of living in a democracy. "My intent is to show my son the fundamental ideal of the FSLN and how it differs from other political ideologies. My hope is that when he gets old enough he can decide for himself the kind of process he wants to support. This is an experience that my father could not have given to me."

Graciela García suggested there will be a legacy to leave to her children, too: "My children understand what is happening in Nicaragua. It is hard to ignore starving children." She makes a point of taking both her son and her daughter to the CEB projects with which she works in Adolfo Reyes. "I think this is a good way to teach them about the work of the community and the past efforts of the Sandinistas that supported them." Graciela believes that in this way she can teach her children about her own concerns and commitments to the poor: "It is a way for me to be there to answer their questions and to advise them. My great hope is that they will try to live out my example in their own lives."

Despite its electoral loss, the FSLN remains a powerful minority in the Nicaraguan legislature. It continues to play the role of intermediary between the government and the popular sectors. "Because the popular church has a foot in both organized and unorganized popular movements, it serves as an important link in the community," explained Father Joseph Mulligan.

In fact, Revolutionary Christians continue to be active in public celebrations like the annual May 22 celebration of the revolution. They also continue to march in public demonstrations in support of strikers, including the student strike in September 1992.

When asked about this participation, Revolutionary Christians explain that they remain committed to assisting the people's movement in Nicaragua. They also offer other examples, like their participation in circulating petitions, writing letters and articles for newspapers, and organizing workshops and colloquia to discuss current governmental and church affairs. When asked about their motivation, Revolutionary Christians return to rhetoric about building the kingdom of God on Earth. Their inspiration remains religious.

"We base our hope on the power of organized groups and our faith in God," explained Julio Sequeira. "We believe that justice is possible, but it will call for greater solidarity among all members of Nicaraguan society. Part of our work will be to continue to support the popular organizations, all those that truly favor the interests of the poorest."

Revolutionary Christians continue to speak of their role as part of the vanguard in promoting a new society. Like their Marxist counterparts, they continue to be highly politicized. Unlike members of the Marxist type, however, Revolutionary Christians continue to be inspired by their faith and are less enthusiastic about working toward a Marxist society. Today they are also increasingly concerned that the struggle for greater equality and social justice remains nonviolent.

Fears about violence are particularly justified as the Nicaraguan economy fails to deliver the recovery that people expected. According to the Reverend Javier Gorostiaga, the Jesuit rector of the University of Central America, the economic situation is the most depressed in decades. By January 1993 70 percent of Nicaraguans were living in poverty and 60 percent remained unemployed. "How can you consolidate democracy under these conditions?" Gorostiaga asked. "We are seeing levels of poverty not seen in the worst time of the Somoza dictatorship or at the height of the contra war."

Since the war's end in 1991, political instability has led some disgruntled former contra members and Sandinista soldiers to take up arms and return to the mountains. In winter 1992, there were increased reports of civilians rearming to protect themselves from acts of terror in the countryside.

Julita Soza suggested that one of her greatest concerns is the fact that the army has been reduced and is no longer well connected to the community: "This frightens me. My fear is that if the army turns against the state the first people to be arrested will be priests and CEB members. I am terribly fearful of civil war and what this would do to Nicaragua."

Despite these fears, Revolutionary Christians place their hope in the power of their faith. "Our Christian commitment helps us to continue the march. It is our faith that makes us walk forward," said Raquel López. "It is our inspiration."

Because violence is an ever increasing possibility, Revolutionary Christians speak of the urgent need for building greater solidarity. Today, Revolutionary Christians see their social role in Nicaragua as supporting organizations that are truly representative and participatory, ones that can peacefully challenge government programs and policies with which they disagree.

Solidarity is the key word Revolutionary Christians use when speaking of their future objective. But solidarity must begin at home. In reflecting upon their problems, members of the CEBs consistently cite their loss of members as a major factor in the struggle to maintain vitality. Graciela García said that she sees a lack of motivation among people in the neighborhood, some of it caused by political differences and some by the fact that the communities continue to be accused of being political and therefore in violation of the church's position. Because the CEBs have been accused of being Sandinista supporters, people who do not want to be identified with the FSLN party are unwilling to join many community projects.

Julita Soza suggested that loss of CEB membership also has to do with economic hardship: "Some people do not have the time to join because they are trying to make a living. In the case of women it is especially difficult because they are also trying to take care of their children."

Others suggested that their loss of active members has been the result of personality conflicts having nothing to do with religion or politics. Graciela García believes that their communities should have visited those people who left. In Adolfo Reyes, for example, the community depended solely on Julita Soza to speak to those who were unhappy. "She just couldn't do it all. We have come to recognize this as a mistake on our part." Today, Adolfo Reyes has organized a visitation commission that works with the neighborhood. The commission speaks to neighbors about the community's projects and encourages them to come to the CEB meetings.

Among some of the revolutionary priests, a constant criticism is that the CEBs are not doing enough to encourage new membership. Father Uriel Molina suggested that most of the communities are paralyzed. He excluded San Pablo: "There the new parish priest is trying to dismantle the community's work and this is an incentive for them to maintain their line in confrontation with him. In San Pablo they are giving seminars, and I am amazed at their autonomy."

Father Molina's criticism appears to be directed at other CEBs where there seems to be a lack of effort in reaching out to young people in the barrios: "The involvement of our youth is critical for reproducing the communities. Today our young people are not interested in reality from a religious point of view because they see the contradictions with the hierarchy, and they are confused."

Dr. Morris Blachman, professor of Latin American studies at the University of South Carolina, suggested that this situation parallels the disinclination among second generations in communities elsewhere, such as those in the Puritan communities in the United States. "This is a fairly typical phenomenon," he explained. "The zeal of the path blazers is not kindled in the hearts of those who follow them."

The visitation commission in Adolfo Reyes has been successful in getting newcomers to CEB meetings, but it has not always been successful in keeping them. This problem became especially evident when two new faces arrived at a meeting one evening in December 1992. At that meeting, two members of the community heatedly argued over a dental clinic that had been established by the CEB. Unfortunately the dentist had not kept many of his promises to the community. Julita Soza, the person responsible for bringing the dentist to the barrio, was accused of mishandling the initial agreement. Before the argument was over, one of the young visitors stood up and stormed out.

The membership problem is recognized as serious, and the CEBs are currently working to build greater interest and involvement in each of their communities. For example, both San Judas and Adolfo Reyes now have a liturgy and entertainment commission. Because Revolutionary Christians remain committed to the Catholic faith, they have involved themselves in commissions that continue to provide Bible study.

In San Pablo as in Adolfo Reyes and San Judas, members of this type have also involved themselves with new pastoral projects, such as training children for First Holy Communion and for Confirmation. In San Pablo and San Judas, Revolutionary Christians are leaders in establishing youth groups that have been fairly successful. San Judas's youth group currently has thirty-three members and San Pablo's has thirty-two members. The youth groups provide Catholic instruction and social events. San Pablo also has a commission for the sick. The commission not only visits those who are ill but also raises funds to assist people with medical care costs.

To keep the work of the CEBs alive, community members of the Marxist and Revolutionary Christian types continue to visit one another, share experiences, and cooperate on certain projects. They also work for regional and international solidarity with other popular organizations. In addition to weekly CEB meetings, the communities have developed monthly representative council meetings. Every Friday, Revolutionary Christians also take part in seminars for their ongoing theological education. On Saturdays they meet for more basic courses while others travel to rural areas to serve as missionaries.

Revolutionary Christians articulate the need for attracting greater interest by broadening their base and moving beyond their pastoral institutions. They also speak of the need for national reconciliation, and they suggest the need for reaching out to those who think differently than they do. To assist with this endeavor, the CNP (Comisión Nacional Permentala), a national network of CEBs and other organizations of the church of the poor, comes together every two months to discuss difficulties and strategies. The CNP estimates that about 275 communities and other groups are part of its national network (Mulligan 1990), involving 4,500 people as active, regular members of these communities.

Father Joseph Mulligan explained that during the revolution there was an exaggerated notion about liberation theology and the strength of the CEB movement. "There has been an exaggerated notion of the breadth and depth of the church of the poor," Mulligan said. "That exaggeration has led many people to conclude that this church has declined drastically since 1979. That isn't the case. But a similar exaggerated notion of the CEBs during the Sandinista period has led people today to think that the communities have fallen apart during the last year. In reality, they were and still are a limited but healthy and significant movement."

Father Mulligan believes that today the grass-roots church is in a time of exile and captivity: "We think of it as being a time of purification and rebuilding. This is the time for gathering the resources that will be necessary for transforming society."

When reflecting on the revolutionary experiment, Revolutionary Christians suggest that the last decade has been one of tremendous personal and spiritual growth. Today, they contend that they are changed citizens. They are also changed Catholics. While members of the Marxist type are formally divorced from the Catholic Church and no longer practice their faith, Revolutionary Christians might be thought of as being separated from the institutional church. They acknowledge their belief that the Catholic Church has failed them. Indeed, they believe that the traditional church, as an important actor in society, has also failed the majority of people in Nicaragua.

Revolutionary Christians admit the fact that they no longer have a direct relationship with the Catholic hierarchy. One might believe from their remarks that they are hinting that a separate church may already be taking form in the Nicaraguan state. Increasingly, they have defied the authority of the bishops by continuing their activity in projects that have been criticized by the hierarchy. In fact, they are often the leaders in autonomous projects and programs in their neighborhoods.

Despite Revolutionary Christians' conflict with the institutional church, Catholic proselytizing continues to be a major objective. They also continue to express their desire to raise their children as Catholics.

When conflicts do arise—when Revolutionary Christians are forced to choose between their community commitments and the institutional church—allegiance appears to be to the community, not to the bishops. Part of this independence appears to be a consequence of the revolutionary experience itself, the rest to the effects of liberation theology. The revolutionary experience has taught Revolutionary Christians about democratic processes. Liberation theology has challenged them to question authority and to think in terms of the collective good.

Members of this type have suggested that the last decade has made them aware of the powerful force that religion can have on political culture. They credit their political consciousness and their desire for greater democratic processes to a new understanding of what it means to be Catholic. Indeed, they are questioning the very essence of what it means to be Catholic.

Whereas the last decade has been filled with euphoria, it has also been one of tragedy and crisis. Today, Revolutionary Christians admit that there is the need for a further maturation of the conscience of society. Father Mulligan has suggested that many Nicaraguans have a political consciousness that is open to revolutionary change, but this is deeply out of step with their traditional Christian consciousness. He explained that the synthesis between faith and social commitment is still a minority phenomenon. The new person so hoped for has yet to arrive in fullness in Nicaragua.

Outside the country there appears to be an exaggerated perception about the numbers and strength of the church of the poor. In summary, it appears that the Christian base communities still represent a small percentage of the Catholic population in Nicaragua. Revolutionary Christians—whose numbers are larger than those of their Marxist counterparts—nonetheless appear to be a minority within the grass-roots church.

Inside Nicaragua, the Christian communities are struggling but are still alive. In the face of much adversity, this struggle attests to their strong roots and dedication. As Father Angel Torelles eloquently expressed: "Our work for social justice will continue. We want a new world, a more beautiful world. Despite the poverty you see here, take home the message that there is love here. There is joy here. There is hope here."

CHAPTER EIGHT

The Reformist Christian Type

IN THE CHRISTIAN base communities in Nicaragua it is not uncommon to hear people speak about the need for creating a "new person." Whereas one typically hears this expression among Marxists and Revolutionary Christians, it is even more common to hear it articulated by members of the third ideal type, Reformist Christians. When asked about this new person, Reformist Christians are likely to suggest that it is someone who recognizes the suffering of others: This new person is someone who willingly contributes to the establishment of a more socially just society, and this new society is a kingdom where suffering no longer exists.

The discussion of a kingdom of heaven on Earth is frequently articulated both by Reformist Christians and by Revolutionary Christians. When Revolutionary and Reformist Christians speak of the kingdom, their vision is of a world where social justice reigns. That is where the similarity ends. For Reformists, the achievement of a socially just society differs from the project of Revolutionary Christians or Marxist members of the popular church. This difference has to do with how members have understood and continue to understand the problems of Nicaragua.

Reformist Christians argue that during the 1970s the church's prophetic ministry was aimed at removing the apparent root of injustice, that of the Somoza dictatorship. But unlike members

144

of the two types already discussed, the challenge for them was to reform or change the political institutions of Nicaragua, not to achieve liberation from capitalist development (see also Shaw 1989: 5).

Reformists differ from members of the other types in another way. As we have seen, both Marxists and Revolutionary Christians explained their inspiration for revolution as a consequence and convergence of two distinct ideologies. First, they pointed to an inspiration based on the tenets of liberation theology. Second, they cited an inspiration based on the objectives of Sandinista Marxism. For Reformist members of the popular church, however, motivation appears to have been more secular in nature. Reformists suggest that while the reinterpretation of Christianity in Latin America may have facilitated a greater consciousness of social injustice, it was the overt corruption of the regime and the social and economic crises they were suffering that ultimately inspired their involvement in the insurrection.

Due to this philosophical position, Reformists gave only tenuous support to the revolutionary reforms of the 1980s. Unlike members of the other types, they were critical of many Sandinista projects that were aimed at a radical restructuring of society. In instances where they gave their support, it was cautiously enthusiastic.

Today Reformists continue to be active members of the Christian base communities. In fact, they appear to represent the majority within the grass-roots church. Although they are sympathetic to the popular church's commitment to the preferential option for the poor, they do not believe this commitment necessitates an obligation to any one political ideology. Unlike Marxists and Revolutionary Christians, they are highly critical of any ideology that seeks to defend one class interest over another. Individuals of this type accept the popular church's doctrinal understanding of the Bible as a message of hope and liberation for the poor, but they express skepticism that these ideals can (or should) be achieved through political means. A good part of this conviction has to do with their reassessment concerning the maturation of Christian consciousness. Like Revolutionary

145

Christians, Reformists within the popular church have acknowledged the need for a greater maturation among sectors of Nicaraguan society. Yet they depart from their counterparts because they are convinced that revolutionary change cannot be led. Increasingly, these Christians have rejected the notion that society can be reformed from the top down, by a revolutionary vanguard.

What is particularly interesting about this position is the fact that Reformists may actually be recovering authentic Marxist theory. Karl Marx argued that conflict between subjective and objective conditions of society would inevitably lead to revolutionary change. On reflection, Reformists have come to believe that in Nicaragua such conditions were never mature enough to allow the successful transformation of their society. This awareness is articulated when Reformist Christians suggest that social justice must come from the bottom up. They believe that all sectors of society must become cognizant of the necessity and desirability for change. Reformists speak of change erupting from the base, like a volcano, not from the trickle-down effects of a waterfall.

Reformists argue that the work for change must begin again at the civic level. They suggest that it must begin with the maturation of Christian consciousness. They believe that their popular church should continue to play a role in this process.

When asked to reflect on the evolution of their church, Reformists explain that the grass-roots church began essentially as a religious organization dedicated to living out a preferential option for the poor. Despite this fact, they believe the church took on a political character as events in Nicaragua changed. Today, they acknowledge this trend as a mistake. Like Revolutionary Christians, they suggest that members of the popular church erred in choosing to neglect Christian instruction in favor of service to the Sandinista regime. While Reformists agree that Christian liberation continues to demand working for greater social justice, they believe that their grass-roots church should focus on this objective at the religious and not the political level.

As a consequence of this philosophical position, Reformists are more likely to identify their church as an essentially religious entity today, one that seeks to preach a religious message and not a political one. Unlike Revolutionary or Marxist members of the popular church, Reformist Christians believe their work should be focused in the private rather than the public sphere. As a consequence, Reformist Christians are less likely than other members of the popular church to be involved in political activity. Instead, their participation is found in activities that seek to further the process of Catholic proselytizing. These Christians are more likely, for example, to be engaged in religious and educational activities in their neighborhoods. Their efforts appear to be focused on raising Christian consciousness, and their activities appear to be aimed at creating a new kind of person in Nicaragua.

Because Reformists understand the divisive effects of favoring one class over another, they are also more likely to avoid organizations perceived to be out of the mainstream: those either too liberal or too conservative. Whereas they appear to be politically cautious, they also articulate support for popular organizations that they perceive are working toward a more democratic, equitable, and socially just society.

Unlike members of the Marxist type who have given up the practice of their faith, Reformists remain seriously religious. And unlike Revolutionary Christians who acknowledge their separation from the Catholic Church, Reformists are much less critical of the traditional church. Unlike members of the other types, they deny claims that a new Catholic Church is emerging in Nicaragua. When asked about the grass-roots conflict with the Catholic hierarchy, Reformists express their continued faith that the institutional church will become more sensitive to the plight of the poor. Indeed, they understand their role as devoted Catholics to be the force that can move the institutional church toward a greater recognition of the needs of a predominately impoverished society.

CREATING THE NEW PERSON

Reformist Christians acknowledge the conflict that occurred between the Christian base communities and the institutional church following the insurrection against the Somoza dictatorship. They argue that the conflict should not have been unexpected. Reformists suggest that the involvement of so many Christians in the insurrection has been misrepresented as unqualified support for the Sandinista guerrillas. Not all Christians embraced the objectives of the FSLN. For many people, the primary aim was to remove the tyrannical government.

It was not surprising to Reformist Christians, then, that the anti-Somoza coalition began to show strains following the Sandinista triumph. Javier Talavera, director of the Interchurch Center for Theological Studies (CIEETS), a Protestant affiliate of the church of the poor, explained that not everyone joined the Somoza struggle. Of those who did participate not all did so out of a political commitment to the Sandinistas. He noted that while some Christians supported the Sandinistas, many who supported revolutionary reforms eventually became disillusioned with the evolution of events. "This was particularly true among groups in the Atlantic region of Nicaragua," explained Talavera. "There, many people became increasingly alienated by the Sandinista government."

Ray Hooker, former Sandinista director of the Autonomous Development for the Atlantic Coast, explained that the east coast of Nicaragua is predominately Protestant and that the region has always been geographically, culturally, and historically different from the rest of the country. "Throughout Nicaragua's history the Atlantic region had been ignored by political forces, but this changed with the triumph of the Sandinistas."

Hooker suggested that for most people in the Atlantic region the anti-Somoza struggle had remained a distant and unimportant event. After the revolution, however, many Sandinista programs were introduced, but not all of these programs were enthusiastically embraced by residents of the coast. "These were positive programs—literacy, health care, construction projects—but all of the decisions concerning them were made back in Managua," Hooker explained. "This eroded indigenous support, particularly as people began to fear that with these projects our people would lose their cultural identity."

Ronald Reagan's commitment to destroy the Nicaraguan

148

Revolution, Ray Hooker suggested, capitalized on the discontent that was brewing in the Atlantic region: "The region was militarized against the revolution. Many of our towns were attacked by the contras and counterattacked by the Sandinistas. Our infrastructure was destroyed; there was great bloodshed; and 40 percent of the population fled. When the Sandinistas forced the evacuation of those who remained in the region, they did so against the will of the people there."

Hooker explained that by the time the Sandinistas became sensitive to these mistakes, it was too late for them to garner popular support. Apparently, similar mistakes were made elsewhere in Nicaragua.

In the mountainous city of Boaco, Mayor Armando Incer acknowledged a similar phenomenon. "Following the insurrection, peace and work are all that the people wanted here. But our city was hit very hard by the contra war," he explained. "Infrastructure was destroyed and people were thrown out of work. City hall was bankrupt—everything was sold off to help finance the war."

The mayor suggested that the city had been critical of the Sandinistas because their war destroyed its financial base. "Our budget comes from cattle taxes. The war destroyed cattle and land, and our inability to produce caused immense suffering and poverty," he explained. "Fundamental things, like light bulbs and a clean drink of water, were luxuries. We understood that change was absolutely necessary for our survival."

The contra war and several policies of the FSLN apparently alienated many Christians. Julio García, general secretary of the Social Christian Party, suggested that while the contra war hurt production, other Sandinista policies were equally disastrous for Nicaraguans. "One of the gravest mistakes the FSLN made had to do with agrarian reform," he said. "It was primarily used for propaganda purposes. While peasants received titles for the land, the government still owned it. They dictated what could be produced and how much it had to be sold for. Other lands became collectives."

García noted that ten years ago Nicaragua was able to grow basic foodstuffs both for consumption and for export. Today, however, Nicaragua is importing basics. Low productivity thus became a very important issue.

Another problem was the great exodus from rural areas to the urban centers. Due to the contra conflict, low productivity meant fewer jobs for peasants. In other areas where productivity remained stable, much of the rural labor force was conscripted to fight in the war. "This practice took many necessary workers and resources away from agriculture activity," suggested García. "That only exacerbated our problems."

Like members of the other types, Reformist Christians believed that differences over economic policy and the contra war divided people in the Christian base communities. In Solentiname, Olivia Guevara explained that during the insurrection the community had been supportive of the guerrillas. Following the revolution, however, some members did not agree with the community's continued support of the Sandinistas, particularly when the civil war began.

"Under the Sandinistas the islands had become the focus of a number of development projects," Olivia remarked. "With the war and the economic crisis of the 1980s, however, many of the projects were abandoned, including the technical school and the factory for educational toys that employed the majority of our people." Apparently, such factors as these worked to undermine support for the government and convinced critics that the Sandinistas were no more committed to the needs of the people than the previous regime had been.

Other Nicaraguans were critical of the Sandinistas from the beginning of their rise to power. For example, following the insurrection, the Tijerino family decided to remain in Nicaragua. During the revolutionary years, Juan Tijerino served as a representative of the farmers to the National Assembly. The family, however, did not formally join the FSLN.

"We did not choose to join the FSLN party," explained Piada Tijerino, "because we believed we would be too tied up in their demands if we joined. My children participated in the literacy campaign and I continued working in the base communities in the area. Juan served in the assembly because this allowed him to be critical of programs and policies that the farmers disagreed with."

Piada suggested that there were many issues with which to disagree: "For about two years, the Sandinistas were making changes, radical changes. There were profound transformations: socialized medicine, literacy programs, education, and land reform. They were trying to achieve all this even with a bankrupt nation."

The family came to believe that these priorities were critical mistakes. "Getting used to change is a difficult thing, particularly among those who are asked to sacrifice. I think the Sandinistas tried to do too much too quickly," Piada said. "We were not even able to catch our breath before the new aggression started. The economic sanctions and the contra war caused the poor to suffer again. The contra war divided families, one son to one side, one son to another side."

Piada Tijerino explained that these were times of great anguish that caused great attrition among the people. "In our own case, we were forced to make a decision. During the contra aggression we made the choice to side with the Sandinistas, but this was not because we supported their political project."

She explained that in the early 1980s the contras crossed the border from Honduras and raped, killed, and burned and destroyed the people's farms. "At that time our family owned 3,000 *manzanas*, the best cattle ranch in the region. During the 1970s, and with the help of the clergy, we established in that region many Christian communities. Together we had built schools and health clinics. But when the contras learned of our participation in these projects, three hundred of them came and set our house on fire."

The Tijerinos remembered that the contra soldiers came and looted the family's home. Before they burned the house down they terrorized the farmhands. "They took their bayonets and decapitated the foreman right in front of the workers!" Piada exclaimed. "We found his body hanging from a tree a few days later."

The Tijerino family said that they were accused of trying to

151

create communist communities. "At this time we became committed to the Sandinistas," Piada continued. "But when Juan became committed to the revolution, he was personally threatened by the contras. They returned and forced us from our land." As a consequence, Piada said, her husband accepted a Sandinista offer to sell the government the land so that it could be protected against the contra aggression.

"My sons wanted to join the Sandinista army and we spent long nights discussing this with them," she remembered. "We told them that we were wealthy enough to send them away to safety, someplace where they could finish their education. But in the end we knew it was their decision, and both boys chose to fight alongside the Sandinista army."

Piada Tijerino suggested that it was the war and the ensuing economic hardship that ultimately accounted for the Sandinista defeat in the 1990 national elections. "When a mother, a woman [Violeta Chamorro] says she will abolish the draft, it was like someone offering to take a thorn from your eye," she suggested. "People were tired; they were wasting away. Many people believed the Sandinista government was moving toward communism and atheism. They were told this by the contras, by the Catholic hierarchy. So many campesinos, with all these things, chose to abandon the FSLN."

Uli Schmidtt, speaking of his religious work in the campo, agreed that in the rural areas of Nicaragua the Catholic Church's position against the Sandinistas had an important effect. He suggested that while the Delegate of the Word program had been very successful in the 1960s and 1970s, no successful CEBs existed in the campo areas in the 1980s. "There were several reasons for this. During the revolutionary process I saw Christians becoming involved in political projects and organizations. In the rural areas, like Estelí, some CEB members left for Managua to join FSLN activities. In other cases the revolutionary organizations absorbed the CEBs and the communities abandoned their pastoral obligations. I think part of this had to do with the fact that there was a lack of centers in the countryside," Schmidtt explained.

152

According to Schmidtt, unlike ecumenical centers in the capital city such as the Antonio Valdivieso Center, the campo suffered from a lack of staff support. "Everything became centralized in Managua," he said. "Regional projects and outreach programs lacked the money, the transportation, and trained personnel to continue religious work in the rural areas."

Schmidtt explained that as the Catholic Church came out against the revolution in the 1980s, the internal struggle within the church had immediate repercussions in the base, particularly in the countryside. "Radical priests were removed from their communities," he said. "This was an attempt by the Catholic hierarchy to marginalize the campo, and it worked to confuse a lot of people. You see, the campesinos are very traditional people. They love the church but at the same time they can be very radical."

Schmidtt's discussion suggests that a dualistic aspect of the campesino exists, a characteristic that often is not recognized. "Internally, the campesino people are very traditional, but politically they can be very revolutionary. I think they were taking in the positive experiences of the revolution and rejecting those parts of it that negatively affected them," he explained. "For example, I think 50 percent supported land reform and education but they also rejected sharply the economic and military policies of the Sandinistas."

Schmidtt remembered that when the pope came to Nicaragua in 1983 his treatment of revolutionary Christians alienated many Catholics in the campo. "About that time the campesinos were rejecting the work of Obando, who was supporting the work of the contra. From 1983 on, I think many campesinos no longer agreed with either side."

Schmidtt's explanation about Nicaraguans who were taking in the positive experiences of the revolution and rejecting those that were negative reflects a common experience articulated by members of the Reformist type. In Managua, Reformists applauded Sandinista policies that helped to further social reforms, but they also spoke critically of the party's economic and military policies.

At a community meeting in San Judas, CEB members were

willing to discuss their disappointment with the Sandinista regime. Most of them criticized the contra war. They argued that the government should have been more receptive toward plans for an early peace. Many others believed that the Sandinistas were intent upon policies that served their own interests.

Indiana Larios remembered that within the community people disagreed over many things: "During the revolutionary process there was great controversy because not everyone understood the problems we faced. Not everyone understood the reasons for the economic embargo and the war. There were disagreements over these things, and both the communities and the Sandinistas lost members as a consequence."

Indiana believed that the Sandinistas did many good things. She pointed to the literacy campaign that taught many people how to read and write. She also mentioned the Sandinista health campaign that brought medical care to many people for the first time. "But I think the Sandinistas also did many bad things," Larios continued. "I think the war was a mistake. I heard people say that there was forced conscription. Boys were rounded up in the streets. In the Atlantic region there were human rights violations. I supported many of the positive efforts of the FSLN, but there were many things that I felt I had to speak out about."

Among members of all types there appears to be agreement that the Catholic hierarchy's position against the regime had an impact. But unlike Marxists and Revolutionary Christians, Reformists do not believe that the bishops took sides with the contras. This appears to be a majority sentiment in the Christian communities. Reformist Christians continue to believe that the Catholic Church did its best to bring peace to Nicaragua. They argued that when the cardinal criticized the Sandinistas it was with justification.

For instance, they point to the suspension of civil liberties during the contra aggression as an example of an abuse of government power. Flavio Tijerino, who identified himself as an early supporter of the Sandinistas, acknowledged the fact that over time he, too, became critical of the party: "I think there was a contradiction between the Sandinistas' objectives and their strategies. I believe this was due in part to the contra offensive but also due to the circumstances of our internal reality. People recognized the increasing vertical and authoritarian nature of the regime."

Flavio noted that following the insurrection he was a vice-minister of culture for the party. "While I was an early supporter of the historic program of the Sandinistas," he said, "I came to oppose their vertical form of control. It seemed a contradiction to democratization. Absolute liberty to question the program was promised. Frank, honest dialogue was assured. But this was not always the case. There was a contradiction between giving people freedom but also forcing them to support policies they ultimately disagreed with."

Flavio suggested that what goes against justice cannot oblige one's obedience. It obliges rebellion, he said. "I came to believe that in the end the Sandinistas failed to raise the national consciousness, the awareness to unite, to defend our homeland."

Reformist Christians argue that the Catholic Church in good faith sought to negotiate with the government. Speaking for himself in an interview, Cardinal Miguel Obando y Bravo suggested that the church's position during the contra war was one that sought peace. He denied accusations that the church had taken sides or that it had abandoned its option for the poor. "I believe in the traditional doctrine of the church that speaks for the poor," the cardinal explained. "The church must speak for the poor and be concerned with their interests. The problem was that in these times people came to believe that there were only two choices: that of Marxism or that of capitalism. But Marxism and capitalism are not the only paths to development. In the doctrines of the church there is flexibility that can be used for the good and prosperity of everyone."

Cardinal Obando stated his conviction that the church must be charitable toward the poor and that it must encourage community members to invest in their neighbors. "But this does not have to be one political way or another," he continued. "The church's position should be regarded as a third alternative."

Like reform-minded clergy elsewhere in Latin America, the

cardinal argued that he had always sought a third way between capitalism and communism. Historically, this has been the position of the church when it has encouraged support for political organizations like the Social Christian and Christian Democratic parties.

This position reflects a salient point within the popular church today. While Reformist Christians remain committed to the poor, they are seeking alternatives to both the Sandinista and the Chamorro visions of government. Unlike their Marxist and Revolutionary Christian counterparts, they remain critical of the Sandinistas.

For Reformists, this is a time of reevaluation. In San Judas, Indiana Larios said that she is dumbfounded by the political climate of the times: "I'm confused about the Sandinistas and frankly I think they are confused, too. I believe there are two tendencies in the party that make them ineffective. I think one side wants to work toward socialism and the greater distribution of wealth. I think there is another side that wants to pursue capitalist development without regard for the poor."

Indiana Larios explained that during the 1990 elections some people in the community believed that the UNO party was going to bring positive changes to Nicaragua. "But I think today we all agree that this has not been the case. People are confused and discouraged," she remarked. "Many people are looking for alternative answers."

Cardinal Obando acknowledged that the situation of the poor in Nicaragua is desperate. But he blamed this situation on the Sandinistas: "This nation has inherited many problems from the Sandinista regime. Just because there is no more war does not mean that there is peace here. With peace one can construct jobs, hospitals, and many other things necessary for development. But these things cannot be acquired so long as the Sandinista party exists. So long as they remain in positions of power, peace will be impossible here."

Today, Reformists in Nicaragua increasingly speak of two governments: one Sandinista, the other Violeta Chamorro's UNO coalition. In the 1990 national elections, the UNO party captured the presidency and the majority of seats in the Nicaraguan legislature, but the Sandinistas retained a strong voice in the National Assembly. As a consequence, the UNO—a fragile coalition party—has been forced to compromise on issues that might have otherwise gone unchallenged. The compromises have ultimately fragmented their coalition's solidarity.

Asked about the political chaos, Reformist Christians expressed their disappointment. They applauded President Chamorro's efforts in bringing an end to the contra war, but they also expressed the belief that she remains handicapped by her party's division. While they articulated support for the president's efforts to work at compromising on other issues, they criticized members of her party who are unwilling to work at accommodation. For example, they pointed to people like Vice-President Virgilio Godoy, who they believe has worked to undermine her efforts.

Reformists argue that the constant struggle for power and the conflicts over the national agenda continue to stagnate progress. They also charge that there is increasing gridlock in the seat of government. Hence, Reformist Christians are frustrated by all this obstruction and by the seeming inability of President Chamorro to force greater political compromises. They contend that the conflict between the Sandinistas and members of the UNO coalition is being felt at all levels of society.

For example, in San Pablo residents complain that the mayor, a staunch conservative, has created a huge bureaucracy to oversee community programs. Many of these projects had originally been controlled by CEB members or by neighborhood supporters of the Sandinistas. Julio Sequeira explained that in 1990 the mayor gave UNO supporters authority to oversee community assignments. "Today, to initiate a project you must go through a long chain of command to receive the necessary approval," Julio explained. "This has created many problems and some conflict because when a project is started, and if you have not gotten the necessary signatures, it comes under attack by the mayor's office.

This frustrates people trying to address a need in the community, and it slows the progress to such an extent that people give up before the work can be completed."

Julio suggested that with some existing programs, like the natural medicine clinic in San Pablo, support has eroded because it has been identified as a Sandinista program and thus has been neglected by the municipal government that remains hostile to anything Sandinista.

"The mayor likes to go to a poor barrio and announce a new project, like the construction of sewers," Julio continued. "He comes with the press, opens a bottle of champagne and says 'this is just the beginning,' but then he never returns. This is the reality here!"

Reformist Christians, like members of the other types, noted that before the 1990 election there were education, health care, and food programs. "We had to stand in line," explained Rafael Valdéz. "But today, while everything is available, there is no money. There is no work, no medicines, no hospitals for the poor. People are increasingly frustrated and many are resorting to violence or crime."

There is a growing sense in Nicaragua that this government is incapable of bringing stability or progress. In San Judas, Indiana Larios explained that the Christian base communities have been affected by two factors: by the fact that the popular church has been identified as Sandinista and by attrition resulting from the economic crisis: "We've lost members because people believed we were political and Sandinista sympathizers. As the Sandinistas lost favor, it became a more sensitive subject to defend their programs or policies. But we also lost people because of the economic crisis here. There is a need to survive, to work. Some people are working two or three jobs to make ends meet. There is little time left for other things."

In Adolfo Reyes, Reformists suggested that after the elections some members of the community were depressed and that an air of despair permeated the neighborhood. Today, however, they believe the community is stronger because its members have overcome the desire to give up on their efforts. They said that they have rededicated themselves to the work that is so necessary for national reconciliation.

Despite this new commitment, most community members believe that the Chamorro government has little sympathy for the poor. A woman in the community offered her sense of disappointment: "Many people believed that the UNO party was going to bring good changes to Nicaragua. This just isn't so. Today we face a severe economic crisis; people are hungry and many are out of work. There is no money for medicine, and we're witnessing a growing division between the rich and the poor."

Another member said that she was particularly worried about the privatization of the hospitals. For the community of San Judas this issue appeared to be of overriding concern because the community is very poor and its residents depend on free clinics.

Because the mortality rate is high in the community, members said they had been trying to find ways of providing inexpensive funeral services for residents of the barrio. As was typical of other CEB projects, a committee was created to investigate the means for creating a carpentry service that could provide inexpensive coffins. A year and a half later, the objective was still not realized. Members of the community explained that the economic situation had deteriorated so rapidly that it was impossible for them to raise the necessary resources.

Throughout the country, the accelerated process of the Chamorro government's economic liberalization policies appears to have come at the expense of the working population. At the beginning of 1991, unemployment affected approximately 400,000 Nicaraguans. By November of that year, the number had risen to 540,000, or 46 percent of the economically active population (*Barricada* 1993: 23). By December 1992, authorities in Nicaragua were estimating that the number had risen to just under 70 percent of the population.

Economic desperation has created a greater sense of urgency in realizing community goals. Despite this sense of urgency, Sister Cecilia García, a Catholic nun who has worked with the Christian base communities since 1987, acknowledged the increasing problems that face the CEBs. She noted that during the 1980s there was more interest among Christians to get involved in community programs: "There was a general sense of enthusiasm among Nicaraguans and a spirit of cooperation. The enthusiasm ended as the contra war dragged on and the economy worsened. While neighborhood projects were suffering from lack of government attention, differences over the proper solutions to the problems of the country further affected our membership."

Sister García believes that today the communities are more polarized. "Since the election we have lost CEB members and neighborhood support for some of our programs. People have become discouraged. There is a lack of trust among Nicaraguans because people believed that all of their problems would be solved by the revolution. When this didn't happen, they lost faith."

Reformist Christians suggested that their communities have suffered because so many of their projects have been focused on the poor. Like members of the other types, they believe that in Nicaragua this focus is interpreted by critics as a sign that the communities had taken sides with one class against another. They also agree that this criticism has been exacerbated by the Catholic hierarchy, who spoke out against neglecting the needs of those who are not poor.

"We see a divided church," explained Flavio Tijerino. "But we forget that this is really a reflection of a divided society. A society divided between the rich and the poor." "The cardinal called the popular church communist," explained Indiana Larios. "But we are following the option for the poor, not some communist ideology. Our faith is tied to action in helping the poor."

Reformist Christians contend that their work is in line with the spirit of Medellín. They believe that their efforts must be at the service of the poorest. "This has always been our motivation," explained Indiana Larios. "Our motivation has always been religious, not the unquestioning allegiance to any political party. When the Sandinistas were committed to policies favoring the poorest, we were supportive. When their policies hurt the poorest, we were its critics."

Not surprisingly, Reformist Christians remain angered by accusations that they have been Sandinista stooges. "What the revolution taught us is that working for one class without being sensitive to the concerns of another only brings conflict," Indiana Larios explained as other women in the group nodded in agreement. "We must find a way for embracing all members of this society. We must work with all Nicaraguans for solutions to our country's problems."

Reformist Christians speak of searching for a third political alternative, an option that can embrace greater democratic values and practices. Unlike members of the other types, they are not convinced that the Sandinistas can provide democracy for Nicaragua. Indeed, these Christians are more likely to reject any extreme political positions, whether on the left or right. They represent an element in the popular church that embraces neither the Sandinistas nor the Chamorro party. Thus they appear to represent a growing segment in society that may be readily captured by a new kind of political organization.

When asked about their position vis-à-vis the church, Reformist Christians deny charges that they have fomented disunity, rejecting any claims that they have been intent on establishing a breakaway church. Unlike Marxist or Revolutionary Christians, Reformists believe themselves to be in communion with the Catholic Church. It is not uncommon to hear them speak of maintaining their space within the institutional church. As a consequence, members of this type are likely to be those who are attending and participating in local parish masses.

Alberto Morales, a theological coordinator with the Antonio Valdivieso Center in Managua, acknowledged the Reformist Christian type in his discussion of the popular church when he suggested the existence of a mainstream group that remains committed both to the work of the poor and to the Catholic hierarchy. "I think there are several trends within the Catholic Church today," Morales explained. "But the majority are traditional Catholics. At the base level these Christians remain paranoid of traditional priests. And while they do not always agree with the church's position on particular issues, I do not think that they act without their priest's consent."

Asked about this group's effect on the popular church, Morales was not encouraged: "I think we are witnessing a situation where the traditional church's hierarchical model is being transposed to the communities. This is particularly true as progressive priests are purged from liberation theology centers. New, more traditional clergy are taking their place in the CEBs, and they are resurrecting the original traditional ways."

Morales's assessment is interesting. It helps to explain the fact that while the popular sector has been in tension with positions taken by the hierarchy, the work of the CEBs continues to be devoted to traditional Catholic practices. For example, the communities of San Pablo, San Judas, and Adolfo Reyes are involved in Catholic instruction, which includes training of children for First Holy Communion and Catholic Confirmation.

But conflict in the CEBs over some of these practices has been evident. In fact, such conflict helps to elucidate the differences exhibited between types within the popular church. One example occurred in December 1992 when the community of Adolfo Reyes planned First Holy Communion for a large number of the barrio's children. On the morning of the service, only half of the children participated. CEB member Yamileth Sequeira tried to explain the lack of participation: "The community was in charge of preparing the children for this important event. One night at one of the meetings there was discussion about the clothes the children would be required to wear for the ceremony. Of course, it has always been traditional that girls wear formal white dresses and the boys, formal black suits. But some of us at the meeting assumed that this formal—and very expensive—dress would not be required of the children's families. After all, most of the families in Adolfo Reyes are very poor and cannot afford such fine clothing."

Apparently, a large debate took place over the dress requirements. Some members of the community believed that in the church of the poor the children should be dressed informally. Yamileth continued: "To our distress, this discussion became very acrimonious and many people were angry, on both sides. Eventually we came to a compromise. This year the children would

Celebration of First Holy Communion in the Christian base community of Adolfo Reyes

dress formally and next year they will dress in everyday clothes. It was the best agreement that we could arrange."

This conflict reflects the increasing tensions between Revolutionary and Reformist Christians in their different understanding of their grass-roots church. Revolutionary Christians involved in Catholic instruction programs are more likely to identify their CEBs as a church of the poor. Reformists, on the other hand, are less supportive of any departure—however subtle—that hints at breaking with Catholic tradition. The consequences of such differences may eventually divide the remaining membership within the CEBs.

The need for accommodation and compromise is recognized among most members of the CEBs. They acknowledge the need for their continued solidarity. Both Revolutionary and Reformist Christians suggested that conflict among members of the popular church must be avoided if they are to continue their work together. When asked about their differences, Reformists ex-

163

plained their devotion to traditional practices out of fear that small departures would be used against them by their critics. "We need the Catholic Church. We need the entire Catholic community if we are to continue reaching out to others," explained Indiana Larios. "We cannot afford to sever our ties because most of this country is traditionally Catholic."

Reformist Christians suggest that their ultimate goal is to increase their membership in the grass-roots church. Members in San Pablo suggested that if they were to gather greater support for projects that assist the poor, the communities cannot appear divided. It is their expressed conviction that in time by working together they can move the church along to a greater awareness of the correctness of their vision.

To advance this objective, Reformist Christians within the CEBs have concentrated their efforts on enlarging their membership. They are the ones more likely to be involved in Christian outreach projects. When asked about this work, they explained that they remain optimistic about their chances for enlarging membership.

They appear hopeful for a couple of reasons. The first has to do with their recognition that it was a mistake for so many of their members to have abandoned pastoral work during the Sandinista years. For example, they noted that many of their former members are now returning to the communities. These are Christians who are rededicating themselves to the religious work of the popular church.

The second reason lies in a new strategy. Today, Reformist Christians are reaching out to an untapped resource: the youth within their neighborhoods. Both San Judas and San Pablo have initiated youth activities that are focused on Catholic proselytizing and greater civic awareness.

In San Pablo, youth members spoke about their involvement in the community. All of them had joined the CEB the previous year. Nineteen-year-old Tatiana Valdéz explained that most of them had become involved as a way to get to know their neighbors better and to enjoy the activities that the CEB offered to them. "We visit the blind; we have parties and spiritual retreats," she explained. "Each week we have Bible study, and we help the adults prepare children for church activities."

Like Reformist Christians, the youth in San Pablo speak of reconciliation within the church and the community. Unlike members of the Marxist and Revolutionary Christian types who speak of the God of the poor, these youth members reflect a growing reformist element.

"We believe that there is only one God who loves both the rich and the poor," Tatiana remarked. "But many poor people believe God is on their side. We reject this understanding. Our challenge is to discover the existence of the poor, to reach out to those in need, to work in building the kingdom of God on Earth." The San Pablo youths spoke about their outreach efforts in helping street children. They are also involved in visitation to the sick.

In both San Pablo and San Judas, youth members agreed that it was important to maintain their identity as Catholics. Many of these young members have followed the path of Reformists and find meaning in the life of the local church. In San Judas, four of the thirty-three youth members explained that their group remains dedicated to Christian instruction and to service in the local church. In addition to attendance at the Sunday mass, many of the males serve as altar boys. Each Saturday the youth members meet for Bible reflection. Julio Ruiz explained that they work at relating the Bible to their reality: "We ask ourselves what it means to be a Christian. We believe it means following in the footsteps of Christ. The life and work of Christ is our role model. This means we are directed to following the Ten Commandments, doing good works for others. In our community it means we must strive to be good role models for others."

The teenagers of both San Judas and San Pablo lament the fact that most Nicaraguan youths are not religious. In San Pablo, Johana Escarlitte explained that teenagers in their neighborhoods are more interested in other things, like drugs and alcohol: "The majority do not care about religion. Our group represents just 2 percent of the youth in our community. During the contra war many Nicaraguans fled to the United States, both rich families and poor families. Many poor people who fled have returned now with many of the same traditional values they left with. These are good values, those that center around the family and the life of the church. But many wealthy families returned with North American values that are not so good."

Another teenager agreed and suggested that part of the problem is the fact that these wealthy children, commonly referred to as the "Miami boys" are returning with a lot of money. "They have returned to Nicaragua with drugs and fast cars. They have a lot of money and a lot of freedom that other teenagers find impressive," said Tatiana Valdéz. "But these boys act irresponsibly on the streets and they get into trouble with the law. Of course, they are Nicaraguans and we are glad that they are back, but we are not happy with the new values they have returned with."

When asked about the lack of adult membership in their community, the teenagers in both San Judas and San Pablo gave several explanations. They suggested a lack of communication and information about the CEBs' work as well as a lack of time or commitment. All of the youth mentioned the fact that many people are frightened off by the magnitude of problems that their programs seek to address. "Many people think that we are simply wasting our time," Julio Ruiz remarked. The other children nodded in agreement.

THE REFORMIST STRUGGLE: A CIVIC PROJECT

Despite the social and economic difficulties of the times—indeed as a consequence of them—Reformist Christians continue to speak of the need for working for social justice. In Adolfo Reyes, Sister García contended that building the kingdom of God is always possible for people of faith. "In this moment, however, no one sees it here," she said. "Christians understand that building the kingdom of God means liberating men from oppression and the conditions of oppression, like hunger and misery. With God in our lives we live with the hope that the kingdom is closer. After all, God promised that he would never forget his people, especially the poorest. In this we have faith."

Nevertheless, Sister García admitted that the community has lost confidence in the Chamorro government's ability to bring about greater social justice. "Poor people only have God. For us—as Christian people—we find comfort in fellowship with one other; this is where God's presence is felt. It sustains us. Our grass-roots church, the church of the poor, has never been very large because it has always been discredited, followed by its enemies. But I believe our communities will survive because God is on our side."

Others, like Flavio Tijerino, were optimistic as well: "I think we are now seeing signs of change, a reevaluation within the Sandinista party to become more democratic. I believe that despite the vertical methods there is a democratic core within the party that will bring good things to Nicaragua."

Piada Tijerino and her family believe that as Christians they must remain active in their communities. "What is important to us now is the ongoing process of revolutionary change," she said. "This means evolving toward a more pluralistic and compassionate society."

Both Piada and Flavio believe this change will be possible with or without the Sandinista leadership. "The revolution is greater than the party," suggested Flavio. "You cannot undo what has been started."

Juan Tijerino predicted that the years ahead, particularly the next decade, will be those of great challenge for Nicaraguans. "We suffered great hardships during the contra war," he said. "Great tracts of land are still mined. The peasant population has suffered all the effects of the war and continue to be uprooted from their cultivations. Now they will have to start from scratch."

Juan Tijerino believes that the wounds in Nicaragua are still deep and that the country's greatest challenge will be to practice forgiveness and healing. Asked about the political reality, he suggested that Nicaraguans would continue to struggle against the resurrection of any model like Somoza's.

What would be the place of the church in these new and difficult times? "The church helped us to prove that Christianity can be lived and is worth living despite the hardships," Juan replied. "I believe we are going to have a church more united, more purified, because we have proven that only with the help of God

167

could we have suffered so much and yet loved each other enough to forgive and reconcile as a people."

The Tijerino family suggested that Nicaraguans had learned some important lessons in the revolutionary process. "We have learned what politics is all about," offered Juan Tijerino. "We have become politicized and now we are the authors of the country. We know now that democracy is not only made up of democratic elections. It is a way of life that must be lived everyday."

Flavio Tijerino agreed: "Democracy must be participatory. I think those who are organized have better prospects to affect their futures. We have the commitment to build a new world. And we have faith in God and in the people here not to betray the hope of so many, many people."

Today, other Reformist Christians articulate a growing confidence in the possibility of building democracy in Nicaragua. Like the Tijerinos, they speak of this process in pluralistic terms. For instance, they speak of the need for allowing expression of alternative ideas and of the need for working toward efforts of accommodation and compromise. The revolution appears to have been instrumental in providing these Nicaraguans with a greater sense of what it means to be political, including the right to organize and the obligation to work for a system of greater social and political justice.

Reformists speak about creating a new civil society that is based on gospel principles. What appears clear is their emphasis on living democratic practices every day. Reformists speak of a living philosophy, a way of being in the world that is both compassionate and inclusive. Their emphasis on living gospel principles reflects a shift in their understanding from one that sees this as a largely political endeavor to one that understands it as a civic project. Hence, unlike Marxists and Revolutionary Christians, Reformists are less likely to be involved in activities such as strikes and political protests. Rather, their energy and time are spent working on religious education and community empowerment projects. It is interesting to note that while all sectors of the popular church acknowledge the fact that the "new person" has yet to arrive in Nicaragua, Reformists appear to be the ones most com-

The majority of Nicaraguans live in conditions of dire poverty. Often children—many abandoned by their families—live in landfills and must search for food and clothing.

mitted to bringing that new person to life. For them, unlike the other types, the new society must begin at the civic level, in the community.

While Marxists and Revolutionary Christians see their role in Nicaragua as giving logistical support to popular organizations (those they believe are truly representative and participatory), Reformists are more likely to be engaged in critical assessment of such activities. They are also more likely to commit themselves to local initiatives, initiatives that address community problems. Reformists recognize the fact that today the continued struggle for social justice is a reality in Nicaragua. They point to the fact that in Managua 54 percent of its 2 million residents are living in overcrowded conditions of extreme poverty, without access to water, electricity, education, or health services. They also suggest that with the privatization of schools and hospitals that number is sure to grow. In light of such circumstances, Reformists speak of the need for continued work in addressing these problems.

For instance, San Judas has a people's drug clinic and a community school. The school was originally founded with the help of the Sandinista government. Today, however, public funding for the school has been ended. Nevertheless, Reformists argue that the need for the school's services has grown. Despite the lack of funds for hiring teachers, the school remains open with the help of volunteers, many of whom are former CEB youth. These are young adults who became involved in Sandinista projects in the 1980s, projects like literacy training and youth activities. Today they have returned to serve their neighborhoods.

These programs, like others, seek to empower people in the neighborhood. The objective is highly focused on "making the people subject" and Reformist Christians only engage in them if the programs enjoy consensus.

A fairly new phenomenon is the growing consciousness concerning environmental issues. Christian communities appear to be reawakening to the notion of the sacredness of the earth, an interest that may stem from the recovery and celebration of popular religion. Today, new CEB activities are dedicated to resource preservation. In the community of Adolfo Reyes, for example, Reformist Christians are involved in educating children and their neighbors about resource and waste management. Simple experiments are used to demonstrate pollution by nondegradable items. One demonstration involved the burying of plastic bags; six months later the bags were recovered intact, leaving the community to discuss the implications.

It appears that environmental consciousness within the communities is enriching people's vision for a new society. Increasingly, there are discussions and demands for new alternatives for economic and political development. Reformist Christians speak of the need for alternatives to development—alternatives based on a new and positive relationship to the environment. For example, such demands have spurred experiments and education pertaining to sustainable agriculture.

Like the members of the other types, Reformists in the CEBs suggest that what continues to unite people are their common problems, despite their political differences. "We are well aware

170

that we—and not some God falling down from heaven—must solve our own problems," suggested Javier Talavera. "A major thrust of liberation theology has been development of a true consciousness of Jesus Christ. Our vision in Nicaragua is to have people live by the gospel as Jesus taught, to be in service to one another."

Reformist Christians note that after the defeat of the Sandinistas they began a theme of resurrection, a theme of hope. They suggest that 1990 was a year for critical reflection for the Christian communities, a time for reevaluation. "This is a time for us to deepen our understanding and commitment," offered a community member from Villa Austria. "This has been a year of searching, reflecting, and preparing for the work ahead. Our faith is our inspiration."

Members of the Reformist type continue to be optimistic. They recognize that the political and economic crises of Nicaragua have generated new possibilities for the grass roots. What is particularly striking about members of this type is that today they are far more likely to insist on autonomy from all political parties and from the state as well. They are also more likely to assert local control over natural resources and development policies. They represent a segment in the popular church where "belief in total liberation via state ownership of the economy, and faith in one party and one truth belong to the past" (see also *Report on the Americas* 1992: 12).

Like their Marxist and Revolutionary counterparts, Reformist Christians continue to believe in the power of the masses to initiate change. Increasingly, they acknowledge the years of revolutionary experiment in Nicaragua as a positive experience. In looking back, Reformists believe that both the liberation theology movement and the ensuing revolutionary process helped to bring a growing consciousness to the plight of the poor. They believe this consciousness must be nurtured and used to support initiatives for future change.

Reformist Christians freely criticize practices and policies that they believe increase the suffering of the poor. But they are also

171

equally as likely to express the need for considering the opinions of the rich. Members of this type believe that true revolutionary change must occur from the bottom up with a new way of living and thinking. They believe that change must be driven by aspirations for dignity, justice, and liberty. But they believe that these aspirations must first be practiced in civic society. As Piada Tijerino suggested, "the Sandinistas tried to do too much too quickly." Today, there is optimism that their grass-roots church can learn from its past mistakes.

For Reformist Christians the mistakes of the past have had more to do with the neglect of their communities than with anything else. They believe that while it is important to support popular organizations, those that demand social justice, they have come to believe that the commitment must first be actualized at home, at the community level.

With the commitment to the liberation of the poor has come tension with the Catholic Church. Reformists maintain their line in favor of the poor but are less willing than members of the other types to defy the Catholic hierarchy. Unlike members of the other two types, Reformist Christians were not radicalized to embrace a classless project or to reject their religion. Unlike Marxist Christians who understand themselves as *divorced* from the Catholic Church, or Revolutionary Christians who acknowledge their *separation*, Reformists continue to speak of reconciliation and the need for accommodation. They argue the need for maintaining their space in the universal church.

Among Reformist Christians is a strong conviction that their presence and their influence will work to reform the church, to push it along to a greater recognition of the needs of the impoverished. Insistently, they speak of the need for working for greater local initiatives. They have faith in the fact that this kind of effort can ripen conditions for bringing the inevitable transformation of a new society.

CHAPTER NINE

The Alienated Christian Type

THE ACRIMONY BETWEEN the traditional Catholic Church and the church of the poor, and between pro-Sandinista and anti-Sandinista forces, left a number of disaffected Nicaraguans. Unanticipated consequences of the revolutionary experience affected the nation's religious and political culture. The decade of turmoil alienated many Catholics from both the institutional and the grass-roots church. It also prompted a search for an alternative kind of religion, one more individualistic and less controversial.

This chapter provides a discussion of those who fit into this final position. Christians of this type include wealthy members of Nicaraguan society, poor and middle-class Nicaraguans, critics of the traditional as well as the popular church, and opponents of the Sandinista party. Many have identified themselves as former Catholics. Others are former members of Christian base communities. Most were early supporters of the Sandinista regime.

Members of the Alienated Christian type offer an alternative analysis of the evolution and revolutionary experience of the popular church. While they share some similarities with Nicaraguans from the previously discussed three types, they differ in several important ways.

Like the other three types, Alienated Christians acknowledge the religious origins of the popular church. They agree that during its evolution the grass-roots church underwent a profound transformation from an essentially religious organization to one political in nature. Unlike their Marxist counterparts, however, they do not believe this transformation involved a de-Christianizing process. Unlike Revolutionary Christians, they do not believe that the grass-roots church became politicized as a consequence of its members' deepening Christian reflection. While they accept the idea that the popular church took on a political character, they are more likely to explain this politicization as a consequence of events in Nicaragua. Here they share the opinion of Reformist Christians, who point to the overt corruption and terror of the Somoza dictatorship. Like Reformist Christians they point to the social and economic crises of the nation as explanations for their participation in the anti-Somoza insurrection.

This philosophical conviction has important implications for them. Like Reformists they believe that religious people joined the insurrection out of dissatisfaction arising from the disorder of the state. They reject the notion that revolutionary participation was inspired from some deeply felt conviction about Christian liberation. Alienated Christians argue that they became overwhelmed by what they perceived as a sharp turn toward politics by the popular church. During the 1980s, many of them became disaffected with the Sandinistas and left the church of the poor. Today, they understand the revolutionary experiment as a failure and the popular church's involvement in that project a mistake.

Alienated Christians differ from their Reformist counterparts because they continue to perceive the popular church as a political organization. They are also more likely to identify and understand it as a separated church, one with its own theological doctrine and pastoral practices. Many of them suggest that the acrimony between the traditional church and the Sandinistas influenced them to leave the Catholic community. Today, many of them are active and devout members of fundamentalist Protestant sects.

A subgroup within this ideal type includes Nicaraguans who

were early critics of the Sandinistas. During the 1980s they identified with and supported the Catholic hierarchy's criticism of the
FSLN. Their rejection of liberation theology and Sandinista socialism influenced them to seek more conservative values in both
religious and political spheres. Today, they continue to identify
themselves as very conservative Catholics.

Religious beliefs have affected all of these people's political
values. Unlike members of the three other types, Alienated
Christians do not appear to be dedicated to living out a preferential option for the poor. Rather, they are more likely to believe
that social injustice and poverty will always be part of the worldly
reality. If asked about this reality, they are likely to suggest that
people should find their solace in God. As Shaw (1989: 22) has
argued, such Christians are essentially indifferent to the vast majority of the poor. Ostensibly, they profess an abiding concern for
the family and private morality. They understand their mission
in overwhelmingly sacramental and devotional terms.

Unlike the three other types, Alienated Christians do not believe that building the kingdom of God on Earth can be achieved
in the secular world. Luis Serra (1986: 56–57), a Chilean social
scientist living in Nicaragua, argues that the values promoted by
this sector include personal resignation, ritualism, apoliticism,
and ultraterrestrialism. Alienated Christians believe that the
kingdom and its attendant justice and abundance will come only
after death (in Shaw 1989: 22–23). What is strikingly different
about this type is its members' sharp turn toward conservative
values and traditions. Some have become apolitical, consciously
removing themselves from the political realm. Others seek an
alternative vision for the future of Nicaragua, one reminiscent
of the former Somocista state. Many have organized internally
in a profoundly clerical and authoritarian manner. They charac-
teristically look to similarly antidemocratic political elites to pre-
serve their privileges and enforce their teachings (ibid.: 23).

Members of the Alienated Christian type offer a fascinating
and divergent assessment of the issues facing Nicaraguans and
the popular church today. They provide us with another means
of comprehending the complexity of issues surrounding the

controversial nature of the popular church and the issues of power and influence in the Christian community.

CATHOLICS IN CRISIS

Luz Elena Mejía was raised a traditional Catholic in Granada, the oldest city in the country. Her family has been in Nicaragua for at least five generations. She explained that her great-grandfather was among the landed elite who served in positions of political authority in the city. Today, she owns three hundred acres of rich farmland outside the city, and her brothers and sisters continue to own additional adjacent acres.

As a child, Luz Mejía studied under nuns at the local Catholic school in Granada. As a young woman she traveled extensively in Europe, living for a time in Paris. She also had the opportunity to study at the Sorbonne. Luz recalled the Somoza years as ones of prosperity both for her family and for her nation.

"Times were good," she explained. "People who wanted to work hard and who tried to get ahead had ample opportunity. There were jobs then, agricultural production was flourishing, and there were opportunities for those in the industrial sector. During the Somoza years a middle class developed in Nicaragua. This is something that has disappeared. During the revolution all of the middle class fled to Miami."

Luz suggested that her family lived well, but she said that she was not blind to the abuses of the Somoza dynasty. She acknowledged the fact that corruption existed and that there were abuses of authority, that Somoza had ruled as a dictator and did not tolerate challenges to his power. She remembered times when political opponents were jailed and when critics in both liberal and conservative circles were censored, even silenced.

During the Somoza years Luz Mejía was not political. Like many other Nicaraguans she believed that the earthquake crisis of 1972 and the pilferage that occurred during the relief effort had monumental impact on Nicaraguan society. Despite her verbal support for the insurrection, she remained apart from active involvement in the revolution.

While some Nicaraguans remained apart from the revolution,

this was not true of Daysi Rocha, who was living in Managua, in the community of Adolfo Reyes. She too had been raised as a traditional Catholic but, unlike the Mejías, her family was poor and she did not have the benefit of a full education. During the early 1970s, Daysi remembered, students and priests came to the barrio to talk about the need for solidarity in opposing the Somoza dictatorship. Moved by those experiences and by the terror of the regime, Daysi actively joined the insurrection. She recounted how she was involved in distributing material for the Sandinista guerrillas and how she had used her home to assist them with the urban offensive. She explained that she was committed to fighting to the death to bring a new way of life to the people of Nicaragua.

Ramón García Chenta, a poor, thirty-two-year-old Managuan, was among those who also worked for the liberation of the Nicaraguan people. As a teenager, Ramón worked with other students and the base communities to support the insurrection. "We were all swept up in the excitement," he recalled. "All of us believed in the liberation cause." After the insurrection, Ramón served in the Sandinista army and fought to defend the state against the contra forces.

Like Luz Mejía, Monsignor Oswaldo Mondragón had been raised in the city of Granada. Like the Mejía family, his grandparents were ranchers. Monsignor Mondragón's grandfather was active in conservative politics, and his family was among those involved in anti-Somoza activities.

After receiving a formal Catholic education, Mondragón had an opportunity to go to Chile in 1966. "There I saw the beginning of the iglesia popular, the popular church," he said. "It was called Christian socialism then. It was there that I enlarged my Christian social conscience with a political commitment" (in Heyck 1990: 207).

In Chile, Mondragón met Paulo Freire, who was working with the poor. "Paulo Freire seemed to me to epitomize a valid liberation theology, one that I could be dedicated to. This exposure gave me a new sensibility, a new horizon and a new enthusiasm for the poor" (ibid.).

Returning to Nicaragua in 1970, Mondragón was called to the priesthood and was ordained a priest by Monsignor Obando. Mondragón explained that during the insurrection he had high expectations; he believed things would improve for the poor. He did not join the armed insurrection but did participate in some underground activities, including hiding guerrillas in the parish church.

Despite their enthusiasm and hopes for the revolution, many of these Catholics deserted the ranks and support of the Sandinistas. Luz Mejía left the country just before the fall of the dictator. She explained that she was frightened by the violence of the civil war and that she fled with her son to Miami. In looking back, Luz said that she had intended to return to Nicaragua, but after the insurrection her frequent trips home to visit her family in Granada led her to believe that the Sandinistas were intent on establishing a communist country. She maintained her permanent residence in Miami until 1992. "My mother also fled to the United States, but my brother remained in Granada to live in my parents' home and to work the family farm. He stayed there to protect my family's interests." Apparently there was great concern that the Sandinistas would confiscate their property. "Nothing was ever taken by the government, but our land and home fell into disrepair. My family did not want to invest in our properties because there were continued threats that it would all be taken by the Sandinistas."

Luz Mejía remembered that after each visit to Granada to see her brother she became more depressed about the situation: "All of Nicaragua was falling apart and no one seemed safe. The Sandinistas were corrupt and they began lying to people." For example, Luz pointed to the fact that the government had promised land to the peasants. "They cheated them out of that promise. The campesinos were given land but most of them never got the title to it. The Sandinistas talked about corruption and yet they were seizing people's property and taking their homes for themselves."

The Mejía family was further alienated when the Sandinistas began drafting young men to fight the contra offensive. Luz's brother's children fled to Mexico. Luz remembered, too, how the Sandinistas harassed the church by threatening conservative priests and by censoring Catholic programs from television and radio. "The Sandinistas made a mockery out of religion!" Luz exclaimed. "When the pope came to Nicaragua in 1983 he was humiliated. His visit was an embarrassment to the world! I was shocked by the behavior of people who called themselves Catholics! It was a humiliating day to be a Nicaraguan Catholic."

Daysi Rocha suggested that the pope's visit to Nicaragua divided people's loyalties to both the church and the state. After the insurrection, Daysi became an active member of the Christian base community in Adolfo Reyes. In the early 1980s she was a staunch supporter of the Sandinista government. Like her neighbors, she volunteered in the Commission for Civil Defense to oversee the safety of the barrio. She also worked on Sandinista construction projects in the neighborhood. But after the pope's visit to Nicaragua, she suggested that the community of Adolfo Reyes became more political. "That is when my problems with the community started," Daysi recalled. "There were very high expectations following the insurrection. I think the Sandinistas wished to help the poor, but the people around them were self-interested. The poor remained poor. Promises weren't kept."

Daysi explained that when the church became critical of the government, the Sandinistas and their supporters became vindictive. "No one in the community was willing to criticize the failures of the government. It became very unpopular to speak out against the Sandinistas." For example, Daysi remembered that when international workers came to visit the community, the members were instructed to discuss only the good things about the revolution: the literacy campaign and health reform. "No one was allowed to talk about the bad things like the forced draft," she said.

Daysi said that relations with her neighbors became strained: "I believe it's very hard when you have a community that supports a political position that you do not agree with. Politics came between us. Everything became politicized, and I came to see the community as an instrument of the party."

Monsignor Mondragón pointed to the harassment of the church as the beginning of his own disillusionment with the Sandinista regime. Remaining in Nicaragua after the insurrection, Father Mondragón continued his support of the FSLN and worked with the Literacy Crusade. This work was soon called into question by his Catholic superiors, who accused the campaign of propagating Marxist ideology. He said that the bishops began to believe that the campaign was a pretext for politicizing religion (in Heyck 1990: 208).

Monsignor Mondragón recalled a time when the church held a mass for Catholic literacy teachers. At that event he remembered that there had been a minor disturbance caused by members of the popular church. When Archbishop Obando arrived to perform the mass for the teachers, Father Mondragón recalled, he was jeered by members of the crowd, behavior that shocked him. Thus began his own reevaluation of the goals both of the Christian base communities and of the Sandinista regime. He recalled that as he became more critical of the regime he was increasingly watched and harassed. He suggested that he was the target of a series of attacks in the Sandinista newspapers and that he was followed by Sandinista spies (ibid.: 210).

These Nicaraguans speak of a divided Catholic community. Daysi Rocha said that she perceives the church as separated into two factions: the traditional and more wealthy sector, and the popular, poorer sector. She accused Cardinal Obando of exacerbating the division. Like other members of her community, she recalled the cardinal's infamous visit to her barrio, where Obando had been asked to bless their newly constructed church. "He came to the ceremony and blessed the building but he wouldn't enter," Daysi recalled. She and other members of her community were shocked. "He used the occasion to make his feelings about the popular church very clear to us. He was unwilling to separate himself from our community but he was also using the occasion to make his disgust absolutely clear."

Daysi believed that the cardinal had missed an important opportunity to work toward conciliation: "He should have been an

180

example for all Catholics. He should have been a force for unity, not insult."

Unlike Daysi Rocha, Luz Mejía spoke positively of Cardinal Obando. She believed that he was right to denounce the politicization of religion and to attack the base communities as instruments of the Sandinistas. She also applauded his early attempts to force the resignation of priests who had been serving in the Sandinista government. "Priests cannot serve two gods," she said. "The clergy that served in the Sandinista government had no business being there, and the cardinal was right to admonish them."

Asked about the priests' unwillingness to resign their posts and their justifications for staying in the government, Luz Mejía expressed an opinion also articulated by others within this ideal type: "Social justice and equality sound good. Working for the poor sounds admirable. But I think a classless society is simply impossible to achieve. There are always going to be classes of people. Look, even in heaven there are classes. After all, the church speaks of archangels and angels."

Despite the fact that Daysi Rocha would like to believe in a classless project, she, too, had a similar point of view. "I think the Catholic Church is trying to help bring social justice to our country," she said. "But it is hard to convince the rich in Nicaragua to give up what they have. When we are born we are equal in the eyes of God. But later we become unequal in money and status. This is what makes for inequality in the world. It is difficult for the rich to treat you with respect if you do not share their status. I think the intention was good but it only divided people."

Both Luz Mejía and Daysi Rocha discounted the idea that building a kingdom of God on Earth can or should be a political project. To support their point of view they spoke of the polarization of society and of the failure of the revolution to bring positive changes. Luz believes that revolutionary reforms contributed to a culture of apathy and dependency.

"Today there are many poor people, but this is because poor people are lazy," Luz explained. "During the revolution the government gave handouts and people have gotten used to that. They believe that the government must provide for them. Poor people refuse to work today. They have had ten years of handouts and if you give them a job they come for a few days and then never show up again. They simply refuse to work." Luz explained that she has had trouble keeping her own maids and gardeners. "People will not work even when a job is offered."

Daysi Rocha did not express the belief that the revolution was a mistake, but she suggested that it had given too much freedom to people who were not yet ready for it. "Our young people used to behave better," Daysi explained as we sat together in the dirt courtyard of her home in Adolfo Reyes. "Before the revolution there was more respect for tradition, for religion, for adults, and for authority. Today our young people don't want to work; many are involved in drugs and alcohol. Our children are less religious today. They do not care about religious things, and they are not in church."

Daysi contended that before the 1980s Nicaraguans did not see as many children on the streets or as many people stealing. "I do not blame the Sandinistas for all of these things," she said, "but I do blame the parents of our children. If the Sandinistas were guilty of anything, they were guilty of encouraging greater freedom to defy the ways of the past. Parents have passed this on to their children."

Monsignor Mondragón suggested that the revolution was a failure for Nicaragua; he pointed to the lack of adequate health care, the lack of medicines, and the lack of teachers and competent professionals (in Heyck 1990: 214–15).

Like Mondragón, Ramón Chenta also lost heart in the revolution. After his military service with the Sandinista army, he said, he had trouble finding work. During this time his attention turned to religion. Ramón explained that despite the fact that he had been raised as a traditional Catholic and had worked with several of the Christian base communities, he underwent a profound religious transformation in the late 1980s.

His epiphany occurred at a revival held at a baseball stadium in downtown Managua. "I remember that night as a special gift from God," Ramón began. "God loved me enough to open my eyes and fill me with his light. I went there because I had just lost my job and I was looking for something to take my mind off my problems."

On that particular night a Pentecostal minister was preaching from the Bible. "He was talking about how God loves his children enough to take away their pain and suffering. He told us that we were important to God regardless of whether we were rich or poor," Ramón remembered. "And you see, I know what it's like to be poor. I've been poor all my life, and my parents were poor and their parents before them. But the Bible says that the meek shall inherit the earth, and I think the meek are the poor."

Ramón Chenta suggested the desire of rich people to enslave and oppress the poor: "Everyone has tried to enslave us: the state, the church, our employers. So poor people, we have become enslaved in our bodies and in our minds. This is bad but also good because it is the only way to salvation. When you are poor you become meek."

Ramón argued that government, any government, attempts to use people for its own aggrandizement. "The Sandinistas were no different from the government before them or the government that has come after them. All of them have used the people for their own purposes."

Ramón said that he believes the new Chamorro government lacks respect for Nicaraguans. "The only exception may be for the rich. The government listens to the rich. But God listens to everyone and he gives men life and gladness. This is something the government is always trying to take away. I think governments are lost and so are the people. But one day God will return and strike down all the nonbelievers, especially those who have profited from the exploitation of the meek."

When asked about the political climate of the times, Ramón suggested that Nicaragua is being punished by God because it has set people against each other. "I served in the army, I fought for the Sandinistas, but I was killing my own brothers," he explained. "Now I recognize that they were using me just like the rich have used others to do their dirty work. The Sandinistas

In this example of the "people's art," the figure of Jesus stands in solidarity with the poor, the indigenous, and the martyrs of the struggle for social justice.

used me; they were liars and thieves, but so were the contras. And this government, it isn't any better. It promises things and doesn't deliver. Just like the Sandinistas."

Ramón articulated a common theme found among members of the Alienated type. He epitomizes a frustrated resignation: "There is no hope in this country, no political hope. There is only hope in God and his promise for eternal life."

Ramón Chenta did not vote in the national elections. He explained his aversion to politics by suggesting that all politicians lie. "I am just a poor man trying to live a good life. God has saved me from my vices. My Bible is my rule book. I seek guidance from it and comfort because God doesn't lie," he said. "I know that if I live a good life, if I don't lie, or cheat, or steal, if I am faithful to God's word, there will be a kingdom to inherit."

Like other Alienated Christians, Ramón spoke of God's kingdom in religious—not political—terms. He does not believe that it can be found on Earth. "Just look around you and you will see the devil's work," Ramón exclaimed as he threw up his hands. "God promises a kingdom but it's not of this world."

Today, Ramón Chenta is an active member of a fundamentalist Protestant church, one of many such churches that are rising up everywhere in Nicaragua and throughout Latin America.

CATHOLIC CONVERTS AND
THE RISE OF PROTESTANTISM

While Nicaragua continues to be a predominately Catholic nation, and while no authoritative data exist about alternative religious membership, most studies suggest that about 14 percent of the population is affiliated with Protestant churches (Berryman 1994: 147).

In Latin America all non-Catholic denominations are recognized as evangelical. The Protestant faith was originally brought to Nicaragua by Moravians, who made initial contact with the population on the east coast.

In 1847, in the Bluefields area, the Moravians began the first serious Protestant missionary work in the country (Haslam 1987: 8). They built schools, hospitals, a nursing program, and a theological college.

This work was followed by the contribution of Baptists. Carlos Villagra, dean of the Baptist Seminary of Nicaragua, explained that in 1852 Baptists came to the country by way of the Corn Islands. "Our work there did not affect the rest of the nation," explained Villagra. "But in 1970 we began an outreach program, and Baptist preachers spread our mission to the Pacific coast."

The Episcopal Church established itself in the nineteenth century on the east coast of Nicaragua, in the Greytown area. Later, the Episcopalians moved their mission to the city of Bluefields. In 1951 the Episcopal Church was established on the Pacific side of the country, opening its first church near Managua.

Despite the growth of Protestantism, it appears that vigorous competition and deep suspicions occurred between the various churches. Darwin López, director of Atlantic development in the Río San Juan region of Nicaragua, explained that it was not until

185

the earthquake disaster of 1972 that Protestant churches in Nicaragua began to reach out to one another. López is a founding member of the Protestant organization CEPAD (formerly, the Evangelical Committee for Aid to Victims), a Protestant organization that often works in conjunction with the Christian base communities.

"On December 27, 1972, eight Protestant leaders met in the capital city," López recalled. "It was there that we learned very quickly that in the face of this crisis we could work together." At the same time there was also increased interaction with the Catholic grass-roots church. "Together we realized that there were economic, political, and social problems that had to be addressed. We came to recognize the limitations of charitable aid and that problems in Nicaragua were more structural in nature." As a consequence of this awakening, the organization agreed to change its name to the Evangelical Committee for Aid to Development. "The name change represented our organization's new priority: to support efforts of local community members to better their material, social, and spiritual resources," López said.

Despite the actions of a few progressive Protestant leaders, however, the majority of Protestant churches did not involve themselves in the ensuing insurrection (Haslam 1987). At the Baptist seminary, Carlos Villagra explained that most Baptists' interest in the liberation movement did not emerge until after the triumph of the revolution. He suggested that early interest in liberation theology was limited to seminary students and those few professors who were coming from Costa Rica to teach at the seminary.

"Our initial interest was strictly theoretical," Villagra said. "It wasn't until 1979 that Baptists were beginning to be questioned and challenged. We began asking our parishioners what they were doing with their faith. We asked them to think about their commitment to the community. Out of these questions we grew to realize that there had to be a greater commitment to praxis [working toward social justice]."

Despite this commitment, progressive Protestants found themselves competing with the fundamentalists. Villagra explained that the last two decades have seen an explosive growth of fundamentalist Protestantism in Nicaragua. Many factors account for this rapid growth. One factor has to do with the historic problem of Catholic resources. The Catholic Church in Latin America has always struggled with a lack of attendant clergy.

Berryman (1994: 154) suggests that in 1987 there was an average of 1 Protestant pastor for every 92 evangelical Christians. In comparison, there has been only 1 Catholic representative for every 3,190 Nicaraguans. Protestant ministers in Nicaragua confirm Berryman's conclusion that the lack of a personal relationship with the Catholic community helped to make Nicaraguans vulnerable to evangelical churches.

The Catholic outreach problem appears to have been further exacerbated by the church-state conflict. Father Alvaro Argüello, a Jesuit priest at the University of Central America, explained that after the revolution a vacuum in religious leadership existed as a result of the anti-Sandinista position of the Catholic hierarchy. "The Catholic Church lost membership among committed revolutionaries," Argüello said. "Many of these people continued to take their religion seriously, but they looked to other churches to fulfill their spiritual needs."

It is possible that changes in the Catholic Church also worked to confuse the laity. Berryman (ibid.: 156) suggests that "Catholicism made a dramatic turn-around on a number of seemingly irreformable points: The Latin Mass was dropped, Bible reading was encouraged, and ecumenism replaced religious intolerance." While Vatican II's reforms were aimed at promoting unity, it is just as likely that such drastic changes also worked to undermine it. This situation appears to have been true in the rural areas of the country.

Uli Schmidt contended that in the countryside Catholics found themselves increasingly attracted to Protestant ministries. He suggested that when the hierarchy came out against the revolution, and as internal struggles continued within the Catholic Church, many people found themselves between two models of the church. "Many people did not agree with either side," Schmidt explained. "But there was no third alternative to cap-

187

ture this dissatisfaction. The Protestant churches gained from this alienation."

Schmidtt argued that in the rural areas of the country the popular church's lack of support and staff contributed to the communities' increasing vulnerability to an alternative religious ideology. "This was particularly true," he said, "as radical priests were removed from their churches by the Catholic hierarchy."

Schmidtt's work in the countryside in the 1980s also suggests that as times became more difficult, popular priests were failing to represent their communities. "Many of the clergy were foreign priests who had not captured in their perspective what was really happening here. They didn't understand nor were they cognizant of the campesinos' growing alienation. The Protestant churches capitalized on this. They capitalized on the despair and sense of fatalism that was growing in Nicaragua."

The evangelical churches that reached out to rural Nicaraguans found that their highly emotional and festive services resonated well with the campesinos' popular culture. The churches' emphasis on miracles and prophecies also complemented the popular religiosity of many rural campesinos (ibid.: 157).

The aggressive rise of fundamentalism sapped the strength of the CEB movement in Nicaragua. Members of the community of San Judas spoke of the attraction of new Protestant churches.

"Today we face a severe economic crisis," explained CEB member Raquel López. "People are hungry and out of work and they are looking for help. Because the government has been unable to meet their needs, and because our own resources are limited, people have turned to these rich Protestant churches. These churches can offer them comfort and assistance with their problems."

Both the traditional sector of the Catholic Church and the Christian base communities lament the increasing competition, but they do not blame the Catholic community for the success of Protestant missionary work. It is far more typical to hear Catholics place the blame on the United States. Both Cardinal Obando and his spokesperson, Monsignor Bismark Carballo, argued that the rise of Protestantism has been the result of U.S. objectives that sought to undermine the strength of the liberation movement. Monsignor Carballo accused the evangelical groups of "polluting" the Catholic ethos of Nicaraguan society. He accused them of bringing such North American values as individualism and materialism to his country. "This has not been a positive thing for our culture," he exclaimed.

While the Catholic hierarchy disparages evangelical values, noted North American excesses are not exhibited in most fundamentalist churches. On the contrary, fundamentalist churches appear to enforce very strict codes of conduct. Moral absolutism has an accepted place in communities troubled by high rates of alcohol and drug use and other antisocial behaviors (see also Berryman 1994). Nicaraguans who adhere to these rules find their family and community relations markedly improved.

Uli Schmidtt suggested that simple, clear rules of conduct are philosophically appealing to the campesino whose life remains so fragile. "There is security in structure and predictability."

Church specialist Clifton Holland suggests that an identification with the United States and U.S. pop culture may help to explain the current growth of Protestant churches (ibid.: 158). Many Nicaraguans equate U.S. culture with money, progress, and modernization. In a climate of deprivation it is probably difficult not to be attracted to such an image. The effective use of television by evangelical clergy has enhanced this image of wealth, and it also offers distraction from the rigors of a hard life. For example, it is not uncommon to observe Nicaraguan families attending church services two or three times a week. The church is a place for them to go for fellowship, entertainment, and diversion. Nor is it uncommon to find rural farm families in front of a television or radio, clapping and singing with the broadcast music.

Hardship is the life experience of the majority in Nicaragua. It is precisely this reality that draws the sharpest criticism from progressive evangelicals. The progressive Christian sector accuses the fundamentalist churches of preaching resignation in the face of so much suffering. Javier Talavera, director of CIEETS, contended that Nicaragua has been witnessing an invasion by foreign evangelicals whose "thrust has been to divide Protestants

189

and to confuse the laity." He accused the fundamentalist churches of being the enemies of change.

Talavera suggested that, like the Catholic community, Protestants are divided. "We have taken a very conservative turn here in Nicaragua, and fundamentalist thought is prevailing. Why?" he asked. "Because Nicaragua is suffering from mass poverty and mass illiteracy," he explained. "People who have suffered the worst effects of the contra war, people who are suffering the worst effects of the economy, are looking for simple answers."

Darwin López agreed with Talavera's assessment and added: "These campaigns are of great concern. Not only do they divide our solidarity, but they distract people from their social problems. We are not in agreement with these campaigns. Foreign ministers come here to preach an endurance of suffering. Our position is that each local church should have responsibility for ministering to its own community. This ministering should be a holistic evangelization, not one that preaches separation of body and soul."

López suggested that the danger is in the alienating form that traditional religion takes: "It can lead to a resigned people who perpetuate their own poverty and suffering. Our communities increasingly recognize the need to reach out to the poor masses who practice this traditional Christianity. We are trying to raise their consciousness and offer them an alternative way of living, one that works for the structural change of our society."

Not far from where the Christian base community meets in Adolfo Reyes, a Pentecostal church has been attracting growing attention. The services are well attended and they are recognizably different in gender membership. Unlike the local Catholic church or the CEB meeting hall, this church has a predominately male congregation. Some of the women at the service are strikingly noticeable by the white veils that adorn their heads. "These women are special," explained Ramón Chenta. "The adornment symbolizes their special enlightenment." He suggested that these particular women have been recognized by the congregation because they have the gift of prophecy: "They are able to see into the future and can speak in tongues."

Like Ramón, these Christians believe that only people who surrender their will to God can achieve this enlightenment. He suggested that the women of his church are enlightened because they come to God "with their heads bowed in willing submission." The theme of submission is what worries the progessive sector. In the face of growing impoverishment, many Nicaraguans appear to be turning inward.

Nicaragua's economic problems generally reflect a larger regional crisis. According to official statistics, more than 40 percent of Latin Americans cannot now satisfy their basic needs for food, health, and housing. During the 1980s the region witnessed a decrease in its participation in the international market, a drop from 7 percent to just below 4 percent. Direct investment stock also dropped from 12.3 percent in 1980 to 5.8 percent in 1989 (Gorostiaga 1991: 33).

Data for 1995 show a continuing trend: The foreign trade gap has expanded since 1990. More foreign cooperation has translated into more imports without economic reactivation. In Nicaragua, the foreign trade deficit is 42.5 percent of the annual Gross Domestic Product; in 1990 it was 32.2 percent (*Envio* 1995: 7).

These facts mean that Latin America has suffered the greatest backward movement in the world, even greater than that of Africa (Gorostiaga 1991: 35). In fact, in Nicaragua it is not uncommon to hear scholars speak of the country's "Africanization." In both religious and political circles there is mounting fear that if this trend continues the tiny nation will no longer be able to feed itself.

Jesuit scholar Alvaro Argüello explained that the Chamorro government's answer to these problems appears to be in greater privatization of the public sector and thus reduction of the government's social welfare role. But privatization has had its costs. It has led to an alarming deterioration of health care services and educational opportunities and appears to have contributed to the problems of mass unemployment. According to the United Nations Development Program's June 1994 poverty study, 74.8 percent of all Nicaraguan families live below the poverty line,

43.6 percent of them in extreme poverty. Overall unemployment (open or hidden) still hovers around 60 percent of the population able to work (*Envio* 1995: 7).

Reynaldo Antonio Tefel, the former Sandinista minister of the Nicaraguan Social Security and Welfare Institute, contended that "what President Reagan's trickle-down economics has meant to the North American economy, the imposed neoliberal model of development has meant to the majority of poor Latin Americans." He suggested that social service cutbacks and bureaucratic layoffs have exacerbated the problems of an already devastated economy.

Alberto Morales, a theological coordinator with the Antonio Valdivieso Center in Managua, suggested that economic hardship is a leading factor in the growth of fundamentalist ideology: "Pentecostalism is growing rapidly. In fact, it includes the great majority of Protestants." He said that he believes the rate of Protestantism is higher than 14 percent and suggested that about 20 percent of the Nicaraguan population now claims to be Protestant. He believes that 80 to 85 percent of these Protestants are neo-Pentecostals.

"This sect is not progressive but is highly fundamentalist," Morales said. "Fundamentalism has profited from the economic hardship here. It is successful because fundamentalist Protestant churches offer two kinds of comfort to suffering Nicaraguans. The first is material comfort. Because they are well financed they are able to sustain large handouts of food, blankets, and shelters. The second kind of comfort is personal. Concern for their well-being creates a personal relationship with many of these people."

Morales suggested that the fundamentalist churches provide for suffering Nicaraguans a climate of concern and nurturance. "Protestantism is essentially individualistic," he said. "Protestant pastors usually know their parishioners by name and this gives poor people a sense of identity and personal dignity. This is one reason why the base communities were so popular, because they were connected to the people at a very personal level. But the

CEBs are more rationalized, and many poor people in this country are more involved in feeling and emotion, not reason. Hungry people are searching for escape, and the CEBs require action and concern."

Morales explained that the relationship between Nicaraguans and the fundamentalist Protestant churches is vertical and authoritarian. "There is an evasion of one's situation," he continued. "There is no questioning of one's situation. The sad fact is, many poor Nicaraguans feel more at home with this."

But not all fundamentalist churches are composed of strictly poor people; evangelical churches have also attracted middle-class Latin Americans. For example, Berryman (1994: 163–65) identifies a different kind of "prosperity theology" that is attracting middle-class artisans, merchants, and professionals. Largely urban in nature, it appears to attract upwardly mobile Christians who are seeking a spiritual, disciplined belief system that can assist them in coping with an increasingly competitive economic environment.

The aggressive rise of Protestantism particularly among the middle class has spurred efforts by the Catholic hierarchy to find ways to maintain its historic hegemony. Catholic officials readily admit the church's vulnerability to Protestant campaigns and have thus responded with their own unique, charismatic program. The program borrows from pentecostal strategies that combine liveliness with moments of intense emotional prayer, personal contacts, and invitation. It invites participants to a deep, spiritual conversion that accepts Jesus as a personal savior and that demands a profound biblical morality.

THE CATHOLIC RESPONSE: A GROWING CHARISMATIC MOVEMENT

Phillip Berryman's work (ibid.: 165) traces the origins of the Catholic Charismatic Renewal program to 1967 at Notre Dame and Duquesne Universities. He suggests that during the following decade the program quickly spread throughout the world. Despite its converts, the movement has remained a largely minority phenomenon in the Catholic community. Berryman suggests that because it is so similar to fundamentalist Protestantism, many progressive Catholics regard it as spiritually alienating.

In Nicaragua, however, the Catholic hierarchy appears to be enthusiastic about a new project known as Light Two Thousand. It is a massive charismatic campaign promoted by the cardinal's office. In an interview in his office, Cardinal Obando explained that the program received the blessing of Pope John Paul at the Santo Domingo conference that met during fall 1992.

"We have suffered from divisions as well as challenges from the rise of so many Protestant churches here in Nicaragua," explained the cardinal. "As a consequence, we have been evaluating the means for promoting Catholic unity. This was a major issue at the Santo Domingo conference. The conference was concerned with the future work of the church and it confirmed a new way of evangelization for us. The church shall pursue new methods and means for reaching out to the community of Catholics throughout Latin America. Its object is to promote solidarity among our community."

The cardinal's spokesperson, Monsignor Bismark Carballo, agreed that the main theme of the Santo Domingo conference was the evangelization of cultures. "The bishops of Latin America have proposed projects for unifying the Catholic Church," Carballo explained. "The Light Two Thousand project will reach out to people through television, radio, and newspapers. The attempt will be more lighthearted, a more cheerful strategy but also more devotional." The monsignor explained that the program will promote Catholicism and that it is meant to "penetrate into the culture of Latin American peoples." Both Cardinal Obando and Monsignor Carballo said that the aim of the program was to revitalize the energy of the Catholic community.

The Light Two Thousand project is being financed by the Catholic hierarchy and, according to critics, by wealthy counterrevolutionaries. According to Javier Talavera at CIEETS, the Catholic program is based on rehighlighting the five hundred years of Spanish conquest. "It is the promulgation that we have been Christianized by the Spanish, a Catholic Crown," Talavera suggested. "The hierarchy has taken up the Protestant method of going from house to house, to television, and to radio to re-Christianize our people. It is a theme that ultimately speaks of a return to tradition."

Jerjes Ruiz, a theologian working with the Baptist Seminary of Nicaragua, believes that the effort is primarily political. He argued that Light Two Thousand is a deliberate attempt by the hierarchy to emasculate the Christian base communities. "This program is not just designed to arrest the growth of the evangelical churches," Ruiz argued. "The Light Two Thousand program is intended to reduce the popular church to a sect."

In spite of the church's attempt to unify the Catholic community, Father Alvaro Argüello believes that the community suffers from more than two divisions. In fact, like others in Nicaragua, he sees several competing tendencies. For example, Jorge Bardequez, theologian and coordinator of pastoral work at the Antonio Valdivieso Center, suggested that his own research supports such a view. "What we see are different trends in Catholicism," he explained. "The traditional-legal one is guided by Cardinal Obando, who is currently aligned with the powerful here. In my own work I have found that this sector is the group that has always been aligned with the bourgeoisie. To the extent that the bourgeoisie went anti-Somoza so did the Nicaraguan church. When this same group of elites went anti-Sandinista so did the traditional church."

When asked to identify this sector of Catholics, Bardequez pointed to a variety of Nicaraguan technocrats and professionals plus the president of Nicaragua, Violeta Chamorro, her minister of state (and her son-in-law) Antonio Lacayo, and her official cabinet. "This tendency represents mainstream Catholicism," Bardequez said.

Bardequez also spoke of a cultural Catholicism that he identified as popular religion: "It is a religion that is related to cultural traditions as well as native beliefs. This group consists mainly of the poor who participate in ceremonies, like the Santo Domingo and Purísima celebrations that mix African and indigenous traditions." When asked to identify this group, Bardequez said that

195

he sees this tendency in a context of a people who still live in a feudal world, particularly the campesino.

"My work also understands the *iglesia popular*—a movement related to the anti-Somoza struggle," Bardequez continued. "This movement involved priests who worked with students in the insurrection." He believes that this tendency was inspired by the conferences at the Vatican (II), Medellín, and Puebla. "This sector represents an alternative to traditional Catholicism. One of the distinctive features of our revolution has been the political action of Christians. But political action supportive of the Sandanistas ultimately brought a struggle to the church between the procontra forces, supported by the bourgeoisie, and the people's revolution that was supported by the popular sector of the Catholic Church." When asked to identify this group, he pointed to the Christian base communities. "I also believe there is a fourth trend in the Catholic community, a charismatic, right-wing Catholic group that is known as the City of God movement," Bardequez explained. "They are very conservative, socially, politically, and religiously."

Bardequez believes that this group is ideologically in line with Cardinal Obando. "But while they are in agreement with the cardinal, they are not always in agreement with the current government. They are a smaller minority, a subgroup, within the Nicaraguan elite. This is a secularized Catholic group whose project is a type of mystical Pentecostalism," Bardequez explained. He identifies them as members of the bourgeoisie, including Minister of Education Humberto Belli and Vice-President Virgilio Godoy.

"The City of God movement is one dynamic arising out of the project of Catholic restoration, the Light Two Thousand project," Bardequez continued. "It is a project aimed at the restoration of very traditional Catholicism." Apparently it has grown out of the attempt for church unity and the reassertion of Catholic hegemony.

According to Javier Talavera at CIEETS, the movement has been financed by wealthy counterrevolutionaries. He believes it is currently under the leadership of Humberto Belli, "who is not always in agreement with the cardinal on matters of politics." But Talavera agrees that the City of God movement is being activated by the Nicaraguan hierarchy as part of its Light Two Thousand program.

Alberto Morales sees similar tendencies within the Catholic community. "This small group of Nicaraguan elites plays with the authority of the church. They use the church for their own interests," Morales claimed. "They are semi-independent and are composed of many government people, including the mayor of Managua, Arnoldo Alemán, and Humberto Belli. I believe many of the people returning from Miami, middle- and upper-class Nicaraguans, find intellectual and religious accommodation with this sector of Catholics."

But Morales also suggested that poor people might be associated with this group. "Poor Nicaraguans returning to the country from Costa Rica, and Honduras, and those from Miami, too, have joined this camp," he explained. "The majority of them have been traditional Catholics, and they are looking for a way to remain dedicated to their faith, but they have had fundamental differences with the institutional church." Morales suggested that this group has felt alienated by the Catholic Church's emphasis for two decades on the preferential option for the poor. "Others have become disillusioned with what they considered to be the overpoliticization of religion in the Nicaraguan state," Morales said.

This tendency appears to typify members of the Alienated Christian type. For example, Monsignor Oswaldo Mondragón identifies himself as a charismatic Catholic (in Heyck 1990: 207). Luz Mejía said that she has become deeply involved in the movement, too. She explained that despite the fact that she had been raised as a traditional Catholic, she had fallen out of practice with her faith.

"I am aware of the reforms emanating from the Second Vatican Council," Mejía offered. "While I think that some of them were good and brought religion closer to the people, there has also been great confusion in the church." For example, she points to the fact that the liturgy—now said in Spanish instead

197

of Latin—has been an important reform. "But I also see sacramental practice varying from church to church," she said. "In Managua, for instance, the priest offers the Communion bread in the parishioner's hand. The local bishops here in Granada do not agree with this practice and refuse to serve the Communion wafer in this way. This can confuse the laity."

Luz also suggested that there is a great deal of confusion over what it means to be a good Catholic. "Catholics among themselves cannot agree," she said. "When the Sandinistas were in power, the cardinal criticized the role of priests in positions of authority in the government. I agreed. Priests cannot serve two gods! And the Sandinista state was a god to the people," Luz said with emotion. "Priests do not belong in politics. It makes a mockery out of religion!"

Luz Mejía believes that these are Catholics who have confused their politics with their religious faith: "I think this is dangerous and an affront to God. Some of these Catholics profess to be Christians, but they lie to the people and confuse those who simply don't know any better. They say that God is on the side of the poor. What does this mean?"

"It is a lie to teach people that God only loves the poor or that he takes sides with them over others," Luz continued. "My God loves everyone, and he knows the suffering of all his people, not just the poor."

It seemed apparent that Luz was now speaking of herself. As a wealthy Nicaraguan and a privileged member of the elite, she appeared defensive about this notion of a God of the poor. The conversation turned on her own spiritual life. Asked about her religious practices, she explained that her discovery of God was a result of much suffering. "Shortly before the insurrection I left with my son for Miami," she said. "When I returned to visit my brother in 1984, my child had an accident here in this house and he broke his leg in several places. There was no adequate medical care in Granada or in Managua and no pain medication was available to give to him." Luz recalled that her son screamed in pain for days. "I couldn't sleep; I couldn't eat; I spent day after day crying in anguish over his pain. They were the worst days of my life."

During this ordeal Luz fled the house, unable to endure any longer her son's agony. "I went to a friend's home to be comforted. When I arrived there she spoke to me about the love of Jesus. I was so distraught I listened. Then we knelt down together to pray, and as we did I felt something move inside of me. I felt all of my pain and agony being lifted from my heart. On that day I was converted. I discovered my faith after my great disillusionment with the Catholic Church," she explained.

From that day forward Luz Mejía said that she was able to cope with her son's injury. She found a way to return him to Miami where he received medical assistance. "Today my son is able to walk," Luz said. "This is a miracle of God."

Belief in miracles, sacramentalism, and ritualism are characteristic of this ideal type. Luz Mejía explained that today she regularly practices her faith at the local San Juan church, but the mass is not traditionally Catholic. Parishioners participate in hand clapping, hand waving, and shouting praise to God, and some even speak in tongues. If one did not know it was a Catholic mass, one might mistake it for a fundamentalist Protestant service.

Luz Mejía's story is not atypical. Many Nicaraguans who make up this type have a similar story about a life crisis that brought them to a renewed interest in a charismatic faith. The crisis has usually fallen on the heels of a growing disappointment in the changes within the institutional church and in the positions of radicalized clergy and other church representatives.

Ramón Chenta's story involved a time of personal disillusionment with politics and the economic stress of chronic unemployment. In the case of Monsignor Mondragón, it was the sense of betrayal not only by radical clergy who were defending some form of liberation theology but also by the perception of the Sandinistas who were regarded as the enemies of religion.

RELIGION AND POLITICS

While the Catholic community suffers from such division, it appears that such schisms parallel the lines of political partisanship that have emerged in Nicaragua since the election of the

Chamorro government in 1990. Division is increasingly evident among political elites. Despite several years of UNO rule, political polarization continues to characterize the Chamorro party. Current accounts suggest that the party has now fractionalized into three parts. Gustavo Tablada, president of the National Assembly and leader of the moderate wing of the UNO coalition, offered his explanation of this phenomenon: "The schism reflects an intense struggle between moderates and hard-liners within the party. The conflict within UNO has its roots in the government's policy of seeking reconciliation with the Sandinistas."

Tablada identified the most militant faction within the party as the group known as the Patriotic Opposition Alliance. This faction is led by Vice-President Virgilio Godoy and former president of the National Assembly, Alfredo Cesar. Political analysts have suggested that this particular group has attempted on several occasions to replace President Violeta Chamorro and her minister of state, Antonio Lacayo. The group also was among those who demanded removal of General Humberto Ortega as commander of the Sandinista army. Their strident demands attempted to end what they saw as their party's alleged cogovernment with the Sandinistas.

Tablada suggested that while the hard-line faction of the UNO coalition attempted to overthrow the government, other factions within the party have tried to promote greater dialogue. He further suggested that the strategy for compromise has been nothing less than an attempt to save Nicaragua's fragile democratic process.

A fragile democratic process does appear to be emerging in the country. After the 1990 electoral defeat of the Sandinistas, many critics were surprised by the FSLN's promise to step down peacefully from its position of power. This step alone was a major achievement toward a democratic process.

Luis Humberto Guzmán, a moderate member of the UNO coalition and a leader of the Christian Democratic Party, suggested that the role of Christian democracy is to further this beginning. He claimed that his party will continue to fight against attempts by others to undermine the democratization process.

"There are some people in places of authority who would like to see us step back in time," he said. "They have attempted to polarize society. We need to work toward a multiparty system. By excluding minority groups we won't guarantee democracy. In order to have democracy we must avoid the collapse of the political system."

While Cardinal Obando has been a supporter of the besieged president, Violeta Chamorro, the Catholic hierarchy has also been openly critical of some of Chamorro's decisions to recognize Sandinista demands. The cardinal's continued condemnation of the Sandinista party as illegitimate and his outspoken advocacy for its removal from power have won him favor with evangelical Catholics. Alienated Christians, like Luz Mejía, suggested that the cardinal is on the right side of this debate.

"I don't believe that there is any real leader here in Nicaragua," Luz argued. "But there are a few people in political positions, like Humberto Belli, who are honest and good men. These men would like to see a different kind of Nicaragua, one that recognizes the mistakes of communism and makes a clear commitment to private enterprise. After all, no one will invest in this economy unless they are convinced that their investment is protected. This won't happen until the Sandinistas are removed from government."

Luz argued that President Chamorro has been wrong in her attempts to meet the Sandinista demands. "Vice-President Godoy and people like Mayor Alemán have a vision for Nicaragua," Luz suggested. "It is one that would instill greater morality, a respect for work, law, and order. Nowadays, there is respect neither for work, nor law, nor order. Everyone here thinks other people owe them something and if they can't have it, then they steal it."

Luz also claimed that she had never seen so much crime and deviance as she sees in her country today. "I think the church is right to come out and speak about this. As the father of the Nicaraguan people, the cardinal should speak out against what he sees as wrong."

Both Luz Mejía and Daysi Rocha believe that the current Chamorro government is incapable of ruling, and both blame the

Sandinistas for this problem. "The current government is just as corrupt as the Sandinistas were," offered Luz Mejía. "Violeta Chamorro is a puppet of the Sandinistas. They are a bad influence in this government, and Chamorro has been unwilling—or incapable—of taking control of the situation. The problem is that there is no real leader in Nicaragua. I believe that too many good men here simply avoid politics. People are very discontented because they recognize the corruption of the government and they know that neither side is honest with the people. What we need is political solidarity, a force that can take control of all of this conflict."

Daysi Rocha believes that things are better today, but she too is increasingly concerned about the breakdown of law and order. "Not everything about the Revolution was bad," Daysi said. "There was reform and social progress. It gave many good things to poor people: education, health care, work. We were very excited because we really believed things would be better and we would be able to show the whole world a new way of living. But the Sandinistas' promises became lies. They were not able to deliver all that they promised, and they took back much of what they gave."

Daysi claimed that while times are bad she also believes that things are better today than they were under the Sandinista leadership. "Today we are happy because we no longer have to worry about the draft; we have peace now," she said. But she also offered an opinion similar to Luz Mejía's assessment of Nicaraguan society: "Today there is a breakdown of law and order. If you are killed, no one will even be punished for the crime. I think there is a need for greater authority here. I would like to see greater punishment especially for the rape of children. There is a lot of that happening here. I would like to see someone like that burned in the middle of town! That kind of crime would stop. If the Sandinistas let this government do what it wanted to, things would be better for everyone."

Like others of the Alienated Christian type, Daysi Rocha has become disillusioned about politics. She feels increasingly estranged from both her government and her community. "When the CEB was first established, we had a good relationship," Daysi said. "We worked together and tried to do many things. But as time went on our loyalties became divided. As I began to recognize the errors of the Sandinistas, I became less enthusiastic about the revolution."

Daysi Rocha explained that with increasing disagreements over politics, she began to see many contradictions in the community. For example, she suggested that while the community was preaching spiritual and moral responsibility there were many hypocrites. During a second interview in her home, she seemed more confident and comfortable in discussing the problems she had with her community.

"The 1980s were difficult times," Daysi explained. "There were differences over the war, the economy, over the role of the church." She suggested that the community was divided over the pope's visit to Nicaragua. Some in the community, she explained, were appalled by the pope's behavior, but others like herself were angered by the disrespect that was shown to the Holy Father. This appears to be one of the striking differences that Alienated Christians have with the Marxist and Revolutionary Christian types. Like others of this ideal type, she exhibits a profound devotion to the pope.

Daysi also recalled Father Miguel d'Escoto's celebrated demonstration against the Catholic hierarchy. She was not in agreement with others in the community who participated in the march for peace. She explained that she found the event alienating and that it was not uncommon for CEB meetings to end with disagreements and hard feelings. "Our disagreements were making me ill," Daysi said, her voice quivering with emotion. "I began suffering from a sense of alienation because most of the time I was not in agreement with the majority of the community."

These were lonely times for her, traumatic years, but despite these feelings she said she felt compelled to remain a part of the community. After all, these were her neighbors and they had worked together on many projects. After the national elections, however, her break with the community became final.

"One of the things that made me the most ill was the national election," Daysi recalled. "At that time there were many foreigners here to observe the elections and I hosted two German women in my home." Daysi recalled sitting with her guests to watch television the night of the election returns. When it became apparent that the Sandinistas were losing, the German women began to cry. "I sat there in silence, feeling very bad because I had cast my vote for the UNO party," Daysi said. She explained that in those awkward moments she began to think she had made a terrible mistake.

"But then I realized that I had voted for my children, I had voted to end this terrible [contra] war," Daysi recalled. "But only a few people in this community understood why I had voted against the Sandinistas, only a few tried to understand. There were others in the community that I knew had also voted for the UNO," Daysi continued. "But they denied it and instead they criticized me!" This contradiction ultimately forced her decision to leave the community. Daysi explained that her health had deteriorated as a consequence of the stress over these disagreements.

Daysi Rocha's situation dramatically reflects the effect that Nicaraguan politics has had on the unity and cohesion of the popular church and of the community. Daysi said that she still loves the church but no longer attends the local masses or the CEB meetings.

"Over the years my beliefs have changed," Daysi explained. "I have learned more about love for my brothers and sisters. I know that I must help others and that even in the community I must make compromises. But it's difficult. It is hard to believe that the kingdom of God could ever be built here. Our hearts are hard. The truth is we do not share nor do we tolerate differences."

Daysi said that today she is no longer political. "Once I wanted change and I helped to bring that change to Nicaragua. But I am tired. I wish that our nation could be what we wish it was: a place of peace, love, and compassion among people. But I don't see it here."

Since the national election, the growing polarization between the two political parties has adversely affected people's relations in other CEBs. The community of San Pablo, for example, has suffered alienation problems similar to those felt by Daysi Rocha.

In San Pablo, Rafael Valdéz suggested that of the 1,500 people in that neighborhood about half are Sandinista supporters and the other half are UNO party members. "Despite our political differences, we try to work together on community projects," Valdéz said. "But this is not always an easy task." Julio Sequeira claimed that some members in the CEB are sympathetic both to Cardinal Obando and to the UNO party. "But the reality is that it has more often divided us."

While Alienated Christians speak of their hopes for a new kind of society, all of them have chosen to remove themselves from involvement in political and community life. Unlike members of the other three types, Alienated Christians have a sense of fatalism and resignation. Many seek solace in their religious beliefs and articulate arguments for greater law and order.

In the meantime, the Latin American church is pursuing strategies for reasserting its authority and religious hegemony. Despite this attempt, many Catholics in Nicaragua are increasingly alienated along religious and political lines.

Alberto Morales suggested that the church's inability to reconcile the growing polarization among the Catholic community will ultimately be fatal for the Catholic Church. "I think the traditional Catholic Church will live for a long time but it has no future because it does not respond to the mix of the people," he said. "It ultimately fails to understand the democratic process that is struggling to emerge in Nicaragua and elsewhere in Latin America."

In Nicaragua, a common perception seems to exist that the hierarchy has failed to understand the increasing dissatisfaction among sectors of the Catholic community. Uli Schmidt suggested that the level of disaffection with the Catholic Church has led people to search for a new way of being Christian. "People are searching for a new way to be spiritual," Schmidt suggested. "They are beginning to form their own picture, one still unarticulated by either the Protestant or Catholic faiths. The picture is still trying to take shape. The perspective has just not yet been comprehended by the community of faithful."

But, Schmidt suggested, no plan currently exists for recovering the liberation movement. "There are no political alternatives either—no alternative model exists here for the poor," he said. "People are divided and confused. Currently there is chaos in the religious life of the campesino. All of the cooperatives that were begun in the 1980s are struggling. They cannot get credit from this new government and there is economic disaster. It is a very exhausting experience to be up against."

At the Antonio Valdivieso Center, Father Uriel Molina, a founding member of the Nicaraguan popular church, spoke openly of the mistakes of the past. He acknowledged errors of the progressive sector and admitted that a major problem has been the lack of a new generation to take over the work for social justice: "The future leaders of Nicaragua, its youth, are no longer interested in reality from a religious perspective because they see the contradictions within the hierarchy. Like so many others, they are confused. The new current of youth—those coming from Miami—speak English and their values are not in line with our culture. They emulate the individualistic values of North America."

Father Molina is not discouraged. His current work in Somoto, in the northern region of Nicaragua, gives him great hope for a revitalized movement. "In Nicaragua there are some CEBs that are struggling to maintain their line in confrontation with those traditional priests who seek to reestablish the church's hierarchical authority," he continued. "We have begun to address the need to return to our theological roots. The CEBs also recognize the need for a reproductive device, and the new youth groups are part of this recognition."

Father Molina argued that in the best of times the CEBs held power but only under the protection and support of the Sandinistas. "Today we no longer enjoy political support," he explained. "Most of the CEBs are paralyzed because they are persecuted by the hierarchy and they no longer enjoy the protection of a government that is at odds with them. The only way out of this paralysis is for the communities to continue reaching out to others of different mind."

Father Molina said that he is initiating new seminars in northern Nicaragua that are not structured around a religious point of view. "I continue to use the method of popular education with small groups, and we begin with questions concerning their immediate political and social reality," he said. "The people in the campo are aware of this government, the reality of this government. They are so aware of the situation. In the rural areas I discover a great difference between the middle class and the poor. The poor give hope a reason to live. The poor are rich in values. In Managua, in the middle class, there is only darkness and despair."

The political savvy of the campesino is the reason, he said, that he has chosen to continue his work in the countryside. When asked about the rise of competitive, fundamentalist sects in the rural areas of Nicaragua, Molina was not distressed. "Fundamentalist evangelicals are aware of the social reality, but they do not see any answers," he suggested. "They are a tremendous force in civil society, and we have to come to recognize this force as positive. Many Pentecostal leaders have actually helped me and my work. Currently, we are working together to share ideas, and in the campo there is currently a reaching out between Protestants and Catholics. We are looking to find compromise and work that we can do together."

Asked about the last ten years, Father Molina was reflective. He said that he believed that the revolution in Nicaragua was made possible by the rationale of the church.

"Even if people are not going to church, many, many are living their faith in the communities with the poor," Molina claimed. "The revolution lost power, but power is just the beginning. For me the revolutionary experience was a success, and it is alive in the movement of the poor, in the movement of women and workers. The people are the subject of the revolution, and poverty will continue to be the struggle."

Father Molina suggested that what is common between all re-

207

ligious faiths is the struggle against the suffering of men and women. "It is possible that a new Nicaragua will move beyond questions of religious differences and find a united, common goal," the priest explained. "In this I have great hope."

For members of the Alienated Christian type the revolutionary experience has been one of great disillusionment. Part of this disenchantment may be a direct result of their own understanding of the problems of Nicaragua. Most believed that once the Somoza regime had been removed from office, social justice, prosperity, and peace would follow. Certainly the counterrevolutionary activities of the contra and the perceived communist, antireligious line of the FSLN contributed to their growing sense of frustration and political alienation.

Unlike members of the other three types, the consequence for Alienated Christians has been their withdrawal from the realm of political and community life. For most of them, the extent of interaction with others is confined to their church; most seek solace in religion. In the case of fundamentalist Protestantism, endurance of suffering, submission, and optimism for reward in heaven are preached. In the case of charismatic Catholicism, attention is diverted to belief in miracles, mysticism, and ritualism.

Unlike the other types, Alienated Christians do not accept the notion that the kingdom of God—a society of greater social justice—is possible on Earth. Most believe a class society is inevitable. For those who are poor and suffering, religion offers a sense of identity and relief from misery. Members of this type appear to be turning away from the problems of the community and focusing more on alleviating their own personal suffering.

Unlike the other three types, Alienated Christians are staunchly anti-Sandinista. They believe FSLN members are corrupt and self-serving and should be forced to abdicate their positions of power. Yet they also have little faith in the Chamorro government.

Alienated Christians articulate support for hard-line politicians on the conservative right. Unlike members of the other three types, they do not seem to appreciate the need for political compromise, the very essence of democratic practice. Their frustration with the economic and political climate of Nicaragua has influenced them to support efforts for greater law and order.

While Alienated Christians have withdrawn from political life, they increasingly look to greater authoritarian methods for dealing with what they consider an increase in societal deviance. The political acrimony, the conflict between the popular church and the Catholic hierarchy, and the aggressive evangelical campaigns have all worked to undermine the CEBs and the liberation movement. But the effects have also encouraged a search among some to rethink both their religious and their political beliefs. Ultimately this may be a healthy process.

There are some people in Nicaragua who believe that a new search for understanding of what it means to be a Christian may in fact lead to a new model of church, one that has yet to be articulated or captured by either the Catholic or Protestant communities. It is to this issue and to a few final thoughts that we now turn.

CHAPTER TEN

The Future of the Popular Church

WE HAVE SEEN that the growth and proliferation of the Christian base communities in Nicaragua developed alongside that of the revolution. But just as the form and substance of the popular church was conditioned by the social, political, and economic forces that helped to nurture it, changes in historical conditions also worked to fragment the progressive coalition.

The response of the popular church to the revolutionary experiment and to the changes taking place both in and outside of Nicaragua was multidimensional. Members responded in ways distinct from one another. The acrimony that developed led some to withdraw their involvement with the grass-roots church. Other members of the Christian base communities struggled to maintain their identity with the church of the poor. Among those that remained, there was disagreement and conflict.

During the insurrection period it was primarily religious factors (rather than class or political ideology) that brought the popular sector together. This is an important insight. Contrary to what has often been suggested, the popular church is not a singular entity, one with its own separate, unified political ideology. Past conceptions of the progressive sector—as a community of faithful who share similar beliefs and political practices—is an inadequate model for understanding the popular church in Nicaragua. Conceiving of the church of the poor as a unitary coalition of progressive Catholics has failed to explain the conflict and contradiction exhibited within the Christian base communities.

With the overthrow of President Somoza in 1979, the social and spiritual cement that unified the popular sector was gone. Dissensus rather than consensus characterized the climate within the Christian base communities during the revolutionary decade of the 1980s. Fundamental disagreement centered around the means for actualizing the popular church's preferential option for the poor. Based on different and competing convictions, the popular church had difficulty finding its role in the revolutionary process.

POLITICAL AND RELIGIOUS DIFFERENCES

Not every member of the popular church enthusiastically embraced the stated goals of the Sandinista party, nor did all of them support Sandinista demands for a new economic order. This fact dispels some generally held notions that the popular church was a Marxist organization. Clearly, a case can be made that the grass-roots church did attract Nicaraguans actively committed to the FSLN. Whereas some members of the popular church were sympathetic to the homegrown Marxist ideology that evolved in Nicaragua, most had never been exposed to, nor had formally studied, Marxism.

Studies of the church of the poor in Nicaragua have tried to suggest an intimate connection between members of the popular sector and pro-Sandinista socialism and revolutionary violence. Examples of these studies include the work of Manzar Foroohar (1989), Roger Lancaster (1988), and Luis Serra (1985). Such analysis is flawed, for it has been inadequate in recognizing the marked heterogeneity of the popular sector.

In addition, critics of the popular church, such as Michael Novak (1986), have not only been disparaging of the avowed Marxist elements in liberation thinking—including the support for class struggle, suspicion of private property, and opposition to capitalism—but, particularly in Novak's case, have conveniently ignored the prodemocratic arguments of leading liberation thinkers as well as the movement's action for peaceful, democratic, and pluralistic change clearly evident in Nicaragua.

Paul Sigmund's treatment (1990) has been more sympathetic. His work recognizes the democratic tendencies of liberation theology, but he nonetheless criticizes these very dynamics by denouncing the movement's avowed ties to violent revolutionary radicalism. Sigmund's depiction of the popular sector as such reduces the two ideologies as separate and openly contradictory.

Buying into the myth of the popular church as a bastion of violent radicalism is clearly misleading. As noted earlier, in Nicaragua the base community model developed as a response to concern for pastoral care and evangelism. As John Yoder's work (1990) has also recognized, the formation of CEBs throughout Latin America had no link to any political theology. The liberation theology movement arose gradually in response to events that included terror and the death of community leaders. Violence was seldom embraced by leaders of the movement. In fact, Yoder (ibid.: 287) properly reminds us that justifying violence (under certain circumstances) has not been part of liberation theology's message. Indeed, most of the causes for which establishment churches have historically justified war are not recognized as valid causes by liberation theology.

The myth that the popular church is a leftist organization also fails to explain why it is that in Nicaragua the progressive church continues to express itself as a religious organization, not a political one. A similar conclusion has been suggested by Daniel Levine (1990a). His work recognizes that such a narrow understanding does not help us to anticipate or appreciate how it is that the movement's primary concerns have moved away from politics to more spiritual, long-term issues of social change. Finally, this misperception also fails to explain why it is that so many members of the popular church have ultimately rejected the vision of the Sandinista leadership.

It is also inaccurate to conceive of the popular church as a community made up exclusively of poor, radical individuals. While clearly the popular church embraces, and is an expression of, the poor community, it is a fallacy to conceive of the poor in

Nicaragua as a group of dangerous political radicals. First, just as the popular church has exhibited differences in ideology, it also is characterized by different socioeconomic levels. It was not just poor people who joined the base communities. Nor was it just poor people who joined the revolution. Both middle-class and elite elements joined the grass-roots church and worked together for sociopolitical change.

Other research has well documented that the heart of the popular church, the Christian base communities, is to be found in the poorest areas of Nicaragua. (Very few CEBs have been established in middle-class neighborhoods and none are found in upper-class communities.) Yet just as the grass-roots church has been characterized by divisions along religious and ideological lines, the poor community might also be understood in the very same way. Not all poor people supported the insurrection. Many poor people who did support it actually became disillusioned with the revolutionary experiment. Many believed that the Sandinista government failed to live up to its promises, and others simply believed that turbulence of the times exacerbated their problems and contributed to their ongoing hardships.

Some Nicaraguans supported the revolution because they grew disgusted with the self-aggrandizement of the Somoza family. They supported the guerrillas because they believed that at that time the Sandinistas were the only viable alternative to the Somoza dictatorship. Thus they joined with others in the base communities to bring a more socially just society to their nation.

Because of the differences in inspiration for the revolution, some community members grew disenchanted with the unfolding events in Nicaragua. Many left the popular church because they believed its long-term support of the Sandinistas was a mistake. Others who were more actively committed to the revolutionary project chose to leave the grass-roots church because they viewed it as an inadequate vehicle for transforming the secular system. Still others chose to leave the popular church because they felt overwhelmed by the political disagreements that erupted.

Some of these conclusions are noted in the work of Philip

Williams (1992). His studies of the popular church in Nicaragua have recognized at least three distinct positions within the progressive sector: those priests and religious who took up positions in the Sandinista government; those who actively collaborated in the tasks of the revolution (mainly priests and religious leaders from foreign countries); and other faithful who shunned direct, active involvement but who were nonetheless in general agreement with the revolution's objectives and programs.

The effect of the Catholic hierarchy in influencing these contradictions and conflicts cannot be overlooked. Williams's (1992) and Phillip Berryman's (1994) work recognize how important this influence has been. Williams has argued that the hierarchy's intolerant attitude toward the popular movement fueled tension within the communities and contributed to an ideological struggle that sapped CEB energy and focus (1992: 134). Berryman has argued that as the bishops took sides against the revolution their position worked to confuse some of the laity and helped to undermine support for the grass-roots church. As noted earlier, some Catholics apparently left the base communities out of deference to the bishops. Others left the communities because they were alienated by the reform movement within the church that was initiated by the Second Vatican Council. Here, Berryman's work (1994) has also recognized a similar consequence—not only in Nicaragua but also in other countries in Central America.

As previously discussed, some members of the Christian base communities became disgusted with what they perceived as the politicization of religion. Still others opted for a less controversial faith. Many of these people were Catholics who turned toward conservative Protestant churches. People who left the base communities also withdrew their participation in the social justice struggle. Today, these Christians no longer participate in community projects, nor are they involved in the political life of the nation-state.

THE CONTEMPORARY CLIMATE

Dissensus rather than consensus more adequately characterizes the contemporary climate within the CEBs. The legacy of dis-

cord concerning the proper direction of Nicaraguan society continues to divide membership and hinder cooperation. Indeed,
in a changing political landscape the spiritual cement that
unified the popular sector is not likely to be reconstituted.
Changing global and internal conditions have placed new constraints, new limits, and new challenges on the popular church
in its struggle to maintain its prophetic voice on behalf of the
poor.

What do these constraints and challenges say, then, about the
future viability of liberation theology and, in particular, the
popular church in Nicaragua? Certainly, as life becomes more
difficult for the majority of Nicaraguans (requiring their attention and energy for more immediate concerns, like employment), potential supporters of the popular church may continue
to abandon the social justice struggle. Others may continue to
turn toward more traditional sources of spiritual comfort and
material relief. Indeed, as we have seen, current support for the
popular church continues to be undermined by the rise of fundamentalist Protestant churches.

In this context of change the Catholic hierarchy may find it
easier simply to ignore the popular church, to discredit its work,
or to co-opt remaining members of the CEBs. The renewed coun-
teroffensive launched by the Catholic hierarchy has effectively
removed sympathetic priests and resources from poor neighborhoods. As the base communities lose committed clergy and necessary resources, the charismatic programs will probably continue to capture the attention of disaffected Christians. This is a
conclusion also suggested by Phillip Berryman (1994: 154–58).

Division and membership drain have significantly weakened
the popular church's strength. As the grass-roots church suffers
from loss of membership—a crucial element in any organization—the tasks before it cannot help but become even more
problematic. Its declining numbers will undermine the future legitimacy of the popular church's work and will facilitate a
growing vulnerability to competing forces—social, political, and
spiritual.

The popular church's vulnerability is further seen in its current greater identity crisis, exacerbated by dissensus in the re-

maining sectors of the progressive community. The religious legitimacy of the popular church is compromised by its own inability to establish consensus over the proper role of the church in the context of change. If the popular church was ever regarded as a homogeneous organization, this certainly is not the case today. While there may be reasons for greater solidarity on the part of those who remain, there also are reasons for greater dissensus. Nevertheless, the fact remains that the majority of participants express desire to remain in the institutional church. They continue to value conventional religious practice, and they continue to raise their children in the church.

Both the work of Scott Mainwaring and Alexander Wilde (1989: 16) and the work of Daniel Levine (1988: 257) properly remind us that breaks in religious solidarity are rarely initiated from the bottom up. As elsewhere in Latin America, no large-scale desertion from the churches nor any formal schism has occurred in Nicaragua (Levine 1988: 257).

Religious discord and turmoil in Nicaragua appear to be a microcosm of society. Chaos within the popular church generally reflects the multipolarization of society. Disagreement between people continues to center on solutions to the country's problems. Disunity in the popular church reflects the general disillusionment associated with Nicaragua's revolutionary experiment and the discrediting of socialist options elsewhere in the world.

Dissensus is further exacerbated by Nicaragua's political impotence in dealing with the painful effects of global recession and structural readjustment programs. As life becomes more difficult, agreement over the proper religious response is fragmented by ideological differences and competing visions for creating a more equitable society.

So long as disagreement and disunity exist, the legitimacy of the popular church will remain compromised. While members recognize and are sensitive to this problem, the potential for Revolutionary and Reformist Christians to put aside their differences and to work together in greater solidarity is unlikely because these two groupings believe their commitment to the poor mandates different things. For some it requires continued support for the FSLN, greater autonomy in social justice projects, and continued political involvement in the life of the state. For some it mandates a withdrawal from politics, greater attention to Christian education, and community work. For others it requires a readiness to defy the demands of the Catholic hierarchy and a willingness to participate in defiant political and religious behavior. For still others it mandates greater reconciliation, compromise, and appeasement. These differences accentuate the problems of solidarity and may continue to erode unity and membership. Compromise is likely to become even more difficult as future events unfold. The popular church may continue to suffer fragmentation and may ultimately be overcome by other, more powerful dynamics. The potential always exists that the entire liberation movement will simply die out, a significant fact in the future challenges to Catholicism.

A NEW KIND OF PERSON

Much has been made of the liberation movement in Latin America. At the height of the liberation struggle in the 1970s and 1980s there was speculation that another historic religious reformation might be in the making. This has not proved to be the case.

Religion specialist Martin Marty has suggested that liberation theology is on the decline worldwide. Yet in spite of the pessimism, some interesting trends are apparent and are worthy of comment.

Despite the loss of membership and prestige of the base communities in Nicaragua, a new kind of person appears to be evolving. Among those who have left the practice of all religious faith is a growing belief that religion may handicap the development of a more meaningful liberating consciousness. Among those who remain in the base communities and retain their Catholic identity there appears to be a reevaluation of what it means to be Catholic. Traditionally, the faithful have always identified themselves as Catholics rather than as Christians. In revolutionary Nicaragua, however, Catholics more often refer to themselves as Christians. Perhaps this identification hints of a subtle change in consciousness not yet well recognized by the literature.

What does it mean to be Catholic? What does it mean to be

Christian? Are the two one and the same? Nicaraguan Christians are asking themselves these questions. Their individual and collective answer will ultimately have consequences for the institutional church. Despite the fact that the base communities have suffered division and membership losses, those who remain active continue to be deeply committed to the work of social justice.

As we have seen, the liberation theology agenda is evolving through a dialectical process to embrace a broader range of social and cultural issues. A purification of sorts is under way in the grass-roots church. Those who remain may make revitalization possible. The reduction of liberation theology and of the liberation movement to violent, revolutionary Marxism, to class struggle, and to anticapitalist fervor has missed the creative potential of the grass-roots phenomenon.

Earlier studies on liberation theology, and on Nicaragua in particular, that have reduced analysis to a rigid class struggle have failed to anticipate the potential for these changes. But indeed, it appears that the liberation movement, which was once highly religious and highly politicized, is transforming into a deeply spiritual and civic movement. The transformation appears more eccumenical and less rigidly ideological. Space has been opened to question all belief systems, both religious and political. There appears to be a growing maturation, one that recognizes the need for questioning all answers.

A similar conclusion has been articulated by Mainwaring and Wilde (1989: 17). They suggest that as progressives have come into contact with the poor and have learned through their experiences, they have come to value spirituality as an integral part of their ongoing mission.

Daniel Levine (1988: 256) has argued that "liberation theology's most enduring impacts are likely to come through the development of new structures, mediating agents, and new styles of leaders." His work suggests that such leaders may ultimately carry this sense of conversion forward. Already we witness in Nicaragua the growing role of women in positions of authority and leadership both in and outside the church. These women's styles are more participatory and inclusive. As many Catholics assimilate the lessons of their revolutionary experience, they have begun laying the foundation for a more democratic and pluralistic society.

In the context of evolving democratic change this development is heartening. On the other hand, Hannah Stewart-Gambino (1992: 8–9) has recognized that (re)democratization has tended to undermine consensus and unity within the church. She argues that "democracy itself presents a challenge to the church" with the reemergence of political parties, unions, and civil organizations that will ultimately compete for membership.

It can be argued that the establishment of civilian, democratic governments in Latin America may ameliorate the very conditions that gave rise to the liberation movement. This may be true. At the same time, however, such a process also opens outlets for CEB members to involve themselves in greater service opportunities. It is crucial to remember that a popularly elected civilian government is just one among many conditions necessary for democracy building. It is not the sole measure of this process.

Democratic theorists recognize the need for moving beyond a purely procedural definition of democracy. David Palmer (1991: 85–86) has suggested that democracy requires a marked increase in access to the decision-making process by local and grass-roots organizations. In that regard, the liberation experience and the leaders that it has produced in Nicaragua may be crucial to the country's future democratic experiment.

Abraham Lowenthal (1991) has argued that democracy is an internal process, rooted in a country's history, culture, and institutions. The strengthening of civil society—one that respects human rights and that nurtures trade unions, professional organizations, and women's groups, among others—is important to this process. The significance and success of this process will be found not only in how readily these groups have access to the government but also in whether the government will be able to respond to their demands. Here, too, the lessons of the revolutionary experience will be crucial.

Gustavo Gutiérrez (1994: 255–57) has argued that in addition

219

to the struggle against misery, injustice, and exploitation, the purpose of Christians who participate in the process of liberation is to create a "new man"—one who is of service to those suffering oppression and injustice, one who understands that love and faith cannot be separated from action. Hence, just as it is possible to suggest that the liberation movement will quietly die out, it is just as likely that the liberation movement will quietly resurrect itself in the collective spirit of a people who recognize the need for a stronger, more compassionate, and more democratic civic culture.

REFERENCES

INTERVIEWS

All personal interviews took place in Nicaragua unless otherwise noted.

Aguirre, Luis. Christian base community member. Personal interview, 5 December 1992.

Argüello, Alvaro. Director, Central American Historical Institute. Personal interview, 19 February 1990.

Barahona, Luisa. Christian base community, youth member. Personal interview, 20 December 1992.

Bardequez, Jorge. Theological coordinator, Antonio Valdivieso Center. Personal interview, 10 December 1992.

Bendana, Alejandro. Secretary general to the Foreign Ministry, Sandinista National Liberation Front. Personal interview, 19 February 1990.

Blachman, Morris. Professor, University of South Carolina, Columbia, S.C. Comments made to author, 25 April 1993.

Carballo, Bismark. Director, Catholic Radio. Personal interview, 23 July 1991.

———. Press secretary for Cardinal Miguel Obando y Bravo. Personal interview, 16 December 1992.

Castillo, Marta. Christian base community member. Personal interview, 28 July 1991.

Castro, Antonio. Personal interview, 29 July 1991.

Chamorro, Jaime. Senior editor, *La Prensa,* Managua, Nicaragua. Interview, 22 February 1990.

Chavez, Francisco. Christian base community, youth member. Personal interview, 23 December 1992.

Chenta, Ramón García. Personal interview, 13 December 1992.

Cuadra, Gilberto. Personal interview, 19 February 1990.

Escarlitte, Johana. Christian base community, youth member. Personal interview, 20 December 1992.

García, Cecilia. Personal interview, 12 December 1992.

García, Graciela. Christian base community member. Personal interview, 8 December 1992.

García, Julio. General Secretary, Social Christian Party. Personal interview, 21 February 1990.

Godoy, Virgilio. Vice-president, Nicaraguan Opposition Union. Personal interview, 21 February 1990.

221

References

Guevara, Miriam. Christian base community member. Personal interview, 17 July 1991.

Guevara, Olivia. Christian base community member. Personal interview, 17 July 1991.

Gutiérrez, Ramón. Christian base community member. Personal interview, 20 July 1991.

Guzmán, Luis Humberto. Member, Nicaraguan Opposition Union. Personal interview, 10 December 1992.

Hooker, Ray. Director, Autonomous Development of the Atlantic Coast, Sandinista National Liberation Front. Personal interview, 23 July 1991.

Incer, Armando. Mayor, city of Boaco. Personal interview, 22 July 1992.

Lacayo, Horacio. Christian base community member. Personal interview, 25 July 1991.

Lario, Luz. Christian base community member. Personal interview, 26 July 1991.

Larios, Indiana. Christian base community member. Personal interview, 19 December 1992.

Lester, Mark. Personal interview, 23 July 1991.

López, Darwin. Director, Evangelical Committee for Aid to Development. Personal interview, 23 July 1991.

López, Raquel. Christian base community member. Personal interview, 20 July 1991.

Marty, Martin E. Professor of Theology, University of Chicago. Personal interview, Statesboro, Ga., May 10, 1994.

Mayorga, Francisco. Economist, Central American Institute of Business Administration. Personal interview, 22 February 1990.

Mejía, Luz Elena. Personal interview, 5 December 1992.

Molina, Uriel. Director, Antonio Valdivieso Center. Personal interview, 15 December 1992.

Montenegro, Eduardo. Personal interview, 16 December 1992.

Morales, Alberto. Theological coordinator, Antonio Valdivieso Center. Personal interview, 14 December 1992.

Mulligan, Joseph. Personal interview, 24 July 1991.

Mulligan, Patricia. Personal interview, 14 December 1992.

Obando y Bravo, Miguel. Personal interview, 16 December 1992.

Ortega, Mercedes. Christian base community member. Personal interview, 23 December 1992.

Roa, María. Christian base community, youth member. Personal interview, 20 December 1992.

Rocha, Daysi Quiutauilla. Christian base community member. Personal interview, 8 December 1992.

Rocha, Pablo. Christian base community member. Personal interview, 23 December 1992.

Ruiz, Jerjes. Professor of Theology, Baptist Seminary of Nicaragua. Personal interview, 24 July 1991.

Ruiz, Julio. Christian base community, youth member. Personal interview, 23 December 1992.

Santana, Arnoldo. Personal interview, 11 December 1992.

Schmidtt, Uli. Theologian, Antonio Valdivieso Center. Personal interview, 16 December 1992.

Sequeira, Amélida. Christian base community member. Personal interview, 17 December 1992.

Sequeira, Julio. Christian base community member. Personal interview, 17 December 1992.

Sequeira, Yamileth Ortega. Christian base community member. Personal interview, 12 December 1993.

Soza, Julita. Christian base community member. Personal interview, 7 December 1992.

Tablada, Gustavo. President, National Assembly, Nicaraguan Opposition Union. Personal interview, 10 December 1992.

Talavera, Javier. Director, Interchurch Center for Theological Studies. Personal interview, 20 July 1991.

Tefel, Reynoldo Antonio. Minister, Social Security and Welfare Institute, Sandinista National Liberation Front. Personal interview, 25 July 1991.

Tellez, Claudia Morales. Christian base community, youth member. Personal interview, 23 December 1992.

Tijerino, Flavio. Former minister of culture, Sandinista National Liberation Front. Personal interview, 22 July 1991.

Tijerino, Juan. Representative, National Assembly. Personal interview, 22 July 1991.

Tijerino, Piada. Christian base community member. Personal interview, 22 July 1991.

Torelles, Angel. Personal interview, 21 July 1991.

Urbina, Dominga. Christian base community member. Personal interview, 5 December 1992.

Valdéz, Rafael. Christian base community member. Personal interview, 15 December 1992.

Valdéz, Tatiana. Christian base community, youth member. Personal interview, 20 December 1992.

Vigil, Miguel. Member, Board of Directors, University of Central America. Personal interview, 24 July 1991.

Villagra, Carlos. Dean, Baptist Seminary of Nicaragua. Personal interview, 24 July 1991.

UNPUBLISHED MATERIAL

Mulligan, Joseph. 1990. "The Nicaraguan Church." Ms., in author's possession.

Shaw, Brian J. 1989. "Praxis, Hermeneutics, Ecclesiology: The Struggle for 'Church' in Nicaragua." Photocopy of typescript, in author's possession.

PUBLISHED MATERIAL

Abbott, Walter M., ed. 1966. *The Documents of Vatican II*. New York: Herdy and Herdy Press.

Arellano, José Palo. 1990. "An Economist Views Medellín and the Present

223

References

Crisis." In *Born of the Poor,* edited by Edward L. Cleary. Notre Dame, Ind.: University of Notre Dame Press.

Arico, José. 1992. "Rethink Everything (Maybe It's Always Been This Way)." *Report on the Americas* 25, no. 5 (May): 21–23.

Bamat, Thomas. 1992. "Will Latin America Become Protestant?" *Maryknoll* 86, no. 7 (July): 9–18.

Barreiro, Alvaro. 1984. *Basic Ecclesial Communities.* Maryknoll, N.Y.: Orbis Books.

Barricada Internacional. 1993. "Hell Breaks Loose in the Church." 13, no. 359 (March): 23.

Berryman, Phillip. 1981. "Latin America: *La iglesia que nace del pueblo.*" *Christianity and Crisis* 41, no. 21 (September): 23–30.

——. 1984. *The Religious Roots of Rebellion: Christians in Central American Revolutions.* Maryknoll, N.Y.: Orbis Books.

——. 1987. *Liberation Theology.* Philadelphia: Temple University Press.

——. 1994. *Stubborn Hope.* Maryknoll, N.Y.: Orbis Books.

Black, George. 1981. *Triumph of the People.* London: Zed Books.

Boff, Clodovis, and Leonardo Boff. 1980. "The Poor, the Church, and Theology." *IDOC-International* 1, no. 2: 85–95.

Boff, Leonardo. 1985. *Church, Charisma, and Power: Liberation Theology and the Institutional Church.* New York: Crossroad.

Boff, Leonardo, and Clodovis Boff. 1986. *Liberation Theology.* Translated by Robert R. Barr. San Francisco: Harper and Row.

Bonopane, Blase. 1985. *Guerrillas of Peace: Liberation Theology and the Central American Revolution.* Boston: South End Press.

Booth, John A. 1985. *The End and the Beginning: The Nicaraguan Revolution.* Boulder, Colo.: Westview Press.

——. 1991. "Theories of Religion and Rebellion: The Central American Experience." *Journal of Third World Studies* 8, no. 2 (Fall): 50–74.

Borge, Tomás. 1987. "The Revolutionary Aim: To Eliminate Sin, Not Sinners." In *Christianity and Revolution: Tomás Borge's Theology of Life.* Maryknoll, N.Y.: Orbis Books.

Borge, Tomás, Carlos Fonseca, Daniel Ortega, Humberto Ortega, and Jaime Wheelock. 1983. *Sandinistas Speak.* New York: Pathfinder Press.

Brown, Robert McAfee. 1966. "The Church Today: A Response." In *The Documents of Vatican II,* edited by Walter M. Abbott. New York: Herdy and Herdy Press.

Bulmer-Thomas, Victor. 1987. *The Political Economy of Central America Since 1920.* Cambridge: Cambridge University Press.

Cabestrero, Teofilo. 1986. *Revolutionaries for the Gospel: Testimonies of Fifteen Christians in the Nicaraguan Government.* Translated by Phillip Berryman. Maryknoll, N.Y.: Orbis Books.

Cáceres, Jorge Prendes. 1989. "Political Radicalization and Popular Pastoral Practices in El Salvador, 1969–1985." In *The Progressive Church in Latin America,* edited by Scott Mainwaring and Alexander Wilde. Notre Dame, Ind.: University of Notre Dame Press.

Cardenal, Ernesto. 1976. *The Gospel in Solentiname.* Translated by Donald D. Walsh. Maryknoll, N.Y.: Orbis Books.

References

Christian, Shirley. 1986. *Nicaragua: Revolution in the Family*. New York: Vintage Books.

Christian Committee for the Promotion of Development (CEPAD). *CEPAD*. 1991. Apartado (Post Office Box) 3091. Managua, Nicaragua. (March–April).

Cleary, Edward L. 1992. "Conclusion: Politics and Religion-Crisis Constraints and Restructuring." In *Conflict and Competition: The Latin American Church in a Changing Environment*, edited by Edward L. Cleary and Hannah Stewart-Gambino. Boulder, Colo.: Lynne Rienner.

———, ed. 1990. *Born of the Poor*. London: University of Notre Dame Press.

Cleary, Edward L., and Hannah Stewart-Gambino, eds. 1992. *Conflict and Competition: The Latin American Church in a Changing Environment*. Boulder, Colo.: Lynne Rienner.

Cockcroft, James D. 1989. *Neighbors in Turmoil: Latin America*. New York: Harper and Row.

Costas, Orlando. 1974. *The Church and Its Mission: A Shattering Critique from the Third World*. Wheaton, Ohio: Tyndale.

Crahan, Margaret E. 1989. "Religion and Politics in Revolutionary Nicaragua." In *The Progressive Church in Latin America*, edited by Scott Mainwaring and Alexander Wilde. Notre Dame, Ind.: University of Notre Dame Press.

Crawley, Eduardo. 1979. *Dictators Never Die: A Portrait of Nicaragua and the Somozas*. London: C. Hurst Press.

De Chardin, Pierre Teilhard. 1960. *The Divine Milieu*. English edition. Edited by Bernard Wall. New York: Harper and Brothers.

"Declaracion de Sacredotes Nicaraguerses." 1968. *Cuadernos de Marcha* 17, no. 3 (September): 31–32.

Dodson, Michael. 1986. "Nicaragua: The Struggle for the Church." In *Religion and Political Conflict in Latin America*, edited by Daniel Levine. Chapel Hill: University of North Carolina Press.

Dodson, Michael, and Tommie Sue Montgomery. 1992. "The Churches in the Nicaraguan Revolution." In *Nicaragua in Revolution*, edited by Thomas W. Walker. New York: Praeger.

Dodson, Michael, and Laura Nuzzi O'Shaughnessy. 1990. *Nicaragua's Other Revolution: Religious Faith and Political Struggle*. Chapel Hill: University of North Carolina Press.

Drury, John. 1970. *Between Honesty and Hope: Documents from and about the Church in Latin America, Issued at Lima by the Peruvian Bishops' Commission for Social Action*. Maryknoll, N.Y.: Maryknoll Publications.

Durham, William H. 1979. *Scarcity and Survival in Central America*. Stanford: Stanford University Press.

Dussel, Enrique. 1976. *History and Theology of Liberation: A Latin American Perspective*. Translated by John Drury. Maryknoll, N.Y.: Orbis Books.

———. 1981. *A History of the Church in Latin America: Colonialism to Liberation*. Detroit: William B. Eerdmans Press.

Engels, Friedrich. 1964. "The Peasant War in Germany." In *On Religion*, edited by Karl Marx and Friedrich Engels. New York: Schocken Books.

225

References

Envio: The Monthly Magazine of Analysis on Nicaragua. 1991. 10, no. 122 (September): 3–13.

———. 1992. 11, no. 133 (August): 24–31.

———. 1995. 14, no. 172 (November): 3–10.

Ezcurra, Ana María. 1982. *U.S. Churches and the Ideological Struggle for Latin America*. Translated by Elice Higginbotham and Linda Unzer. New York: Circus Publishers.

———. 1984. *Ideological Aggression Against the Sandinista Revolution: The Political Opposition Church in Nicaragua*. Translated by Elice Higginbotham and Bayard Faithfull. New York: Circus Publishers.

Fonseca, Carlos, ed. 1980. *Ideario politico de Augusto Cesar Sandino*. Managua: Secretaria de Propaganda y Educacion Politica, Frente Sandinista de Liberacion Nacional.

Foroohar, Manzar. 1989. *The Catholic Church and Social Change in Nicaragua*. Albany: State University of New York Press.

Gibellini, Rosino. 1987. *The Liberation Theology Debate*. New York: Maryknoll Books.

Gilbert, Dennis. 1986. "Nicaragua." In *Confronting Revolution*, edited by Morris Y. Blachman, William M. Leogrande, and Kenneth Sharpe. New York: Pantheon Books.

Girardi, Giulio. 1989. *Faith and Revolution in Nicaragua: Convergence and Contradictions*. Maryknoll, N.Y.: Orbis Books.

Gorostiaga, Javier. 1991. "Latin America in the New World Order." *Envio: The Monthly Magazine of Analysis on Nicaragua* 10, no. 121 (August): 31–43.

———. 1993. Quoted in the *Washington Post*, 9 May, A29.

Grubb, Kenneth G. 1937. *Religion in Central America*. London: World Dominion Press.

Gutiérrez, Gustavo. 1986. *A Theology of Liberation: History, Politics and Salvation*. Edited and translated by Caridad Inda and John Eagleson. Maryknoll, N.Y.: Orbis Books.

———. 1990. "The Church of the Poor." In *Born of the Poor*, edited by Edward L. Cleary. Notre Dame, Ind.: University of Notre Dame Press.

———. 1994. "Notes for a Theology of Liberation." In *The Roman Catholic Church in Latin America*, edited by Jorge I. Dominguez. New York: Garland.

Harris, Richard L., and Carlos M. Vilas, eds. 1985. *Nicaragua: A Revolution under Siege*. London: Zed Books.

Haslam, David. 1987. *Faith in Struggle: The Protestant Churches in Nicaragua and Their Response to the Revolution*. London: Epworth Press.

Herring, Herbert. 1962. *A History of Latin America*. New York: Knopf.

Heyck, Denis Lynn Daly. 1990. *Life Stories of the Nicaraguan Revolution*. New York: Routledge Press.

Hodges, Donald C. 1986. *Intellectual Origins of the Nicaraguan Revolution*. Austin: University of Texas Press.

Hollis, Christopher. 1968. *The Jesuits: A History*. New York: Macmillan.

Holy Bible. 1972. Revised Standard Version. Nashville: Thomas Nelson.

References

Hundley, Raymond C. 1987. *Radical Liberation Theology: An Evangelical Response*. Lexington, Ky.: Bristol Books.

John Paul II. 1979. Mexican address. In *Puebla: A Pilgrimage of Faith*. Boston: Saint Paul's Edition.

LaFeber, Walter. 1984. *Inevitable Revolutions*. New York: W. W. Norton.

Lancaster, Roger N. 1988. *Thanks to God and the Revolution*. New York: Columbia University Press.

Landsberger, Henry A., ed. 1970. *The Church and Social Change in Latin America*. Notre Dame, Ind.: University of Notre Dame Press.

Leff, Enrique. 1992. "Environmentalism: Fusing Red and Green." *Report on the Americas* 25, no. 5 (May): 35–37.

Lehmann, David. 1990. *Democracy and Development in Latin America*. Philadelphia: Temple University Press.

Lehmann, Paul. 1963. *Ethics in a Christian Context*. New York: Harper and Row.

Lenin, V. I. 1963. "The Attitude of the Worker's Party to Religion." In *Collected Works*, vol. 15 (March 1908 to August 1909). Moscow: Foreign Languages Publishing House.

Lernoux, Penny. 1979. "The Long Path to Puebla." In *Puebla and Beyond*, edited by John Eagleson and Phillip Scharper. Maryknoll, N.Y.: Orbis Books.

———. 1982. *Cry of the People*. New York: Penguin Books.

———. 1989. *People of God: The Struggle for World Catholicism*. New York: Viking Press.

Levine, Daniel H. 1981. *Religion and Politics in Latin America: The Catholic Church in Venezuela and Columbia*. Princeton, N.J.: Princeton University Press.

———. 1988. "Assessing the Impacts of Liberation Theology in Latin America." *Review of Politics* 50, no. 2 (Spring): 241–63.

———. 1990a. "Considering Liberation Theology as Utopia." *Review of Politics* 52, no. 4 (Spring): 603–20.

———. 1990b. "How Not to Understand Liberation Theology, Nicaragua, or Both." *Journal of InterAmerican Studies and World Affairs* 32, no. 3 (Fall): 229–45.

———. 1990c. "The Impact and Lasting Influence of Medellín and Puebla." In *Born of the Poor*, edited by Edward L. Cleary. Notre Dame, Ind.: University of Notre Dame Press.

———. 1995. "On Premature Reports of the Death of Liberation Theology." *Review of Politics* 57, no. 3 (Winter): 105–31.

———, ed. 1986. *Religion and Political Conflict in Latin America*. Chapel Hill: University of North Carolina Press.

Lewis, Oscar. 1959. *Five Families*. New York: New American Library, Basic Books.

———. 1961. *The Children of Sanchez*. New York: Vintage Books.

Lowenthal, Abraham F. 1991. "Can Democracy Be Exported?" In *Setting the North-South Agenda*, North-South Center, University of Miami. Boulder, Colo.: Lynne Rienner.

227

References

Macaulay, Neil. 1971. *The Sandino Affair*. Chicago: Quadrangle Books.

McGrath, Marcos. 1990. "The Medellín and Puebla Conferences and Their Impact on the Latin American Church." In *Born of the Poor*, edited by Edward L. Cleary. Notre Dame, Ind.: University of Notre Dame Press.

Maciel, Creuza. 1990. "Grassroots Communities: A New Way of Being and Living as a Church." In *Born of the Poor*, edited by Edward L. Cleary. Notre Dame, Ind.: University of Notre Dame Press.

Macridis, Roy C. 1992. *Contemporary Political Ideologies, Movements, and Regimes*. New York: Harper Collins.

Mainwaring, Scott, and Alexander Wilde, eds. 1989. *The Progressive Church in Latin America*. Notre Dame, Ind.: University of Notre Dame Press.

Medellín, La Iglesia Nueva. 1968. Montevideo, Uruguay: Cuadernos de Marcha.

Millet, Richard. 1982. *The Death of the Dynasty: The End of Somoza Rule in Nicaragua*. Maryknoll, N.Y.: Orbis Books.

Montgomery, Tommie Sue. 1982. *Revolution in El Salvador*. Boulder, Colo.: Westview Press.

Mulligan, Joseph E. 1991. *The Nicaraguan Church and the Revolution*. Kansas City, Mo.: Sheed and Ward.

Neal, Marie A. 1990. "The Context of Medellín and Puebla: World Church Movement toward Social Justice." In *Born of the Poor*, edited by Edward L. Cleary. Notre Dame, Ind.: University of Notre Dame Press.

Nelson-Pallmeyer, Jack. 1990. *War Against the Poor: Low-Intensity Conflict and Christian Faith*. Maryknoll, N.Y.: Orbis Books.

Novak, Michael. 1986. *Will It Liberate? Questions about Liberation Theology*. New York: Paulist Press.

Núñez, Emilio A. 1985. *Liberation Theology*. Translated by Paul E. Sywulka. Chicago: Moody Press.

O'Brien, Conor Cruise. 1986. "God and Man in Nicaragua." *Atlantic Monthly* 258, no. 2 (August): 50–72.

O'Shaughnessy, Laura Nuzzi, and Luis Serra. 1986. *The Church and Revolution in Nicaragua*. Athens, Ohio: Ohio University Press.

Palmer, David Scott. 1991. "Democracy and Change in Latin America." In *Setting the North-South Agenda*, North-South Center, University of Miami. Boulder, Colo.: Lynne Rienner.

Planas, Ricardo. 1986. *Liberation Theology: The Political Expression of Religion*. Kansas City, Mo.: Sheed and Ward.

Portantiero, Juan Carlos. 1992. "Foundations of a New Politics." *Report on the Americas* 25, no. 5 (May): 17–20.

Randall, Margaret. 1981. *Sandino's Daughters*. Vancouver, Canada: New Star Books.

———, ed. 1983. *Christians in the Nicaraguan Revolution*. Vancouver, Canada: New Star Books.

Report on the Americas. 1992. 25, no. 5 (May): 12. North American Congress on Latin America.

References

Richard, Pablo. 1987. *Death of Christendom, Birth of the Church*. Maryknoll, N.Y.: Orbis Books.

———. 1992. "Liberation Theology Today: Crisis or Challenge?" *Envio: The Monthly Magazine of Analysis on Nicaragua* 11, no. 133 (August): 24–31.

Rodriguez, Manuel. 1981. *Gaspar vive*. San Juan, Costa Rica: Artes Graficas.

Rosenberg, Tina. 1992. *Children of Cain: Violence and the Violent in Latin America*. New York: Penguin Books.

Runciman, W. G., ed. 1978. *Max Weber: Selections in Translation*. Cambridge: Cambridge University Press.

Schall, James V. 1976. "From Catholic 'Social Doctrine' to the 'Kingdom of God on Earth.' " *Communio* (Winter): 287–300.

———. 1982. *Liberation Theology in Latin America*. San Francisco: Ignatius Press.

Secher, H. P. 1962. *Max Weber: Basic Concepts in Sociology*. New York: Philosophical Library.

Segundo, L. L. 1976. *The Liberation of Theology*. Maryknoll, N.Y.: Orbis Books.

Serra, Luis. 1985. "Ideology, Religion, and the Class Struggle in the Nicaraguan Revolution." In *Nicaragua: A Revolution under Siege*, edited by Richard L. Harris and Carlos M. Vilas. London: Zed Books.

———. 1986. "Religious Institutions and Bourgeois Institutions in the Nicaraguan Revolution." In *The Church and Revolution in Nicaragua*, edited by Laura Nuzzi O'Shaughnessy and Luis Serra. Athens, Ohio: Ohio University Press.

Sigmund, Paul E. 1990. *Liberation Theology at the Crossroads*. New York: Oxford University Press.

Smith, Christian. 1991. *The Emergence of Liberation Theology*. Chicago: University of Chicago Press.

Sobrino, John. 1978. *Christology at the Crossroads*. Maryknoll, N.Y.: Orbis Books.

Sollod, Robert N. 1992. "Point of View." *Chronicle of Higher Education*, 18 March, A60.

Der Spiegel. 1991. "A Quiet Revolution in Latin America." *World Press Review* 38, no. 3 (March): 30–31.

Stewart-Gambino, Hannah. 1992. "Introduction: New Game, New Rules." In *Conflict and Competition*, edited by Edward L. Cleary and Hannah Stewart-Gambino. Boulder, Colo.: Lynne Rienner.

Thompson, Kenneth, and Jeremy Tunstall, eds. 1971. *Sociological Perspectives*. London: Penguin Books.

Tijerino, Doris. 1979. *Inside the Nicaraguan Revolution*. Vancouver, Canada: New Star Books.

Torres-Rivas, Edelberto. 1989. *Repression and Resistance: The Struggle for Democracy in Central America*. Boulder, Colo.: Westview Press.

Vanden, Harry E., and Gary Prevost. 1993. *Democracy and Socialism in Sandinista Nicaragua*. Boulder, Colo.: Lynne Rienner.

References

Vilas, Carlos M. 1990. "What Went Wrong?" *Report on the Americas* 24, no. 1 (June): 10–18.

——. 1992. "What Future for Socialism?" *Report on the Americas* 25, no. 5 (May): 13–16.

Walker, Thomas W. 1981. *Nicaragua: The Land of Sandino*. Boulder, Colo.: Westview Press.

——, ed. 1982. *Nicaragua in Revolution*. New York: Praeger Press.

Weber, Henri. 1981. *Nicaragua: The Sandinist Revolution*. London: Unwin Brothers.

Webster, John C., and Ellen Low, eds. 1985. *The Church and Women in the Third World*. Philadelphia: Westminster Press.

Wiarda, Howard J., ed. 1992. *Politics and Social Change in Latin America*. Boulder, Colo.: Westview Press.

Wiarda, Howard J., and Harvey F. Kline, eds. 1990. *Latin American Politics and Development*. Boulder, Colo.: Westview Press.

Williams, Philip J. 1989. "The Catholic Church in the Nicaraguan Revolution: Differing Responses and New Challenges." In *The Progressive Church in Latin America*, edited by Scott Mainwaring and Alexander Wilde. Notre Dame, Ind.: University of Notre Dame Press.

——. 1992. "The Limits of Religious Influence: The Progressive Church in Nicaragua." In *Conflict and Competition: The Latin American Church in a Changing Environment*, edited by Edward L. Cleary and Hannah Stewart-Gambino. Boulder, Colo.: Lynne Rienner.

Woodward, Ralph L. 1976. *Central America: A Nation Divided*. New York: Oxford University Press.

Yoder, John. 1990. "The Wider Setting of Liberation Theology." *Review of Politics* 52, no. 2 (Spring): 285–96.

Zwerling, Philip, and Connie Martin. 1985. *Nicaragua—A New Kind of Revolution*. New Haven, Conn.: Lawrence Hill.

INDEX

Adolfo Reyes, 43, 44, 48, 50, 51, 61, 65, 67, 68, 72, 101, 102, 105, 119, 124, 131, 136, 177, 190; establishment of, 33; revolutionary activities, 71–72, 101, 118; effect of liberation theology, 43–44; effect of student movement, 48; National Guard, 65; radicalization of, 67–68; effect of FSLN electoral defeat, 126; criticism of Obando y Bravo, 129–30; membership loss, 139–40, 158, 166; Catholicism, 162; environmental projects, 170; conflict in, 179. *See also* Christian base communities

Aguirre, Luis, 130, 131

Alemán, Arnoldo, 197, 201

Alienated Christians: type, 10; Sandinistas, 174, 208; Catholic Church, 174, 208; Protestantism, 174; on social justice, 175; on the poor, 175; values and beliefs, 175, 199; the Bible, 183–84; Kingdom of God, 184–85, 208; beliefs of, 199; politics, 184, 202–3, 205; on revolutionary experience, 208; political apathy, 208; on Chamorro government, 208; Anti-Somoza activities, 177; Antonio Valdivieso Center, 153, 161, 192, 195, 206

Aragón, Rafael, 69

Argüello, Alvaro, 94, 187, 191, 195

Autonomous Development for the Atlantic Coast, 148

Baltodano, Alvaro, 75

Baltodano, Modesto, 127

Baptist Seminary of Nicaragua, 185, 195; liberation theology, 186

Bardequez, Jorge, 195, 196

Belli, Humberto, 95, 196, 197, 201

Bendana, Alejandro, 81

Bible, 19, 20, 145; new conception of, 36; utilized by the CEB, 36–37; inspiration, 67; literacy campaign and, 88; Alienated Christians, 183–84

Blachman, Morris, 139

Bluefields, 185

Boaco: consequences of contra war in, 149

Borge, Tomás, 53, 54, 55; meets Ernesto Cardenal, 58–59

Campesino movement: reasons for, 64

Capitalism, 155; denunciation of, 16

Carballo, Bismark, 90, 123, 188; and base communities, 93; sex scandal, 103; on Protestantism, 189; on charismatic campaign, 194

Cardenal, Ernesto, 26, 114; pastoral method, 27; attracts Sandinista attention, 58; in Cuba, 58; spokesperson for Sandinistas, 60; appointed as minister of culture, 82; defies hierarchy, 91; and Pope John Paul II, 104

Cardenal, Fernando, 59; involvement in student movement, 47–48; Gaspár and, 63; declares himself Marxist-Christian, 60; Los Doce, 75; effect of revolution on, 92

Casadaliga, Pedro, 117

Castillo, Marta, 129, 130

Castro, Antonio, 43, 44, 116

Catholic Church, 12, 23, 73; notion of social justice, 56; fears of separation, 89; Christian base communities, 100–101, 119–20; base community conflict, 127–30; in San Pablo, 103; and Sandinistas, 103–4; membership loss, 114, 187–88; division in, 122, 130; criticism of, 130–31; elites, 132, 147; campesinos, 153; liberation clergy,

231

Index

Index

Index